FROM C◀SC◀DE TO CONVERSATION

Unlocking the collective
wisdom of your workforce

KATIE MACAULAY
with BEN HALL and ELOISE HINDES

ab

First published in 2014 by AB Publishing UK LLP, London.

All quotations have been translated into English.

The views of all contributors are their own and do not necessarily reflect the opinions of their organisations.

British Library Cataloguing in Publication Data. A CIP catalogue record for this book is available from the British Library.

ISBN 978-0-9575724-1-6

Book design led by Joel O'Connor
Printed and bound in Great Britain by Newnorth Print Ltd, Newnorth House, College St, Kempston MK42 8NA

www.cascadetoconversation.co.uk
www.abcomm.co.uk

For Sam and Harry

Contents

Foreword

This book pulls together a broad range of expert inputs from diverse sources as well as from Katie's own direct experience as a practitioner and in leading her agency, AB. It is not just another attempt at a 'how to' guide for internal communication or engaging employees. This book stimulates and provokes thinking, and it does so from a variety of perspectives, rather than telling you what to do.

A famous author once wrote, "the people of the world are islands shouting at each other across seas of misunderstanding"; something I suspect we can all recognise from our own experiences.

There is no such thing as 'no communication' – silence, inaction or passivity all radiate messages from which others infer, often inaccurately, some meaning. Mutual understanding can only come from dialogue. Conversations allow both the exchange of information and the checking that a message has been properly understood. As such it is a valuable prize for any organisation; that's why this book makes this its focus.

Philosopher Thomas Carlyle probably wasn't thinking about how a Finance Director might feel when seeing their organisation's finite resources being squandered when he wrote "nothing is more terrible than activity without insight", but it neatly links the benefits that come from genuine conversations and improving organisational performance.

Using appropriate language is, as you'd expect, a vital component in nurturing useful conversation. Some of the best advice I received on this was from a friend and fellow communicator who shared the following motto: eschew obfuscation. We have tried to ensure this book takes that advice.

You may or may not agree with the points put forward – I certainly agree more strongly with some than others – and you may well feel that a concept that has inspired you isn't included. That's very likely as you'd need many volumes to get anywhere near exhausting the numerous influences on internal communication and employee engagement.

So, if you feel challenged, delighted, infuriated, excited, ambivalent, puzzled or inspired then become part of a conversation, visit the website, and give Katie some feedback.

KEN HUNTER

KEN HAS MORE THAN 30 YEARS' EXPERIENCE IN CORPORATE, INTERNAL AND CHANGE COMMUNICATIONS. HE HAS WORKED IN-HOUSE AND AS A CONSULTANT INTERNATIONALLY AND ACROSS A BROAD RANGE OF SECTORS.

Introduction

In 1999, I was working as a consultant in the Square Mile for a large British bank. One morning a conscientious junior press officer alerted the corporate communications director to something she had found on the internet. "It's a website about us, and…" she hesitated, "I'm afraid you won't like what it's saying." I joined the crowd of curious onlookers who had gathered around her computer screen. As she started scrolling, the director looked on, more and more exasperated. "This is ridiculous! Can't we block it or close it down?" He was greeted with an uneasy silence. Here we were, a well-trained army of communicators who crafted and controlled the message. We considered ourselves to be at the top of our game. Now, without warning, the game had changed.

What had once been in the hands of a few was now in the hands of the many. For as long as anyone could remember, individuals near the top of the hierarchical pyramid drove the agenda, shaped the message and issued statements. We would broadcast our communications with confidence and authority to those inside our organisations and the world at large. Our words were filtered, honed and manipulated until perfectly safe and sterile. If real people had started speaking in the same corporate twaddle, we would have worried for them. Any response from employees was limited and intermittent, often restricted to an annual engagement survey. If something went disastrously wrong, we might reconsider what we were saying or introduce a new 'speak up' mechanism. But while we tinkered with language and channels, the corporate monologue went on largely unhindered. In truth, calling this 'communication' may have been an overstatement.

The premise of *From Cascade to Conversation* is that broadcasting to employees is now dangerously archaic. People everywhere have found their voice. They have both the desire and ability to converse across time and space. Employees no longer passively receive the message, but look to share and shape it. Broadcasting is the antithesis of how individuals choose to communicate. Continuing with the corporate soliloquy will increasingly fail to meet expectations.

We know instinctively that a meaningful dialogue is more rewarding than a one-way pronouncement or directive. Everybody likes to be asked for their views, especially when they feel these are understood and valued. Employees are far more likely to listen and engage if we sense the speaker has a genuine desire to be understood. This is why entering a dialogue with someone, rather than issuing a set of instructions, is more successful when initiating behavioural change. A genuine conversation is likely to lead to a deeper appreciation of the message. Corporate communicators have been saying this for years. Yet it seemed, to our great frustration, few were listening.

Back in 1990, William Kahn, a US professor in organisational behaviour, espoused the commercial benefits of having 'engaged' employees. We are more energised and productive when fully engaged. Problems seem less insurmountable. We choose to give discretionary effort that so often makes the difference. Conversation has the power to do more than drive individual performance. It can unlock the collective value of an entire organisation, turning workers into a true work*force*.

In a tough, competitive market, business as usual is not enough. Organisations need to be constantly innovating. If we look solely to our strategists or management consultants for this thinking, we ignore the hundreds or thousands of people who know our organisations best; who create our products and deliver our services every day. Tomorrow's successful organisations will be listening to the wisdom of their crowds. Conversation is a rare win-win. It is emotionally engaging for the individual and commercially beneficial for the organisation.

In an era when deference is on decline and trust in short supply, conversation has the power to restore much needed faith and confidence in our leaders. It strengthens relationships through mutual respect, openness and honesty. Conversation demands leaders practise an underused skill, active listening. The authors of *The Cluetrain Manifesto* put it this way: "Here's some advice on entering the conversation: Loosen up. Listen up. And shut up for a while. Listen for a change."[1]

Corporate disaster strikes when good people fail to speak up or when their message falls on deaf ears. When leaders demonstrate a willingness to hear the candid views of others, and reciprocate in the same way, this is a message in itself. Employees feel their opinions count, distant figures of authority become real people and executives acquire insight it would have been impossible to get any other way.

Economic, social and technological trends are converging to make the shift from cascade to conversation inevitable. Stifling the discussion or putting our hands over our ears will not make it go away. "Shutting down a discussion board can be like shutting down a city's red-light district: generally you're just pushing the temptation to another part of the city,"[2] says

David Weinberger. Better to hear what employees are thinking – good and bad – within the walls of your organisation where encouraging an open, healthy debate is a sign of corporate confidence, and you can at least take part in what is being said.

However obvious or inescapable the move from to monologue to dialogue, it will not prove easy or comfortable for all. Changing the relationship with our internal audience threatens those attached to conventional command-and-control. Increasingly, though, success demands greater collaboration. The authors of *Wikinomics* believe this will only come from "ceding some control, sharing responsibility, embracing transparency, managing conflict and accepting that successful projects will take on lives of their own".[3] New skills may be required of the many individuals wedded to the way things used to be.

This book is intended to give leaders and communicators the inspiration, insight and confidence to step away from the podium, put down the megaphone and end the corporate soliloquy. It stems from my profound belief that conversation works.

In writing it, my colleagues and I have drawn on personal experience, research and discussions with fellow practitioners. Many writers before us have tackled the weighty subject of achieving corporate success through greater employee participation. We have thoroughly enjoyed reading their work, and many of their ideas are mentioned throughout.

In the spirit of collaboration, we invited others to contribute to the discussion. At the end of each chapter, we are 'in conversation' with those who share varied, first-hand experiences of fostering and maintaining conversations in the workplace.

This book is in two parts. The first five chapters lay the groundwork for a new type of communication inside organisations. The next five explore what this shift means for the content we write, the channels we build, the measurement we undertake, and the skills needed of leaders and practitioners.

In *chapter 1: In the beginning there was broadcast*, we return to our roots. We examine the history of employee communication and engagement. Why did the work of early visionaries take so long to take hold? We investigate the management theories, social trends and technological changes that have led us to this point.

To ensure we all share the same definition of 'conversation', *chapter 2: Why conversation works* explores its meaning in an organisational context. Why is it so intrinsically valuable and what conditions are needed for it to flourish? We outline the vital role practitioners must play in ensuring the conversation remains productive and worthwhile.

"Here's a definition of that pesky boardroom elitist phrase, *knowledge worker*: a knowledge worker is someone whose job entails having really interesting conversations at work,"[4] says David Weinberger. In *chapter 3: No one is as smart as everyone*, we show how successful organisations are beginning to realise that *every* employee is a knowledge worker. Collaborative relationships do more than drive the so-called 'soft' intangibles of engagement and satisfaction. We look at how they can stimulate innovation, provide vital insight and generate commercial value. Former Hewlett-Packard CEO Lew Platt famously admitted: "If only HP knew what HP knows, we would be three times more productive."[5]

In *chapter 4: What does success look like?*, we identify some common traits in organisations already using meaningful employee conversations to drive performance. But we urge that these case studies be seen as sources for inspiration rather than imitation. In our 'search for excellence', as Tom Peters called it, we also caution against overlooking signs of success closer to home. We urge practitioners to examine – and learn from – the good practice that undeniably already exists inside their own organisations. We also examine the causes of corporate failures – hoping to learn from the mistakes of others.

Chapter 5: Preparing organisations for conversation, recognises that even if you are convinced by our argument, others may not be. We give guidance on overcoming the many obstacles communication practitioners are likely to face in the drive to create a more consequential dialogue with employees. We identify the preconditions for conversation and explore ways not just to initiate new dialogue but ensure it is maintained.

"The moment people talk of 'implementing' instead of 'doing', and of 'finalising' instead of 'finishing', the organisation is already running a fever,"[6] says Peter Drucker. *Chapter 6: From the corporate to the employee voice,* examines the causes of 'corporate speak' and its impact on the audience. Corporate platitudes, bland announcements or double-speak destroy trust, thwart understanding and limit success. We identify the fears and obstacles to adopting more humane voice and look at the potential rewards of communicating with people like people.

Chapter 7: Why paper isn't dead, investigates the role of printed communications. We look at how this infrequent, fixed and one-way medium can become conversational. We discover why the traditional skills of the newspaper journalist – the ability to find, write and verify a great story – are becoming more, not less, important.

We cannot expect our new enterprise social network to flourish if our organisations are not inherently social. In *chapter 8: Conversations via a screen,* we look at the impact of digital technologies. Conversation using the medium of the screen breaks the rules of traditional broadcast communication. It is fundamentally human, open and collaborative.

In *chapter 9: Face-to-face conversation*, we look at our leaders' inclination and ability to converse in person and practical ways we can help. We examine the role line managers play today in maintaining a dialogue with employees and how we can better support them. The drive for greater transparency means there are no longer hiding places left for those in authority. Employees expect their leaders at all levels to look them in the eye and tell them the truth. This starts when standing in the same room.

Chapter 10: Measurement through conversation explores the thorny issue of evaluating employee communications. Is the drive to calculate a return on investment helpful or even possible? We argue measurement and research should be used less to justify our existence and more to gain a greater insight and understanding of our audience. We explore the benefits and limitations of standard quantitative approaches and the underused measurement potential of conversation.

One book cannot do justice to a topic as vast and significant as the way we communicate at work. I will have succeeded if this book sparks fresh discussions about the role and approach of communications in today's workplace.

At the heart of this book lies a deceptively simple idea. A genuinely open conversation has the power to change minds, solve seemingly intractable problems and form deep bonds with others. Let us use that power to make the world of work more meaningful and beneficial.

Chapter 1

In the beginning there was broadcast

A LONG TIME COMING

The notion that organisations should do more for their employees than simply issue instructions emerged in the 1890s with paternalistic employers like the Cadbury family. These devout Quakers were among the very first to consider their employees to be more than just a 'living tool'. Their concerns focused on welfare and moral wellbeing, as opposed to a commercial advantage. The debate shifted in the 1920s when a handful of farsighted academics and researchers realised that to optimise employees' output, something more than regular rest breaks, payment and fair working conditions was required. Employees, they claimed, had to feel in some way emotionally connected to their work and to those around them – their colleagues and managers. Although research was undertaken and papers were published, it would seem, for many decades, few organisations – if any – were listening. We can only speculate why. Perhaps two world wars, periods of extreme boom and bust, the demise of manufacturing, trade union activity, the rise of globalisation and several technological revolutions gave organisations other things to worry about. More likely, any commercial advantage businesses could secure from climbing into the minds of their employees did not seem worth the effort. It took 170 years after the birth of the industrial revolution – and another revolution in technology – for that economic advantage to be widely accepted as real and meaningful.

There has been a frustratingly slow but nevertheless important shift in management theory towards a view of workers as sentient human beings whose output is influenced by their perception of themselves, the tasks they perform and their attitudes towards co-workers, managers and leaders. This realisation came first to employees themselves who felt compelled to form trade unions in order to protect and promote these human needs, the value of which were widely unappreciated by industry.

Employee communications – a necessary activity within all organisations whether public, private, large or small, follows a similar trajectory. A few lone radicals dared to suggest it should be an involving and two-way dialogue – a genuinely open and honest exchange of views – but for much of the 20th century, employee communication was the opposite. It was about broadcasting information from the top of the organisational pyramid downwards. For too long employee communication was synonymous with outputs such as newsletters and newspapers, then magazines, intranets, microsites and e-zines. As David MacLeod's notion of employee engagement – "how we create the conditions in which employees offer more of their capability and potential"[1] – has slowly taken hold, the scope of the communicator's work has broadened. We are beginning to become strategic advisers; helping to develop 'employee value propositions' and design engagement programmes. However, while we have raised the profile and value of employee communications among senior executives, much of what we are doing remains broadcasting under a different name. Information is still flowing predominantly one way. We might encourage feedback, and measure attitudes, but all this surveying and 'pulse checking' is not conversation.

A genuine and seismic shift in the theory and practice of employee communication has started to take place in recent years with the development of social media and the proliferation of personal devices connected to the web. Our desire and ability to communicate has changed. We have become active participants in countless daily exchanges with those we hold dear and those we have never met. We are not passive consumers of content. We subscribe, unsubscribe, follow, like, rate and comment. Information is not handed to us fully formed and fixed, we seek it out to digest, share and shape it. This has significant implications for employee communication, which must now genuinely leave its broadcasting legacy behind and facilitate open conversation.

Employee engagement and communication have both reached a turning point. The stage is now set for a new era of mass collaboration, when organisations will rely far more on the initiative and ingenuity of their people to stay in business because almost everything else can be copied. Quickly, communication will be propelled into a new, more commercially significant role, more akin to research and development. It will become the means by which the world's most successful organisations find and keep their competitive edge.

DIM THE LIGHTS, LADIES

One of the first of that handful of farsighted academics to demonstrate a link between dialogue and increased productivity was Elton Mayo. In 1924, Mayo was involved in a series of experiments conducted at the Hawthorne Works, a Western Electric factory near Chicago. The plant primarily produced telephone and other electronic equipment, made by assembly lines of predominantly female workers. Initial studies were conducted at the plant by Clarence Stoll and George Pennock, who "were engineers, and treated the row of women like an engine in its test bed, tweaking the conditions to achieve maximum output".[2] Stoll and Pennock endeavoured to understand whether changing the level of lighting inside the factory would affect the output of the workforce. They were following a model of scientific management called 'Taylorism' that sought to maximise efficiency within industry. However, their findings failed to provide such a simple optimal condition. When the lighting was dimmed in the test room, the productivity of the female workers increased. But when the lights went up, productivity increased still further. Other incentives such as financial rewards and rest pauses were manipulated at regular intervals. Although output levels varied, whatever the change – even when it was reversed – the productivity trend was almost inexorably upwards. This flummoxed the researchers who called in academic consultants, including Mayo, to investigate.

Searching for an answer, Mayo looked at the supervisor of the test group. He was relaxed and friendly; he got to know the operators well while conducting the experiments. He was not too worried about company policies and procedures. In turn, the women of the experiment enjoyed a novel sense of involvement. They became active participants in the project and consequently formed a social group. This was in stark contrast to how they had been managed previously – and how the other 200 employees in the factory were being treated. Mayo concluded it was this supervisory style that was driving up productivity. The women's output depended more on co-operation and a feeling of worth than on physical working conditions. According to Edwin Gale, the experimenters "had bridged a social abyss and discovered a new alchemy. Treat working people with respect, understand their thinking and group dynamics, reward them appropriately, and they will work better for you".[3]

Between 1928 and 1930, the research continued with an extensive interview programme involving 21,000 employees. According to Jeffrey Sonnenfeld, "the interview program suggested a great motivational value to directly soliciting the opinions and perceptions of workers".[4] Today, it is hard to believe that Mayo's conclusions were anything more than self-evident. Yet, in the context of the era, they were revolutionary. Increasing human output was not a science, dependent on the size of the shovel or the light in the room as previously thought; it was driven by social and psychological factors. In fact, Mayo's conclusions were so revolutionary that it took another 60 years for them to become part of mainstream management theory.

IT'S OK TO BE NEEDY
The Hawthorne project is a footnote in history compared to the work of American psychologist Abraham Maslow. His 'hierarchy of needs' can be almost guaranteed a mention in any management-training course, although for many years it appears that the mentioning was more thorough than the listening. One of the pioneers of modern leadership studies, Warren Bennis, believes few paid attention to Maslow at the time he was writing, because "a rather complacent industrial America, famously supreme since WWII, was not particularly interested in business books, especially by a psychologist who had no business expertise to speak of".[5] Yet Bennis argues Maslow's theories were decades ahead of their time. In 1943, Maslow's article 'A Theory of Human Motivation', described the five sets of needs he argues we all have. As each need is satisfied, we feel a desire to fulfil the next. It starts with physiological needs, our primary needs to eat and drink, for example. Our next need is for safety, shelter and security. Then comes

belonging – the need to feel part of a group and to be accepted. After that is self-esteem – our desire to feel good about ourselves and be recognised for our achievements. Our ultimate need is self-realisation or actualisation. When all other needs are met, we look for personal fulfilment, to grow and develop. There were no pyramids or triangles in the original paper but thanks to the management theorists who were later inspired by his work, a triangle or a staircase sliced into five parts has become synonymous with Maslow.

Maslow has his critics. What about the famished poet who would rather write than eat? What of the mountaineer who disregards safety in his determination to reach the summit? Since the 1940s, his hierarchy has been debated, relabelled, flipped on its head and turned sideways. But for all of that, Maslow put forward a theory that helped spark a more human, enlightened view of industrial relations. In his view, employees were not work-shy creatures who feared or loathed hard labour; who needed to be controlled, coerced and monitored to achieve anything. Instead, they each had individual psychological needs that required recognition and fulfilment. If employers satisfied these, they would create employees willing to give far more of themselves to their roles.

Maslow's work had a profound impact on major management figures writing in the second half of the 20th century. In 1960, Douglas McGregor published *The Human Side of Enterprise* in which he contrasted traditional managerial styles with a people-centric approach inspired by Maslow. McGregor believed "many of our attempts to control behaviour, far from representing selective adaptations, are in direct violation of human nature".[6] McGregor, like Maslow, believed employees at every level were much more than cogs in a machine and that "the distinctive potential contribution of the human being in contrast to the machine, at every level of the organisation, stems from his capacity to think, to plan, to exercise judgement, to be creative, to direct and control his own behaviour".[7]

To gain more from their people, organisations had to think again about the command-and-control of employees and instead adopt a management style that was more discursive and involving. McGregor worried at the time that "if there is a single assumption which pervades conventional organisation theory it is that authority is the central, indispensable means of managerial control".[8] Like Maslow, many think McGregor was ahead of his time. Forty years later, Peter Drucker wrote that "with every passing year, McGregor's message becomes ever more relevant, more timely, and more important."[9] Bennis agrees. In the foreword to the 25th anniversary printing of *The Human Side of Enterprise*, he writes: "This book, more than any other book on management, changed an entire concept of organisational man and replaced it with a new paradigm that stressed human potentials, emphasised human growth, and elevated the human role in industrial society."[10]

GETTING ENGAGED

Thanks to writers such as McGregor, a distinction was finally being made between a 'transactional' contract with an employee, in which he or she receives money in exchange for performing a specific set of tasks, and a more complex 'relational' contract, where an organisation offers opportunities for an individual to feel fulfilled, but expects more in return. Although a few visionary management theorists may have agreed, businesses were not rushing to put the theory into action. Indeed, if we fast-forward 30 years to the 1990s, William Kahn, a US professor in organisational behaviour, seems to echo their familiar theme. In the *Academy of Management Journal*, Kahn introduces the notion that people 'perform' their jobs and the more they draw on themselves to do this, the "more stirring are their performances".[11] Kahn is credited with coining the phrase 'the engaged employee', which he defined as those who conduct and express themself "physically, cognitively, or emotionally during their performances".[12] He set out the psychological conditions for such personal engagement – a variation on Maslow's hierarchy of needs. We need to feel our work is meaningful to us, it is safe to invest ourselves in the work and that we are available to do so. According to Kahn's research, "managerial reluctance to loosen their control sent a message that their employees were not to be trusted and should fear over-stepping their boundaries".[13] A manager's role should instead be to give employees the respect, freedom and confidence to feel safe enough to invest themselves fully in their work. A draconian, command-and-control culture saps personal initiative and responsibility – leading to an underused workforce.

By 2011, the concept of employee engagement had reached mainstream politics when Prime Minister David Cameron gave his backing to a new independent Employee Engagement Task Force. This was to spearhead a movement bringing together the experience of leading practitioners, the ideas and research of leading academics, and the findings of think tanks, to share learning, ideas and practical guidance on 'the what, the why and the how' of employee engagement.

SEARCHING FOR EXCELLENCE

This task force, which became the Engage for Success movement, was necessary because although the theory was clear, the practice had been a long time coming. In his best-selling book, *In Search of Excellence*, Tom Peters profiled companies achieving success through a people-centric approach. Like Mayo, Peters told us "attention to employees, not work conditions per se, has the dominant impact on productivity".[14] Annoyingly for Peters, many of the companies he wrote about in 1982 when the book was published took a wrong turn later – Sears, Xerox, IBM, Kodak, Hewlett-Packard. However, at the time his work taught us lessons about leadership, communication and, by implication, why so many organisations were finding it so difficult to achieve the same levels of excellence. As well as being close to the customer, these companies perceived their workers differently – not as innately lazy, uninterested or dumb, but quite the opposite; as the root source of quality and productivity gains. They built a culture of autonomy and entrepreneurship within the framework of strict and defining core values. He quotes a manager at General Motors: "Our control systems are designed under the apparent assumption that 90 per cent of the people are lazy ne'er-do-wells, just waiting to lie, cheat, steal, or otherwise screw us. We demoralise 95 per cent of the work force who do act as adults by designing systems to cover our tails against the 5 per cent who really are bad actors."[15] Peters concluded that the better performing companies did not design management systems for the lowest common denominator. "The excellent companies are the way they are because they are organised to obtain extraordinary effort from ordinary human beings."[16] Once again, it was being suggested that command-and-control should give way to something more fluid. Organisations needed "simultaneous loose-tight properties".[17] Peters believed "autonomy is a product of discipline. The discipline (a few shared values) provides the framework. It gives people confidence (to experiment, for instance), stemming from stable expectations about what really counts".[18]

Peters told us that you need a special mix of ingredients inside an organisation if it is to truly engage its employees, not least a defining and commanding vision and set of values.

"Men willingly shackle themselves to the nine-to-five only if the cause is perceived to be in some sense great."[19] You need a prevailing attitude among managers at all levels that competitive advantage and order are created not by issuing dictates but through trust and understanding. It is no wonder organisations were struggling to adopt this approach as it turned previous management theory on its head. McGregor explains "conventional organisation theory teaches us that power and authority are coextensive. Consequently, relinquishing authority is seen as losing the power to control. This is a completely misleading conception".[20]

DEALING IN KNOWLEDGE

As the 20th century drew to a close, corporates had only learned so much from writers like Peters. Few had moved away from their hierarchies or command-and-control cultures, although advances in information technology were forcing some to accept a new reality.

The Austrian economist, Fritz Machlup, is widely credited with having first used the phrase 'knowledge economy' in 1962. Four decades on, technological change that Machlup could barely have imagined was making his phrase a global buzzword. Successful and profitable organisations were making money from developing, sharing and selling ideas. To compete in this new economy, an organisation needed knowledge. A workforce that produced insight and ideas as opposed to widgets was clearly not an extension of the machinery. Indeed, inside these organisations there may be little or no machinery to speak of, just the same computing power that exists in many people's homes. Knowledge workers could not be managed like the workers of yesteryear with the provision of regular breaks, reasonable working conditions, fair pay, clear direction and benevolent management. These new 'proactive employees' were not, in writer Donald Campbell's view, employed simply to execute a manager's instructions fully and consistently. Instead they were employed for their sound judgement; they questioned and challenged authority because it was their job to do so. Firms attempting to harness the intelligence and creativity of these employees had to encourage "open communication, build trust and co-operation, and engage in consultation".[21]

If this sounds familiar it is because Mayo's work at the Hawthorne project reached the same conclusion nearly a century earlier but it was only now that businesses were really forced to sit up and take notice. In these industries their most valuable asset was highly mobile, even volatile, and in scarce supply. It left the building every night to hopefully return the next morning. To make matters worse, it was not enough to simply hire this talent and sit back. Breakthrough ideas came from creating an environment of collaboration, creative freedom, stimulation and inspiration. From 2010 onwards, despite widespread economic gloom and high rates of unemployment, there has been a war for talent as organisations struggle to find and keep the brightest and best. For a century, the gurus of management science had described how best to engage employees for maximum productivity. Now there is a subtle but vital shift in the argument. Properly engaging employees is not a 'nice to do' – a way to produce a little more each hour – it is the only way to stay in business. Peters quoted Thomas Watson at IBM, who reached this conclusion earlier than most, and explained: "Our early emphasis on human relations was not motivated by altruism but by the simple belief that if we respected our people and helped them to respect themselves, the company would make the most profit."[22]

BECOMING SOCIALLY ADEPT
In 2012 the McKinsey Global Institute published a report

entitled 'The Social Economy', charting the unprecedented speed and scale with which social technologies had been adopted. It had taken commercial television 13 years to reach 50 million households, the internet three years, Facebook one year and Twitter just nine months.[23] The report found 70 per cent of US corporates were using social media as a means of communication. It argues that social technologies promise to extend the capabilities of such high-skill workers "by stream-lining communication and collaboration, lowering barriers between functional silos, and even redrawing the boundaries of the enterprise to bring in additional knowledge and expertise in 'extended networked enterprises'".[23]

Social technologies make organisational boundaries more permeable, allowing individuals from outside the enterprise to participate in tasks that are traditionally performed by employ-ees. This is already apparent in the crowdsourcing of customers who are solicited en masse for contributions to new services, ideas or content.

Social is a feature not a product, claimed the McKinsey report. It has inexhaustible applications, freeing people from the limitations of the physical world to interact instantaneously on a global scale. Euan Semple, author of *Organisations Don't Tweet, People Do*, believes "it is easy to dismiss what is happening as technological – to label it 'digital' – and to miss the real point – the changes we are seeing are cultural." What we are witnessing is not a "technological revolution followed by a social change, but a social revolution made easier by technological change".[24]

TURKEYS DON'T VOTE FOR CHRISTMAS

There is now so much evidence of the benefits for organisa-tions treating employees as value drivers – as assets rather than costs – that the intellectual argument for this approach has been largely won. At the same time, technology now allows organisations the practical tools to reach out to their employees in new, more involving and interactive ways. So, why are organisations still holding back from truly engaging with their employees?

Perhaps we should not be surprised that our leaders have not rushed to embrace openness, inclusivity and power sharing within their organisations. As a leader, if your control is no longer based on issuing commands but on your relationship with, and influence over, your workforce, what control do you really have? If your importance to the firm rests on your ability, contribution and potential, not your grade, job title or pay scale, how truly important are you? If your decision-making must be open and transparent, can you cope with the increased scrutiny that will surely follow? Not every leader is equipped to operate in this new world order. Much of what they must do and how they must behave is a communication challenge. Our duty is to guide leadership teams through this new, uncharted territory and towards a promised land of profitable, innovative collaboration.

COMING FULL CIRCLE

There are parallels between the rise of employee engagement as a robust and commercially beneficial approach to managing people and the emergence of employee communication as something more than a broadcasting function. Once again the story starts with a few lone radicals daring to suggest that organisations should do more than bark instructions to their workers. One of the first was the American Alexander Heron who, in 1942, wrote a book on internal communication entitled *Sharing Information with Employees*. Heron was so far-sighted that his manifesto for employee communication is, even now, yet to be fully realised. Seventy years ago, Heron believed that employee communication should be "a two-way sharing of information; it is not a persuasion or propaganda campaign; it requires the freedom and opportunity to ask questions, get answers and exchange ideas".[25] The communication itself "should be a continuous one, a method of conduct rather than a campaign [...] it must not become an institution apart from the actual work or operation of the enterprise".[26] In contrast, much of what organisations have done since the industrial revolution is simply distribute information. Later, industrial editors and corporate communicators created something of an institution around this, but how much of this activity materially affected 'the actual work or operation of the enterprise'?

One of the first employee newsletters, *The Lowell Offering* (1840-1845), was written, edited and published by its readers – female operatives working at the New England Lowell Cotton Mills. It is unfortunate that 170 years later so many employee publications still lack anything close to such readership involvement. In their paper 'Tracking the rise and rise of internal communication from the 1980s', Kevin Ruck and Heather Yaxley note: "In reviewing the history of the house organ, it is curious that industrial editing was dominant for so long as it was very often management propaganda that did little to engage employees."[27] Vanity publishing may go some way to explaining this longevity.

FROM INDUSTRIAL EDITOR TO CORPORATE COMMUNICATOR

Internal communicators' first professional body in the UK, the British Association of Industrial Editors, was formed in 1949. A clue about the skills and activity of our profession at the time is in the name. Editors wrote corporate communications in various forms, often newsletters, and sent them to press. The early agencies specialising in helping corporates to communicate were formed in the 1960s. One of the first was

AB, founded by Anthony Buckley in 1964 and the agency I run today. The titles in our basement are a testament to that early period. They are largely tabloid newspapers for employees in companies still thriving today such as British American Tobacco, Initial and BP, and others long since gone, such as United Distillers, Allied Domecq, Allders Department Stores and Allied Lyons. They make for amusing reading with their 'page three lovelies' and rigid typeset design. But we would be wrong to dismiss them simply for looking dated. What AB and other agencies were doing was revolutionary – applying a Fleet Street approach to company newspapers. These were the first professionally created employee publications written and produced by trained editors, journalists, designers and photographers. AB's journalists could not have quite the same 'publish and be damned' mentality we like to think the national press enjoys. In reality, national newspaper editors have owners, shareholders and advertisers to consider. AB had, and indeed continues to have, corporate clients with a party line to communicate and plenty of sensitivities they would prefer to avoid or gloss over. But here was both the frustration and fascination of the job – guiding, cajoling and persuading private and public sector organisations to be open and honest with their employees. It is a challenge many of us still face today.

From the 1980s to 1990s, Kevin Ruck believes that "the scope of practice widens considerably as more channels become available, planning and measurement emerge, and there is more focus on persuasion during times of industrial unrest and change (e.g. privatisation in the UK)".[28] Certainly during this time, employee communication was becoming a more recognised and valued activity, although it was not widely seen as a discrete profession. The title of a handbook from the period, *Employee Communications in the 1980s: A Personnel Manager's Guide*, written by Michael Bland, gives this away. Employee communications was the responsibility of an 'editor' who sat within the personnel department. Bland's book is, among other things, a stark illustration of the sexism of the age. He suggests that you survey your workforce before deciding whether to picture a "scantily-clad girl" or "a full frontal nude" in your company's tabloid. According to the author: "A hint of nipple peeping through a wet blouse does a lot more to men than [a] starkly clinical set of mammaries... Keeping a few clothes on will also save you no end of trouble with the more prudish older female staff."[29] But amid these howlers, Bland also makes some more convincing points, writing that: "Many companies who pride themselves on their elaborate 'communication' are really only good at sending it one way. It's like a tennis player without an opponent, serving aces and priding himself on his great game."[30] In 1980, Bland had spotted the same problem Heron had identified back in 1942; we needed to stop broadcasting and start a conversation.

HELLO? ANYONE OUT THERE?

Bland was complaining in the 1980s, "all the resources go in the management-to-employee direction. The PR department, the company newspaper, the audio-visual equipment, communication budget, all are concentrated with passing stuff down the line rather than back up it again."[31] How much has really changed? Too often, when employees are invited to speak up today, this is another monologue rather than an exchange of views. Despite many feedback mechanisms and surveys, employees still do not know if anyone is really listening; whether their views have been understood, or if anyone cares about them. The standard measurement tool for the corporate communicator was, and still often is, the all-employee engagement survey, frequently another one-way communication exercise. Despite being branded 'Your Shout' or 'Speak

Up', they rarely contain open questions and may only happen annually. The delays associated with processing results means that any subsequent action is so removed from the asking, that employees often find it hard to connect changes to their original feedback. The instantaneous nature of social media makes this annual check-up and delayed response look highly antiquated. David Fairhurst, senior vice-president of people for McDonald's, questions the approach: "Why would you wait months to understand the mood of your employees, when in just a few seconds you can understand reactions to what is happening, not what has happened?"[32]

HONOURABLE INTENTIONS

As the acceptance of the commercial advantage of an engaged workforce gained ground in the late 1990s, partly thanks to the work of Kahn and others, it was not coincidental that employee communication teams grew in size and stature. We were bringing the organisation's strategy to life in new, more meaningful ways, broadening the scope of our work to face-to-face events, team briefings, film and business TV, intranet sites and behavioural change programmes. The content pumped down these channels was also changing; we were communicating not just what was happening and when, but also why. We conveyed values and shared the CEO's vision – when he or she had one. We looked for the great stories that brought this vision to life and tried to help employees feel a sense of belonging, explaining how their contribution counted. Our intentions were honourable. Whether we had read the management theories or not, we wanted to help employees connect with their organisations on a more visceral level, the argument being that the deeper the connection, the deeper employees' commitment and the better their performance. More often than not, we also tried to make it an interesting read.

James Surowiecki, author of *The Wisdom of Crowds*, believes there was a paradox at play during the 1990s. We were paying greater attention to bottom-up mechanisms and pursuing decentralisation while also treating our CEOs as superheroes. For a communicator, both then and now, it is hard to resist the lure of an enigmatic CEO, who can and wants to communicate. But it was dangerous to rely on a cascade of one to many – from the CEO to 'the troops' – and wed ourselves to the madness of the organisational 'organogram'. Despite our shiny new pipes, communication was still flowing, or sometimes trickling, down the hierarchy. We might have identified a few 'local champions' to add context and meaning to our message but we were not yet thinking of the organisation as it really was; a central nervous system of connected and disconnected individuals. Peters quotes HP's founder David Packard on this very subject: "If an organisation is to work effectively, the communication should be through the most effective channel, regardless of the organisational chart... I've often thought that after you get organised, you ought to throw the chart away."[33] In the view of communication experts Janet Fulk and Gerardine DeSanctis, "yesterday's organisation reflected the metaphor of a tree – with a common trunk of communication linking progressively smaller branches up to a peak representing top management control – today's organisation is more like a nervous system: a multi-centred entity with governance and operations managed differently at different centres".[34] In this new environment, without rigid and steep hierarchies, information is exchanged mutually, regardless of grade, seniority and position. Many communicators spent too long 'segmenting audiences' and 'mapping the process' according to sender, receiver, gatekeeper, stakeholder and so on. Instead, we should have concentrated more on ways to give everyone permission, confidence and space to converse with –

and hopefully influence – each other.

YOU'VE GOT (TOO MUCH) MAIL

The impact of digital communication on the communicator's toolkit was initially felt with email, which arrived in the early 1990s. This gave executives and communication teams a new means of disseminating yet more information. In those early years, emails were often sent from an anonymous 'outbox' to vast and poorly maintained distribution lists. Replies were not expected or encouraged. Email was the perfect broadcast mechanism and, for many, it still is. It is fast, inexpensive and easy. Today we ask employees to be candid; how many of these impersonal, broadcast emails do they delete before opening? If there was an 'unsubscribe' button, would they use it? The percentage of unread, unwanted email is very high. If a significant percentage of recipients would elect not to receive these emails, communication teams need to ask why.

For those who can remember working life before email, it is a business tool without precedent. It has enabled us to work with greater speed and agility. But an exchange of emails is not a real conversation. More often than not, it enables us to avoid a conversation. Few employees have been trained to use email effectively. Too many organisations need to weaned off an over-reliance on email and as communicators we need to look for more collaborative and social solutions.

FALLING THROUGH THE NET

Soon after email came intranets. These closed networks promised much. They were heralded as 'business tools' rather than communication channels that (we were all told) would increase operational efficiency, reduce email traffic and help us collaborate in new ways. A few intranets delivered at least parts of this dream but many did not. Many became dusty libraries of old, uncatalogued information with poor search facilities.

As communicators, any failings of the intranet were all too often seen as 'not our problem'. Few of us built, owned or controlled them – certainly not beyond the home page. Our internal communication budgets did not stretch to overhauling them, and even if they had, we lacked skills and confidence in internet protocol and information technology to rebuild them. Slowly that began to change. Even if we could not own or run these channels, at the very least we needed to become advisers, to guide their development. In some cases communications teams have helped intranets become what they should be – a core, multi-media channel carrying live news updates, detailed profile pages for employees to encourage interaction and co-operation, places for discussion, and a well maintained and structured corporate library of tools and information. But most intranets continue to fall far short of this ideal. They do not drive operational efficiency and, sadly, they have not reduced email traffic. Few we see today are places for collaboration.

EMBRACING OUR SOCIAL SELVES

With the rise of social media, traditional borders between the internal and external are being dismantled – intranet and internet are less clearly distinguishable. Increasingly, the sites we build for employees are now accessible from any device connected to the web, even if some keep their content password-protected. At the time of writing, Asda, Royal Mail, Post Office and Tesco all have websites for employees than can be seen by anyone. This new approach uses transparency to the organisation's advantage. It says if you want to go looking for information about us, whoever you are, feel free – we have nothing to hide; indeed, whatever you do find will reinforce our good name and values.

As communicators, we once gave our audiences labels

– employee, franchisee, shareholder, customer, regulator, prospect. Now people are more likely to skip between groups or have the social technology to spread their sphere of influence far wider than their immediate peers. 'Social' does not only rely on transparency but on an authentic, accountable voice. It frequently exposes information, values and even individuals that may have before been hidden behind a corporate edifice. It also exposes those leaders whose position relies on people not knowing. According to Euan Semple, a boss might be nervous of social media because they understand its potential only too well: "Once people learn that they can find each other, share their knowledge, and work together the roles of many managers will change if not disappear. This is frightening. However, good managers will make the effort to adapt and will continue to add value in the more networked world we are moving into."[35]

CONTENT IS NO LONGER FIXED AND FINITE

The 2012 McKinsey report on the social economy states: "In addition to enabling people to interact socially...social technologies allow anyone within a group to create, add, or modify content and communications."[36] Wikis, blogs, shared workspaces, ratings and reviews, social gaming, forums and social networks mean that content is no longer a fixed and finite product. It is fluid, dynamic and less able to be contained and controlled. This is not without precedent; the report compares it to the oral tradition where stories were passed informally from person to person across a community and through time, reshaped by each generation. Communication should, as it traditionally was, be a conversation rather than a monologue, over which its originator (in this case the organisation) has less control. Some leaders are nervous of a communication free-for-all, not admitting even to themselves that employees have always been free and perfectly willing to converse openly, at least in private. By the turn of the 21st century, although technology was enabling faster, more fluid and less structured communication, both organisations and audiences were not yet taking full advantage of the opportunities this offered. We were all still shouting into a dark room; no one was quite sure who was there or who was listening. The most strategic conversations continued to take place behind closed doors – often on the executive floor – while employees aired their views, to each other, in the pub after work, round the water cooler or with their trade union representatives. Today, with digital and web technology more pervasive, workers can do this publicly on any website, blog or online forum beyond the reach of their corporation. The era of command-and-control – at least of the message – is finally dead.

According to Semple: "The trouble with much corporate training on this issue is that it is still very focused around delivering 'content' to people who then 'consume' it rather than about informed conversations between people learning from each other and passing on the latest knowledge."[37] This has implications for the corporate communicator; rather than drafting every corporate message as a fait accompli, he or she might be better kick-starting a discussion about it. If this becomes a genuine discussion, where both sides are listening, the result will be a more effective and meaningful message. Knowledge and experience will have been shared and understanding deepened, which is entirely the point of all good communication.

EMPLOYEE COMMUNICATION ON THE PRECIPICE

We have witnessed the gradual development of employee communication from publishing to a broader, more strategic role, which by the late 1990s encapsulated employee engagement, change management and the 'employee value proposition'. John Smythe, author of *The Velvet Revolution at Work*, believes that today internal communication "lies at a crossroads between being the radio station of the powerful and being a contributor to sustaining a healthy workplace where expression and constructive challenge by employees is encouraged and enabled"[38]. We have seen how internal communicators have moved beyond writing, subbing and proofreading. We have become digitally savvy. We have developed our powers of persuasion. Executives have proved increasingly open to receiving our advice on how best to inspire and influence their workforce, provided we demonstrate at least a modicum of business acumen. We have a sophisticated array of channels at our disposal. We understand the importance of feedback and dialogue. We know information should not flow one way. Our executive teams listen – in the main – to our advice about how to craft the message. In the interests of transparency, we are breaking down barriers between internal and external communication. We are able to question decisions before they are made, not simply window dress them afterwards. We are making our communications more social and authentic – losing the corporate-speak for something that sounds more like people talking.

In short, we are heading in the right direction. The next step is not just to make corporate communication sound like people talking, but to actively engage people in true conversation.

In conversation with Tony Buckley

Anthony Buckley founded the internal communications agency, AB, in 1964. A young entrepreneur who had already managed a City of London printing company at just 22, Tony later rented a desk and telephone in an office above Ronnie Scott's Jazz Club in Soho, London. There he started a company that would produce newspapers and magazines for hundreds of thousands of employees around the world.

He offers a stark insight into the state of internal communication when he entered the industry: a post-war London full of managers failing to connect with their employees.

Your experience was in mass circulation in an industry where newspapers were in their prime. What made a successful Fleet Street publisher consider internal communication?
There was a huge gap in the market. I've never been a journalist, but as a publisher I could see how organisations could benefit from the impartiality of qualified journalists. I looked at the people creating in-house titles and I knew we could do better. Approaching it in a different way was a niche I could develop.

Back then there was not the plethora of consumer magazines we see on newsstands today. Tabloid newspapers were in
their prime and that is why, when proposing a new or revised
publication for a client, it was often in a tabloid format similar
to the Daily Mirror or Evening Standard – it was a style readers
knew well.

**In those early days, what was wrong with how companies were
communicating with their people?**
Many senior managers deemed it was sufficient to make an
announcement on a noticeboard or with a memo. That was not
engagement – it was certainly not conversation. I felt faceless,
corporate announcements were detrimental to the morale of
the employees. That is not to say management teams of the
time were actively choosing to communicate poorly or disengage with their people. They just did not have the skills – they
were there to run companies. Communication did not come
naturally to them.

Many did not realise there were teams like ours – with
qualified journalists and typesetters who could put an entire
publication together from start to finish. Fewer realised our
publications could act as a bridge between management and
the frontline.

**A bridge should benefit both sides. Many companies still strug-
gle with genuine two-way communication between frontline
staff and management; so how difficult was it to make two-way
communication a reality back then?**
I think a communications company like ours has a privileged
position. In the early days, we tried to gain the respect of both
sides for everything we published – those who sent the message
and those who read it. Later, management teams became more
aware that the workforce was more than just a group of people

fulfilling a specific task or purpose. They realised it would be beneficial to truly engage with them – to help them understand what their company was trying to achieve. Educating clients about employee engagement was undoubtedly one of our biggest challenges. Pitching for internal communication was more about helping the client to realise the value of engagement rather than dazzling them with fancy designs.

Without engagement there is no real communication. It has to be reciprocal. No management team is an island, its workforce can always add something positive. That was the moment of realisation for many clients and it was always very rewarding for us as internal communicators to watch it happen.

Get it right and ideas cross-pollinate from one part of the company to another. This often led to financial savings or operational efficiencies. It was not just about people at the coalface feeling valued. There can be real commercial power in the ideas of everyone on the payroll.

This approach was not just novel for management teams; how about employees – how did they feel about being targeted in this way?
It was alien to them, to put it bluntly! And that made it all the more challenging to get readers to trust us. The constant challenge for an agency like ours is maintaining our integrity as an impartial, objective commentator in the eyes of employees when they know their corporation pays us. In some ways it was more of a challenge to win the trust of audiences than it was the buy-in of management.

The key turning point was when readers realised the in-house title was there for the good of the company as a whole, not just the management.

There can be situations where employees feel very strongly about something but they do not speak up because they fear for their jobs. We acted as an independent third-party, mediating the debate. Of course, there is never any guarantee that a management team will act on the information it hears or that employees will always understand the company line, but getting both sides to at least listen to, and hopefully understand, each other can be of huge worth.

What did success look like for you in AB's early years?
Successfully swimming against the tide of a company's financial department! Internal communication was often the first thing to get hit when budgets needed trimming. We lost some lucrative pitches for new business because senior management saw the title we offered as completely separate from what they were doing day-to-day, when we saw it as integral.

All organisations have their own constant, captive audience. This is a great luxury in the publishing business. Companies do not have to rely on people going out and actively picking up or purchasing a newspaper or magazine – it is delivered directly to readers. It was very satisfying to see leaders realise the potential of their in-house title.

Success was getting people to listen to each other and building that bridge between the frontline and the top of the hierarchy. I always had faith that AB would succeed because there's always a place for impartial experts, especially when these specialists are a family of journalists with the utmost integrity, like those who have come and gone at AB over its 50 years.

Chapter 2

Why conversation works

MAN THE SOCIAL ANIMAL

Few of us need convincing of the power of a conversation. Humans have an innate desire to share information – not merely to preach or present but to *converse*. We are wired to expect a response from others. Imagine what would happen if you passed a colleague in the corridor, smiled a 'hello' and he blanked you. You would probably be both annoyed and curious. What's up with him? Have you upset him? Should you check he's ok? This need for a response is evident even when we are in broadcast mode, speaking to a group, for example. It becomes difficult to present when there is no response from the room. Comedians call it 'dying on your feet' for good reason. It is also what makes the ability to talk interestingly and fluently to the dead eye of a camera lens so difficult. As a presenter, I look for – *long for* – at least a few people in the audience who are responding to what I am saying. It might be a knowing smile, a slight nod of the head. However solitary it may feel to stand at a lectern, a speaker is never isolated from the room. The interaction with the audience starts as soon as you get up from your seat.

Of course, a genuine conversation should be a very different kind of an exchange to a presentation. We have all been on the receiving end of a monologue dressed up as a conversation. An exchange where you feel that your presence is purely perfunctory has none of the benefits of true conversation. We are far less likely to listen and engage if we feel there is no chance to contribute and collaborate.

Even in a genuine exchange of views, misunderstandings can occur. Everything we say is interpreted through the eyes and ears of others. What is received and understood is not within our control. That is why, if you ask for six views on the success of a group discussion, you are likely to receive six differing answers. The interpretation of what took place is filtered through a personal lens born from our history and experience. We can aid understanding with a considered choice of words, body language and tonality, but every conversation is a leap of faith. We can only hope we are conveying the meaning we intend. Yet, despite the ever-present danger of misinterpretation and misunderstanding, we connect with each other every day.

WHAT IS CONVERSATION?

A real conversation is a genuine exchange of information between two people or more. It is not people talking *at* each other – each following their own train of thought, barely listening or reacting to the other. Meaningful and effective conversations will be taking place every day inside your organisation. Your business would collapse without them. But as a communicator or leader, it is not practical or desirable for you to influence or manage a million daily exchanges. This book is about cultivating, guiding and managing the conversations that are central to the success of your organisation. In their book, *Talk, Inc.*, Professor Boris Groysberg and consultant Michael Slind call these 'organisational conversations'. [1] These are conversations with purpose. The reason for their existence is linked to the aspirations of the organisation – they fulfil a strategic goal. These are the conversations that build trust between colleagues; that lead to more ingenious ideas and sharper solutions; and that feel motivational for those involved. As well as being a more effective way to communicate, there is an amazing by-product from having the right kind of conversations at work – they drive engagement and productivity.

Consequential and constructive conversations make work a less transactional experience, encouraging us to give more of ourselves in our roles. William Kahn, an authority on employee engagement, tells us: "Meaningful interactions promote dignity, self-appreciation and a sense of worthwhileness."[2] This is exactly what Elton Mayo discovered in the 1920s earlier during the Hawthorne experiments. Genuinely soliciting the opinions and perceptions of his test group of female workers increased motivation and, as a consequence, output. If this was true for factory workers, it is doubly true for today's knowledge workers. Brainpower does not come to life with the flick of a management switch. It needs to be developed, coaxed and stimulated. Having a workforce of knowledgeable people operating in neutral cripples your greatest commercial asset. In *The Wisdom of Crowds*, James Surowiecki writes: "Intelligence alone is not enough, because intelligence alone cannot guarantee you different perspectives on a problem."[3] There are many reasons to collaborate, which we address in the next chapter, but all collaboration is in essence a structured conversation.

LEARNING TO LISTEN

There are plenty of books on social etiquette – this is not one of them. Most give hints and tips on body language, making eye contact, asking open questions and avoiding sensitive topics. However, the skill that matters most – the one that needs regular practice and deeper consideration especially in a corporate setting – is the ability to listen.

David Weinberger is author of the brilliantly titled *Too Big to Know: Rethinking Knowledge Now that the Facts aren't the Facts, Experts are Everywhere, and the Smartest Person in the Room is the Room* and co-author of *The Cluetrain Manifesto*. He tells us "conversations occur only between equals."[4] So, while hierarchies and seniority are often vital to the smooth running of an organisation, when it comes to conversation, your pay grade and rank are best left outside the room. Keith Sawyer, author of *Group Genius,* advises managers who really want to engage in conversation "participate in the same way as everyone else by listening closely and granting autonomy and authority to the group's emergent decision processes".[5]

The best conversationalists are the best listeners. Accordingly, Tom Peters tells us "excellent companies are better listeners".[6] Leaders who take organisational conversation seriously know when to stop talking and start listening. In Groysberg and Slind's view, real attentiveness leads to real intimacy.[7] Nancy Klein goes further, and believes that good listeners lead to more articulate speakers: "When you are listening to someone, much of the quality of what you are hearing is your effect on them. Giving good attention to people makes them more intelligent. Poor attention makes them stumble over their words and seem stupid. Your attention, your listening is that important."[8]

As business consultants, the deep and undivided attention we give clients, our probing for information and obvious desire to truly understand their problems, builds intimacy and trust. This transcends the non-disclosure agreement and results in a very privileged peek inside the client's mind and their organisation. We often joke that we feel like therapists. An outsider's perspective helps us to enter conversations on an equal footing with both CEOs and frontline staff. By being outside the internal hierarchy, it is easier for us to create an atmosphere of attentive openness. For those within the hierarchy, and particularly those trying to change a culture of command-and-control, they have to work – and listen – even harder to establish intimacy and build trust.

Management scholar Edgar Schien suggests that the way to escape hierarchy is though the 'humble enquiry'. It is through asking questions that leaders can "build relationships that are based on mutual respect and the recognition that others know things that we may need to know in order to get the job done"[9]. He worries that the "social art of asking a question has been strangely neglected"[10] in favour of more sophisticated ways of barking commands. A question at once places a leader in the more vulnerable role, asking for help and recognising the expertise of another. Schien urges leaders to adopt "an attitude of interest and curiosity"[11].

SEARCHING INSIDE OURSELVES

To listen – really listen – takes time and practice. Mindfulness is one way of teaching us how to do this, to check understanding and listen openly without judging. Mindfulness is not a new concept but is currently in vogue as our world gets noisier. It is a technique that uses breathing and meditation to clear the mind and be present in the moment. The United States military, educationalists and a growing number of businesses are training people in mindfulness. The principles and practice of 'mindful leadership' are taught at Harvard, while Oxford University's dedicated Mindfulness Centre is carrying out research into its clinical and general health benefits.

Google engineer Chade-Meng Tan has created a mindfulness programme to boost emotional intelligence, which has been taught at Google since 2007. It claims remarkable results – increasing people's creativity, helping to form stronger bonds between colleagues, encouraging collaboration and ultimately, driving productivity. In 2012, Tan published *Search Inside Yourself*[12] – a book based on the programme. Both the book and programme are divided into three key stages:

- Attention training – creating a quality of mind that is calm and clear
- Self-knowledge and self-mastery – increasing perception of your own cognitive and emotional processes, resulting in an ability to view yourself objectively from a third-party perspective
- Creating useful mental habits – developing new, instinctive thoughts that are unconsciously picked up by others and that build goodwill and trust.

In a chapter entitled 'Mindfulness Without Butt on Cushion' (Tan has a very particular sense of humour), he describes how to use mindfulness techniques to bring wandering attention back to the moment in everyday situations, most especially at work.

In extreme circumstances, the ability to listen is a matter of life or death. As a hostage negotiator working with the Metropolitan Police, United Nations and FBI, Richard Mullender developed finely tuned listening skills. It is unlikely that Mullender would attach the label 'mindfulness' to the skills he teaches. For him, listening well has saved lives. He is a self-proclaimed 'Formula One listener'.

Mindful listening, however it is referred to, is about adopting a "generous attitude to someone who is speaking"[13] and having the right mental state while listening. Tan writes: "Remind yourself that this person is valuable to you, entitled to your attention and the space and time needed to express herself or himself."[14] As you listen, give your full attention to the speaker. If you find your attention drifting, gently bring it back to the speaker as if she or he was an object of meditation. As Mullender explains: "There are no shortcuts or models that will let you get away without paying full attention."[15] Try not to 'over acknowledge' what the speaker is saying – you may inadvertently influence them. If they fall silent, do not rush to fill the void. I particularly agree with Tan and Mullender on this point. Many years of reporting have taught me that what someone says after a moment of contemplation is often the most important and poignant.

Having mastered mindful listening, the next step is mindful conversation. This involves 'closing the loop of communication' by giving feedback to the speaker on what you thought you heard – checking you have understood him or her correctly. In practice sessions, the mindful listener says: "What I hear you say is…" The high-pressure negotiations that Mullender has experienced in his working life mean he places particular importance on checking understanding. He advises you phrase this 'check' in a way that places the blame for any misinterpretation squarely with the listener. By telling someone they feel a certain way, you are likely to infuriate and isolate them if you get it wrong. But by asking, or suggesting how you *think* they might be feeling, if you do get it wrong, it becomes their responsibility to explain themselves more accurately.

Listening in this way also involves 'dipping' or checking in with ourselves. According to Tan, the main reason we do not listen to others is our own feelings and internal chatter – often a reaction to what has just been said – detract us. Tan says the best way to respond to these internal distractions is to notice and acknowledge them. "Know they are there, try not to judge them, and let them go… If they are willing to go."[16] This practice can also be used when we are speaking. It helps us to understand what feelings are arising as we are talking.

LISTENING FOR VALUES

Mullender believes "people always give themselves away by the words they use".[17] He feels it is easier to modify our body language to appear more confident or self-assured but harder to modify our words – get someone talking for long enough and their words will eventually betray them. The words we use reveal our personal values and priorities. Mullender, unlike Tan, is purely pragmatic in his motivation for unearthing these. "The moment I have your values, I can impose them back on you. You will not change your behaviour by adopting my values, but you might change your course of action if your current behaviour conflicts with your own values."[17] The best way to convince a pacifist to buy a gun, for example, is to construct an argument using his or her values – *who better to own a gun than someone who would never use it?*

Speaking to a roomful of communicators, Mullender gave the dramatic example of a domestic siege situation where a violent husband, suspecting his wife of adultery, beats her, ties her up and pours petrol over her. After talking to him for sometime, the highly agitated husband says to Mullender: "Tell me what you would do? You work hard, you earn a living, you look after your family and this is what happens! What am I supposed to do?" This is the moment the man reveals who he really is – someone who loves and looks after his family. With the man's values revealed, Mullender can use those values to his advantage. His response to the man was: "I don't want to speak with the angry man who's threatening to set fire to his wife. Let me speak to the man that loves and cares for his family." By uncovering the values of an individual, it is far easier to engage with them at a deeper level, and ultimately persuade them to your way of thinking if necessary. Mullender's experience reminds us that listening hard for someone's values can be far more revealing than merely observing their behaviour and leaping to our own conclusions.

This turns on its head the notion that employees can or should adopt corporate values and behaviours. As communicators, many of us have tried to 'bring to life' a series of often anodyne corporate values by asking employees questions like: What does 'challenging' mean to you? Mullender's approach suggests we are wasting our time. We should jettison these corporate values and instead listen for those in the room. These are what drive everyday behaviour and beliefs. We should turn the question on its head: How can the corporate strategy harness the values that already exist? What if employees need to change – to become more flexible or differently skilled, for example? The same rule applies: do not impose values from outside. A blue-collar, highly unionised workforce may believe in loyalty, hard work and fair play. A white-collar workforce may believe in professional recognition, development and self-fulfilment. Both may need to change, but as Mullender argues, framing the message in the values, language and beliefs of the employees concerned will get the job done more effectively. In fact, when people are faced with the uncertainty and anxiety of change, it is the very worst time to ask them to adopt values that are not their own.

Mullender takes the idea of non-judgemental responses further than Tan. He believes that any declarations of empathy are inherently presumptive and provocative. "The worst thing I can say to a hostage taker is 'I understand'. Of course I don't understand... Our personal world view has been shaped by things that have happened to us as children and as adults... our experience has meant we have developed coping mechanisms that enable us to survive. For me to believe that I can understand you so well that I can even understand your coping mechanisms is arrogant beyond belief."[18] In corporate life, I have met leaders who too quickly say 'I understand how you feel' to an assembled group of employees when they only visit them twice a year, have a series of short, superficial conversations, give rehearsed answers to planted questions, then leave. In these circumstances, saying 'I understand' is purely antagonistic. Entering into a genuine dialogue to gather and test understanding is far more beneficial to both parties.

I WISH I HADN'T ASKED

It is important that managers and communicators are not just listening actively, but are also being seen to be listening. Internationally renowned psychologist Daniel Goleman says: "People who seem easy to talk to are those who get to hear more."[19] The better leaders want to understand and show they are open to hearing feedback. Having learned about the views and concerns of their workforce, they demonstrate this understanding by replaying these views, even when they are negative. *You told us that we handled that change process badly. We rushed it through without proper consultation. You felt unnerved and frustrated. Some of you felt it was the worst experience of your careers.* Having asked for feedback, leaders should not bury it, even if the response is not what they were hoping for.

As their advisers, we should encourage our leaders to acknowledge what they have heard openly and publicly, and give recognition to the feelings being expressed by the words employees have used. This will help the workforce feel understood and, while it may not address the root cause of their unhappiness, it shows that speaking up is worth the effort, their message got through.

Employees quickly stop contributing their views – negative or positive – if there is no one 'looping' their feedback by checking and reiterating what they have said. When they stop talking upwards, managers should not imagine that their employees have suddenly stopped talking altogether. By creating blocks to communication within the organisation, companies leave themselves liable to forcing conversations outwards, where there is little or no shield from the public eye. Websites such as glassdoor, ratemyemployer and thejobcrowd give any employee a forum to discuss their company. Many large organisations have dedicated unofficial websites where employees can rave or, more likely, rant. This forces both problems and great ideas away from the gaze and control of leadership, which means they are less able to address either.

When we undertake our Acid Test audit – a series of open questions about the health of an organisation asked in confidential, face-to-face interviews – we insist that everyone being interviewed, from the CEO to the most junior employee, receives a full and frank report on our findings. Clients often hesitate, which is curious given that we are only replaying what the participants already think and feel. Similarly, when delivering feedback from our Acid Test audit to a senior team, we can see immediately who round the table finds the mere act of listening to feedback rather uncomfortable. The better leaders acknowledge their colleagues' disquiet but say everyone must listen because disagreeing with feedback does not invalidate it. As Aristotle wrote: "It is the mark of an educated mind to be able to entertain a thought without accepting it."[20] But it takes courage, confidence and patience to listen to views we find hard to accept.

Leaders find it particularly difficult to deal with critical feedback because, as head of the organisation, they may feel personally culpable for any weaknesses or failing. They may also fear criticism will spread and once-happy employees will be negatively influenced by hearing the concerns and troubles of their colleagues. The 'let's keep a lid on it' approach is naïve and counterproductive. People talk and rumours spread however many controls you try to impose. As communicators, our message to leaders must be 'tell it like it is'. In this way you will build credibility and trust. You may disagree with the feedback you hear, but do not dismiss it. Show you have heard; then explain the counter view. You may still have to plough on – the factory may close, the team may be restructured – but managing change is easier when there is open dialogue and trust.

COMMUNICATING INSIDE OUT

I guarantee there have been times when your senior colleagues have resisted talking to employees. When the topic is sensitive and the deadline looming, executives can quickly retreat, especially from those who might hold an opposing view. In the run-up to a significant event or when a major announcement is due – an acquisition, merger or sale, for example – executives often lock themselves away in an 'echo chamber', a phrase used by David Weinberger to describe places where "like-minded people listen only to those people who already agree with them".[21] Here, they hone an 'approved' message with colleagues who know better than to challenge. In these situations, an announcement is often made to both internal and external audiences at roughly the same time. Our job as internal communicators is to help contextualise it for employees – to give the announcement personal meaning to those affected. *Yes, the business did make £3bn profit but unfortunately you work in a loss-making part of the business, which has suffered in recent years from fierce competition.* The extent to which our efforts are successful depends on how often we step out of our echo chambers to consult with our audiences before the announcement.

In most UK FTSE organisations, senior management spend time briefing analysts ahead of a major announcement so that on the day of the full or interim results, there are few surprises for the market. Sadly, the same time and effort is rarely spent briefing staff. The reason given is often the Stock Exchange 'close period', which is typically one month preceding the release of quarterly results or two months before annual results. The close period is intended to prevent insider trading – or people acting on information not yet in the public domain. Athenahealth, a US company, got around statutory constraints by making its employees legal 'insiders' before an initial public offering. John Hallock, director of global corporate communications, knew it was risky but embraced that risk "and the responsibility that comes with it. It's core to our internal communications strategy".[22] The company takes employee engagement seriously, publishing its internal transfer and promotion rate on its website (25 per cent), and a comprehensive benefits and perks package for potential 'athenistas'.

It is time to see employees as the principal audience – a constituency that, above all others, holds the key to success. As Gary C Kelly, CEO of SouthWest Airlines, explains: "We take good care of our staff. Our staff take good care of our customers. And our customers take good care of our shareholders."[23] Whatever role an employee might perform today, he or she has the potential to be a spokesman, salesperson and manager of your organisation. Many companies today consciously turn their employees into ambassadors. Nike has 'official evangelists'. Hewlett-Packard has 'demo days' where employees are invited to perform demonstrations of HP products in stores, and Body Shop asks staff to test and review its products for customers. Steven Van Belleghem, author of *The Conversation Company*, argues: "In our modern society every employee of a company is jointly responsible for the experience of the consumers."[24] In his view, marketing is too important to be left to the marketeers alone.

However, employees should not be treated as insiders when

the going is good then shut out when things become difficult. If a leadership team is trusted, it may be granted some leniency if, on occasions, its communications falters. But employees are harsh critics and trust needs to be fostered and maintained continuously. As communications consultant Gary F Grates explains: "When you're an employee, you see the warts. You see under the rug."[25] At a recent HR conference, I was astonished to discover that I felt more passionately about certain retail brands as a customer than some of their senior employees. The brand promise could be maintained for a customer like me who might visit a store once a month, but not for those who see behind the scenes every day. Yet, if you can make an advocate out of someone who knows your company intimately, the stories they tell, and the passion they convey, will be hugely persuasive.

TRUST IN ME

Trust is a recurring motif in studies about leadership and team success. Patrick Lencioni's *Five Dysfunctions of a Team* starts with the absence of trust. It is the root cause of all other dysfunctional behaviour. Without trust, team members protect themselves from others; they tread warily and do not want to be seen as vulnerable. Real issues are not openly addressed because no one will admit to a weakness or failing. Instead, people busily protect their own patch and egos, often ignoring 'the elephant in the room'. Entering into an open and honest dialogue, where we show vulnerability or a human failing, may build trust but it becomes harder as we climb the corporate ladder. The ascent to the top can be combative, leaving leaders cautious, wary and cynical. As a result, once in a position of authority, some leaders rarely let down their guard. The cultural impact can be significant – a downward spiral of circumspection where leaders do not know who to trust, nor do they invite trust from others. One manifestation of this is micro-management – a surefire way to disenfranchise and disengage those most capable members of a team.

Forming bonds and building trust are not the only reasons conversations are valuable in the workplace. They help us test our thinking. Great ideas rarely spring fully formed from our minds. We test, analyse and rehearse our ideas on others. It is their reactions – especially those we feel are our equals or we want to impress – that shape our thoughts. We put forward the beginnings of an idea for feedback and critique. We do this because we know it is better to get more than one perspective on a problem. The idea of the lone genius creating something amazing in a moment of revelation is false, says Keith Sawyer. Sawyer researched various companies looking for those lightbulb moments – radical breakthroughs, such as the invention of TV, the airplane, email, and even the board game Monopoly. All emerged from collaboration, and for him what drives this collaboration is conversation.[26] Having people at all levels willing and able to converse openly – sharing, critiquing and building on each other's ideas – creates an intelligent organisation, one that is able to learn from itself and grow.

STEP AWAY FROM THE MEGAPHONE

In many organisations, a hierarchical, command-and-control operation is being replaced by a more collaborative style of management. Instead of handing down commands or impos-ing formal controls, many leaders are interacting with their workforces in ways that call to mind "an ordinary conversa-tion between two people",[27] say Groysberg and Slind. These 'ordinary conversations' have a number of organisational benefits. The authors believe that through conversation, a big organisation can "retain or recapture much of the nimbleness, the cohesiveness and the raw productive energy of a well-oiled small company".[28] This is because organisational conversation closes the distance – both physical and psychological – between people, particularly between managers and their reports.

To truly close this gap, as well as listening attentively, leaders need to let down their guard. Groysberg and Slind give examples of leaders who have shared highly personal stories with their employees. By making themselves demonstrably vulnerable and open, these executives were able to begin to gain the trust of their frontline. To launch its diversity and inclusion campaign, senior managers at the US company Exelon recorded very personal videos of what diversity means to them. A senior financial executive, for example, talked about his experience of class prejudice in childhood. Howard N Karesh, director of communication at the company, says that when a senior executive shares a clearly private moment with employees it is "very, very powerful".[29] I saw this work equally powerfully inside a UK bank when one of its senior executives became the sponsor of an LGBT campaign. As a well-known figure, his insight and personal perspective positively influenced how people thought of him and the campaign.

ORGANISATIONS THAT TALK TOO MUCH

There are organisations that like to deliberate and discuss, where employees who want to get something done, particularly against a tight deadline, complain that there is too much debate and not enough action. In partnerships, for example, or cultures built on consensus, the frustration for many is that decisions must be pondered and approved by a vast array of individuals often tangential to a project before it can proceed. Conversations in these organisations can feel frustrating and be seen as thwarting progress.

When discussions happen at the wrong time and when their purpose is unclear, they can do more harm than good. In these circumstances, we often see 'design by committee' where a once good idea gets diluted, distorted and eventually becomes unrecognisable thanks to endless rounds of reviews and revisions. To avoid this, be precise about which individuals need to be involved in a project (and its associated discussions), when, and for what purpose. Some people may need to contribute their ideas, others may need to give their approval to proceed, and others may need to know as a courtesy 'for information only'. Be clear on who does what to avoid an unruly, free-for-all discussion that leads nowhere. Give everyone a timetable of activity and alert them in advance to their role in your project. This will help set expectations.

Work with the corporate culture rather than against it. If your colleagues need time to assimilate and accept a new idea, invest time in developing and sharing the 'back story' – the context and background that led to this new development. If your colleagues are naturally wary of change – as most of us are – ask for their concerns first, before you proceed. Show you have listened and accounted for their concerns before presenting a potential solution. Conducting an initial research project to fully understand how your audience is currently thinking and feeling might save time later. And, when inviting people to converse, always keep the objective of any discussion clear and compelling. There is also a time to say when the decision has been made and that that particular conversation is over.

WHY A FAIT ACCOMPLI IS RARELY A DONE DEAL

Not every interaction with a member of staff can and should be turned into a discussion, but an order or announcement is rarely the right approach unless, for example, you want people to evacuate a burning building. It is not always more time-

consuming or onerous to involve employees in the communication process – it can actually save time. Our personal experience of being managed tells us much about the benefits of a
conversational approach to almost every situation. Presenting
people with a fait accompli may seem quicker but our brains
need time to process and assimilate information before we can
act. Involve people earlier and you get this assimilation process
under way sooner. Then, when it is time for action and the
announcement comes, employees will be ready for it. How
much better to be able to make that earlier announcement
in a different way: *As we discussed throughout the year, the
company as a whole has been performing well and our profit for
the year is £3bn. However, you told us that things in your part
of the business could be better – your order book is down and
it feels like overseas competitors are stealing your customers...*
In this example, the conversations that took place throughout the year means the announcement is expected and can be
relayed in the language of the receiver not the broadcaster.

   Stopping to ask how a team or division is feeling and engaging people in discussion and debate is never wasted effort. As
a communicator, the knowledge and insight you glean will
be invaluable and simply taking the time to ask, helps build
trust. I saw this in practice while working with a major credit
card company's lost-and-stolen call centre team. Initially, when
callers rang, they were immediately shepherded through a long
list of questions about where and when the card had been stolen
or lost. After a rethink, when callers rang to report a theft, for
example, this response was changed to: "I'm very sorry to hear
your card has been stolen. Before we cancel it, are you ok?
Do you need us to contact anyone?" This dissipated the rising
panic many callers were feeling. As a result, they answered the
other standard questions more quickly and the company saved
time and money. Asking a co-worker or customer how they are

feeling is not time-wasting – it's simply getting to the heart of what matters. It is amazing how often observing basic courtesies eases the interaction between people.

LET'S GET TO THE POINT

While it should be stimulating and enjoyable to engage in conversation for its own sake, in business our discussions need a defined, commercial purpose. There are many productive reasons to converse with others – to deliver information; to create understanding; to gather feedback; to collaborate and create; to test thinking. Whatever the purpose of the discussion, it needs to be defined, commercial and clear to all. We are not advocating businesses turn themselves into 'talking shops' where things gets discussed before – or in place of – action. Our role as corporate communicators is to make the conversation productive. We are guardians of the organisation's voice, promoting and maintaining language and behaviour that aids productive dialogue. Equally, we should seek to minimise the opposite; language and behaviour that stifles feedback, generates mistrust and creates a chasm between leaders and employees. The journalistic heritage of our profession is a strength in this regard. As well as a passion for words, we are a trusted source of the truth – detached, objective and knowledgeable. Whether or not we started our careers as reporters, when people duck a difficult issue, deliberately avoid giving a straight answer or fail to ask or answer the most pertinent question, we typically feel a journalistic tendency to wade in. In this way, we are not only the eyes and ears of an organisation but also its conscience.

Conversations happen every day inside your organisation. These are conversations that, thanks to advances in technology, no one can control and that spread far beyond its boundary walls. As Boris Groysberg and Michael Slind explain: "At the nearest water cooler, or at the virtual rumour mill, employees chat about the state of their organisation, and that chatter has a bearing on the company's operational performance."[30] It is far better to hear, participate in and hopefully influence these discussions than simply turn a deaf ear. Organisations that wish to move from yesterday's hierarchical, command-and-control culture to a more inclusive and dynamic one must learn the new rules of corporate communication. Leaders should listen first, check they have understood both meaning and emotion, demonstrate this, then seek to influence through a conversation. It might appear to be more taxing than barking a command and walking away – or giving a speech and answering a few planted questions from the floor – but the impact is significant. Leaders learn more, employees contribute more and organisations become greater than the sum of their parts.

In conversation with Richard Mullender

Richard Mullender spent 30 years as a police officer and detective. He ran the Advanced Interviewing course for the Metropolitan Police – the highest standard of training at the time – and spent five years as a hostage negotiator. He has also worked internationally, in peacekeeping operations in Afghanistan. Since retiring in 2007, Richard has worked with corporate clients, using his unique insight, skills and experience to help organisations improve their communications. Mullender focuses on the power of listening, which he believes is one of the most formidable tools in the world.

Why is listening so powerful?
The average hostage negotiation lasts between eight and 12 hours. At the end of it you have to be driven home because, quite frankly, you're knackered. Active listening is exhausting. It requires absolute concentration – it's not like the listening most of us do in our ordinary lives. For a hostage negotiator, listening can be the difference between life and death; it's that powerful. Think of it as the difference between you driving your family saloon and Sebastian Vettel driving his

Formula One racing car.

With so many years of adrenaline-fuelled work under your belt, what attracted you to the private sector?
As a police officer and detective, I always enjoyed interviewing prisoners and suspects. In short, my job was to make someone talk. I realised early on that I wasn't bad at it. However, as I advanced through the ranks, I missed that hands-on experience.

Fortunately, a former colleague proposed setting up Scotland Yard's first hostage negotiation department – it was a perfect opportunity. Many of the skills I'd gained interviewing suspects were transferable; the key difference in hostage situations is the intensity of the situation. You can't afford to miss a word. I spent five years negotiating nationally and internationally. Closer to home, I worked on many suicide cases with people standing on bridges. I also used my background in advanced interviewing skills to help design a course for future negotiators. I stepped into the world of business almost by accident. Again, it was a former colleague who made me realise my skills were transferable.

How did you find the transition from hostage negotiator to corporate trainer?
To be honest, I got properly beaten up in the beginning! The simple question that floored me was, 'how do you make us money?'. Having worked in the public sector where saving lives was the ultimate goal, any financial gain from our work was not immediately clear to me. Initially, we received pretty terse feedback in fairly colourful language, but it was incredibly useful. It gave me a benchmark I still use today: how do I make or save you money? If I'm not doing either of those, then I am of no value to you.

How easy was it to apply the skills you learned from hostage negotiations to corporate settings?

It became evident very quickly that, in the private sector, people were not as good at listening as I'd expected them to be. That was surprising. Initially, I tried traditionally teaching methods. But when I ran a small hostage negotiation scenario at the end of the course, I realised my students had missed absolutely everything I'd tried to teach them. I was perplexed as to why people found active listening skills so hard to master. This forced me to take a long, hard look at how I was delivering the training. I played the part of one of my students and listened to each of the scenarios I'd given them. I wrote down what I knew were the 'hooks' – those crucial pieces of information that enable me to understand what is *really* being said.

I realised the words and phrases I knew to be important fitted into specific categories. Once I'd identified them, it became easier to explain to people what words to listen for. Once you start using this listening technique in everyday conversations, it's incredible how much information people divulge.

Can you give an example?

Let's imagine someone says: "Things have been bad recently." This tells you nothing specific about how they are feeling. As a listener, I need to dig deeper:

- Things – what are these 'things'? How important are these 'things' to you?
- Have been – is this an ongoing problem or is it resolved?
- Bad – what do you mean by 'bad'? Is your 'bad' worse than my 'bad'? How worrying to you are these 'bad' things?
- Recently – do you mean yesterday, last week or last year?

Having identified the key words, the control of the conversation shifts to you, the listener. You must choose which words you want to analyse. You can do this by simply repeating it aloud; implying you want to know more.

At this point, you should be thinking about the outcome of the conversation – what do you want to gain from it? Do you want to identify or resolve a problem, for example? Analysing a conversation in this way, and the meaning behind the words someone is using, helps you to understand their values and beliefs. Once you know these, you can use their values to your advantage. With practice, this becomes a powerful skill. In terms of information and influence, you can get both from almost every conversation.

What are the mistakes people most often make when trying to be become better listeners?
To really listen, understand and interpret, you have to be in a conscious state. Most of us listen in a subconscious state without concentrating on what is really being said. You have to do more than *hear* the words; you also have to interpret them and form a hypothesis about their meaning; you have to test that hypothesis with your response, then note their reply. All of this gives you the insight you need to influence people using your understanding of what *really* matters to them. Listen, understand, influence. That's the path.

What happens inside organisations where there is the perception that management is unapproachable and fails to listen? How do you overcome these hurdles?
If you know employees don't trust a management team based on what may have happened in the past, tackle this head on. The problem won't go away until you do. Ideally, there should be an acknowledgment of these issues, which serves as

an introduction to how things will change in the future. Put yourself forward as someone employees can talk to about their issues. Talk to them about the trust and confidence you want to build. Make it personal – lay your values down. It's the same as dealing with someone threatening to jump off a bridge: if they don't trust the police, then I need them to forget I'm with the service – it's just me they're talking to.

Chapter 3

No one is as smart as everyone

NOT SO SPLENDID ISOLATION

Meaningful and productive conversations are already happening en masse inside your organisation; without them it would not function. The challenge is how we can promote, harness and manage them – ensuring that they happen at the right time, between the right people and around the right subjects. As James Surowiecki, author of the unsurprisingly pro-collaboration work *The Wisdom of Crowds,* writes, "the only reason to organise thousands of people to work in a company is that together they can be more productive and intelligent than they would be apart".[1]

Tomorrow's organisations – the smarter ones at least – will be climbing into the minds of employees to find and keep their commercial advantage. Why would we bother to gather hundreds of intelligent, diverse employees into an organisation, only to keep them segregated? What we need is collective brain power. Not lone experts, with their heads down, toiling away in splendid isolation, but a smart ecosystem of diverse individuals with their heads up, constantly looking around them for input, support and inspiration – and ideally finding it.

Smart companies are realising that conversation and collaboration create value. Meaningful interaction between employees is creating smarter processes, innovative products, more efficient operations, better lead generation and more effective marketing strategies. The rewards can be great as the more collaborative enterprises make the whole equal more than the sum of their parts. "The wisdom of crowds has a far more important and beneficial impact on our everyday lives than we recognise, and its implications for the future are immense,"[2] claims Surowiecki. As communicators, we are ideally placed to take on a new role marshalling the crowd towards smarter, more collaborative ways of communicating, because as Keith Sawyer, author of *Group Genius*, tells us "the engine that drives collaboration is conversation".[3]

NOT ALL COLLABORATION IS THE SAME

'Collaboration' has long been used, both at work and in society, as a general term for many different styles and methods of human co-operation. This chapter will explore three distinct but related forms, which both leaders and communicators can use to great effect.

The first is aggregated knowledge, most useful for gathering opinions and predictions on clear and unambiguous questions, such as which product is likely to sell best. Here averaging out the opinions of large groups is likely to provide better intelligence than relying on the preferences of a few.

The second type is characterised as 'crowdsourcing', searching for insight from a broader group of employees than is usually consulted, and so increasing the possibility of uncovering a creative gem. This can be especially powerful when individuals on the frontline are asked to solve problems as they are often closer to the issue and have the most relevant knowledge, but are too frequently excluded from the conversation.

Finally, there is what Sawyer calls 'group genius'; his idea being that "when we collaborate, creativity unfolds across people; the sparks fly faster, and the whole is greater than the sum of its parts."[4] This is social collaboration, where employees join forces in real or virtual groups – what IBM calls 'jams' – to solve problems or innovate. In his article 'The Proactive Employee', Donald Campbell describes these as 'involvement initiatives', where a wide group of employees combine their talents and expertise.

OXEN, GOOGLE AND MILLIONAIRES

The cousin of Charles Darwin recorded the power of crowd averaging in 1906. Francis Galton, an 84-year-old British scientist who had devoted his working life to studying heritage and eugenics, believed that very few people had the characteristics he deemed necessary to keep societies healthy. His experiments on individuals – testing their sight, hearing, colour sense and reaction time – led him to believe "the stupidity and wrong-headedness of many men and women" left them "scarcely credible"[5].

However, in 1906, at the annual West of England Fat Stock and Poultry Exhibition, Galton came across a weight-judging competition. Eight hundred people had attempted to judge the weight of an ox after it had been slaughtered and dressed. As this was an agricultural show, some of the guesses had come from farmers and butchers with insider knowledge, but many were men, women and children simply enjoying a day out. Galton was immediately interested in the guess of the average voter, assuming it would be wildly inaccurate given his belief that the average individual was capable of very little. He borrowed the tickets from the competition and ran a series of tests to calculate the mean – the collective wisdom of the crowd. The crowd's guess was 1,197 pounds, and after it had been slaughtered and dressed, the ox weighed in at 1,198. The crowd had given a near perfect answer. Galton wrote: "The result seems more creditable to the trustworthiness of a democratic judgement that might have been expected."[6] For a scientist who had spent his life trying to prove the exact opposite – the total lack of 'democratic judgement' – this must have hurt.

Surowiecki believes that what Galton stumbled across that day was a simple but powerful truth, that "under the right circumstances, groups are remarkably intelligent, and are often smarter than the smartest people in them".[7] What is more, to be collectively intelligent a group does not need to be made up of particularly smart individuals. When our personal judgements are aggregated in the right way, our combined intelligence is often excellent regardless. Average performance is certainly not optimal in every circumstance, and Surowiecki acknowledges that if you were to ask 100 people to run a 100-metre race, the average time would be a long way from that of Usain Bolt. But ask 100 for the answer to a problem, and it seems that the average answer will likely be at least as good as the smartest answer. A series of psychological experiments in the 1920s and 1950s repeatedly demonstrated this phenomenon, that the average decisions of the crowd are frequently more accurate than the response of a single individual.

This kind of aggregated wisdom is already helping to run the world. Every time Google instantly provides the information you search for, it is a testament to the genius of the group. Google's search algorithm, PageRank, created by the company's founders Sergey Brin and Larry Page, ranks a page higher when other pages link to it. In short, it aggregates our use of the web. There are no Google experts reviewing the quality and content of each page. Instead, according to Google, its search algorithm "capitalises on the uniquely democratic characteristic of the web by using its vast link structure as an organisational tool".[8] Each link, from page A to page B, is a 'vote', with careful weighting that credits popular pages with greater influence. This means many of us take part in a global collaboration project almost every day, every time we google we are harnessing the collective wisdom of every search that has gone before and contributing to every search that follows.

To take a more prosaic example, in the TV quiz programme *Who Wants to be a Millionaire?*, a contestant unable to answer a question is given several options, including 'ask the audience' and 'phone a friend'. When members of the TV studio audience are asked to provide the answer, their most chosen answer is right 91% of the time. When a friend is asked, however carefully picked by the contestant, his or her answer is right only 65% of the time.[9] It seems you are better banking on the wisdom of crowds than the knowledge of a pal.

How might we use this intelligence inside our organisations? Surowiecki tells us of InnoCentive, a spin-off of pharmaceutical giant Eli Lilly, where a diverse group of employees was asked to form an internal market – the ultimate knowledge aggregator – to buy and sell potential new drugs. The company wanted to assess whether its employees could accurately predict which drugs would be likely to get Federal Drug Authority (FDA) approval. They created an internal market around six experimental products, allowing employees to 'invest' in those they expected to do well. When trading opened, the market quickly and successfully identified the winners and losers by sending their prices soaring and plummeting respectively.[10] InnoCentive was so convinced by the potential of collective intelligence, that it now operates as an 'open innovation' company, posing research and development challenges on behalf of 'Seeker organisations' to over 300,000 independent 'Solvers'.

As communicators, we can use the power of the crowd

to provide answers to a diverse range of questions using quantitative research techniques, such as polls and surveys, to generate estimates and predictions with greater accuracy. This type of collaboration is not explorative or social. Indeed, as we will see later, it is far better if respondents remain independent from each other and give their own personal view. It is more suited to closed or definitive questions – *which, where, when or how much* – rather than problem-solving, which is likely to require analysis and debate. We might ask the workforce which of our services will be in more or less demand in five years? Which geographical regions will see the most growth? What is the optimum price, colour or name for a new product? Normally these are questions for small teams of experts or external consultants. I am not suggesting such expertise is now redundant, but seeking the collective wisdom of your entire organisation is beneficial on two counts; it provides additional fresh perspectives on key questions and sends an important message to the crowd – your opinion counts.

ASK SOMEONE WHO KNOWS

There is an urban myth about senior executives at a major toothpaste company visiting one of their production facilities. While on the factory floor, they engage in a heated conversation about how to increase stagnant sales. Listening into their conversation somewhat exasperatedly is a woman who has been working on the production line for more than 20 years. Eventually, she plucks up enough courage to tell her managers: "I know exactly how to increase sales – and what's more the answer is straightforward." With rather low expectations, they entice her to tell them more. "It's very simple," she replies. "Make the hole at the end of the tube bigger."

There are various versions of this story, and plenty of others like it, such as the employee at Swan Vesta who saved his company a fortune by suggesting they only put sandpaper on one side of the matchbox. A manager of a Canadian road maintenance company told me his own story at a conference in Toronto. Each year there was an employee whose job was to grit the roads by shovelling a special mix of sand and salt off the back of a moving truck on to tarmac night after night. For years this employee watched, as the grit would roll off the road into verges and kerbs creating unnecessary waste. Then he had an idea: mix an adhesive substance into the grit to make it sticky and it would stay put. The idea saved his company millions. The salutary lesson behind all these tales is that the very best people to solve a problem are often the last ones to get asked.

Our second type of collaboration is about widening the circle of expertise and asking a broader selection of people to contribute their views and opinions. We must recognise the value of employees stepping out of their designated roles and lending their weight to innovation or problem-solving initiatives. Donald Campbell believes this recognition is already growing, and "the emerging view of the proactive employee is of an individual highly involved and committed, an independent contributor with initiative and a well-developed sense of responsibility".[11] He argues this contradicts previous views of employees, where firms had no use for the whole person and wanted only those aspects of the individual necessary for the effective performance of their specific tasks. Charles Heckscher and Laurence Prusack believe, given today's marketplace, "businesses need a lot more than minimal co-operation and mere compliance. They need everyone's ideas on how to do things better and more cheaply. They need true collaboration".[12] Our experience supports this, and it is clear many of today's more enlightened companies do not want employees who just follow instructions and do only what is asked of them. They want employees who 'go the extra mile' – who participate, contribute and perform beyond what is written in their job descriptions. The good news for these organisations is that a virtuous circle can be created. Employees who are encouraged to contribute and participate more actually perform better and become more engaged. By asking employees to get involved, drawing on their expertise and experience to solve a problem, not only might you solve it more effectively, but you also drive participation and therefore engagement.

We have seen this kind of collaboration used to good effect inside a large financial services organisation. The company wanted to highlight risk and security issues internally, such as the importance of ensuring your security pass is always visible, of properly logging off your PC and not leaving documents unattended or publicly visible. Rather than design another awareness-raising campaign, we helped launch an initiative asking employees to submit their ideas for a short film warning about these risks. The best storyline was made into a film and shown internally with the winners attending a special 'Oscar' awards night and screening. The traditional approach – asking us for design concepts – would have worked, but there was an authenticity about these employee-generated ideas that res-onated with the audience. When we need to generate ideas, as communicators, we should cast our nets internally, asking employees to submit their own suggestions. Turning this approach into a competition is likely to generate even more interest. Where better to look for a bright idea than among those with insider knowledge and personal experience?

This idea is not a new concept, nor is it reliant on new tech-nologies or bigger budgets. In the 1990s, the BBC show *Sid's Heroes* was already inviting groups of frontline employees to improve the way their companies operated – with the caveat of changes having to be possible without additional funding.

In the book that followed, author and presenter Sid Joynson wrote that everyone involved in the experiment and watching the show "started off thinking [these employees] were just ordinary people, and ended up understanding that they were all heroes and could make a major contribution to the running of their companies".[13] Like Campbell, Joynson believed British companies had a 'blind spot' when it came to the benefits they could derive from treating people as people and not as "some mechanical part of the process".[14] The series of six half-hour programmes featured what Sid called 'grassroots experts' – machine minders, administrators, production line workers and janitors working in small groups to address specific issues. One team in a hospital in Chester looked into why 60 medical case notes were disappearing each week. By 'walking the process' – following the journey records made around the hospital – employees were able to reduce lost medical files by more than 50 per cent. Likewise, low morale and slow production at a shoe factory in Lancashire was improved when employees turned old assembly lines into smaller cells. Blue-collar workers in an electric wiring factory in Wales were able to find ways to increase production by 250 per cent in nine months. These huge gains in productivity and efficiency were achieved at minimal or zero expense because existing resources were being used to solve the problem. Although Joynson does not use the word collaboration, but 'teamwork', he emphasises the importance of managers giving employees the remit to solve their own problems together. He writes: "Teamwork brings great advantages. It pools the collective, intuitive knowledge of the team members and can produce brilliant solutions to the most intractable problems. It also builds strong motivation – far stronger than can be given by mere cash incentives."[15]

CO-CREATING A SOLUTION

Talking to employees should be a common sense approach for organisations not a radically new concept, but it is strange how in the melee of corporate life, common sense can often be in short supply. There is a story of a management consultancy called into a large, established technology company to solve the problem of poor knowledge sharing. The client wanted the organisation to break out of its 'silo mentality' and after careful analysis, the consultancy's key recommendation was to build a coffee shop on the ground floor of its headquarters. This would give employees an opportunity to brush shoulders and talk, to huddle informally in small groups and simply get to know one another, at least by sight. No doubt other measures followed but this was the most natural, obvious way to get the ball rolling. This is a perfect example of our third type of collaboration, which relies not on looking for the common or cleverest answer, but on social collaboration – people joining forces to share and build on each other's information and expertise.

Social collaboration is used to innovate or drive creativity and requires strong meaningful connections across the workforce. It is far less predictable and quantifiable than other forms of collaboration, which is why it often makes management nervous and wary. A leader's role in such social collaboration, as we shall see, is to create the right environment. Providing a clear, compelling goal, a guiding framework and then getting out of the way. Tight supervision and control quells people's collaborative spirit.

Even without leaders who actively encourage it, social collaboration is almost certainly happening inside your organisation – perhaps unnoticed. According to Sawyer, all creativity derives from it; people simply fail to recognise the influence of social interaction on the formation of their ideas. Individuals are often not consciously aware of the social and collaborative encounters that lead to their insights and, as a result, those encounters get overlooked. Sawyer writes: "Many creative collaborations are almost invisible – and it's these largely unseen and undocumented collaborations that hold the secrets of group genius."[16]

In *Collaboration*, Morten Hansen explains it is an ideal way to drive innovation. It "recombines existing resources – products, expertise, technologies, brands, ideas – in order to create something new from something old. This practice leads to more innovations, done more cheaply".[17] It can also drive sales, through increased cross-selling, sharing of customer information and the bundling of products together for customer convenience. And it can improve operations by finding ways to reuse existing ideas – "good solutions and expertise that are created, proven, and used in one part of the organisation can be transferred to other units, lowering the costs of operations."[18]

As a clear example of the benefits that can be derived from this special kind of human co-operation, Hansen considers the difference between what happened at Apple and Sony during the development of the iPod and Connect, its Sony equivalent. While Apple's Jeff Robbin enthused about an organisation where "there were no boundaries. The software guys, the hardware guys, the firmware guys, everybody worked together. It was a pretty amazing experience",[19] Sony executive Phred Dvorak paints a very different picture. In contrast to Apple, "Sony had long thrived on a hyper-competitive culture, where engineers were encouraged to outdo each other, not work together."[20] The domination of the iPod (and consequently the iPhone and iPad), and the financial disaster of Connect, suggests a clear business case for a more collaborative approach.

Companies like IBM are so keen to exploit the potential of this collaborative approach, that they have long made

structured collaboration 'Jams' part of their business practice. In 2003, the organisation held a Values Jam, allowing
employees a chance to redefine core IBM values. While many
companies involve the frontline in the creative of values, their
participation often ends there. Instead IBM began using its
workforce for more fundamental business brainstorming. In
2006, its Innovation Jam "brought together more than 150,000
people across 104 countries, including IBM employees, family
members, universities, business partners and clients from 67
countries".[21] Following the suggestions and ideas generated at
this event, the company invested $100 million to launch 10
new IBM businesses. Its model for 'crowdsourcing' internally,
and with key stakeholders, has since been adopted by organisations across the globe, and used when considering issues from
urbanisation to climate change.

Of course, as IBM recognised, frontline employees are
not the only grassroots experts in a business. Your customers
and clients also have a valuable contribution to make – when
asked. In *The Conversation Company*, Steven Van Belleghem
explains that a progressive "company builds a bridge between
its staff and its customers on a foundation of structural collaboration".[22] In his view, every organisation has untapped 'conversation potential'. We should not impose an artificial limit
of an organisation's own boundary. Individual organisations
should be looking to collaborate with a host of others such as
professional bodies, academia, their suppliers and trade unions.
A continuous dialogue between employees and external stakeholders builds a stronger company. This idea was underlined
by the 2008 McKinsey global survey, which showed that companies whose internal and external worlds are closely linked,
grow faster.[23]

Today, many companies are taking the concept of
collaboration with their consumers further still, and asking

them to create new features for their products or design a new product altogether. The approach is often called 'crowdsourcing', and the organisations using it are diverse. Anheuser-Busch, the brewer of Budweiser, asked its consumers to help develop a new beer brand. Nokia's Ideas Project uses the consumer experiences of participant-innovators to generate new product ideas, and shares revenues generated from these ideas with participants. Unilever has an open portal for anyone with an innovative idea. This 'submissions portal' states: "We have world-class research and development facilities, making breakthroughs that keep Unilever at the forefront of product development. But we know that the world is full of brilliant people, with brilliant ideas – and we are constantly looking for new ways to work with potential partners."[24]

Coca-Cola has six Research and Development departments globally linked to external 'hubs' that connect the company with partners, entrepreneurs, tech start-ups and university researchers. Global R&D Officer Nancy Quan says: "We can't just sit in a silo in Atlanta – we've got to be out closer to the consumer and have a clear understanding of what's happening in the world around us. We believe our reach is one of the key strengths of our business, so we spent time putting together what we call a 'Distributed, Connected and Shared' R&D model. The magic comes when everything connects – both internally and to the outside world."[25]

Crowdsourcing, especially among customers, would have appalled Henry Ford, who is purported to have said: "If I had asked my customers what to build, they would have said a faster horse." But Don Tapscott and Anthony Williams, authors of *Wikinomics*, suggest Ford may have been wrong. "It took car manufacturers more than a decade to 'invent' the pick-up truck after American farmers had spent years ripping the back seats out of their vehicles to make room for their goods and tools".[26]

It seems it is worth listening to today's consumers, who are a connected network of questioning, demanding individuals with a wealth of data at their fingertips. Even if you prefer not to go as far as asking customers to redesign your products, a closer, collaborative relationship can only pay dividends. In a conference in New York in 2013, Shelly Lazarus, Chairman Emeritus of the advertising agency Ogilvy & Mather, eloquently explained how too many leaders are 'hermetically sealed'. She said: "We all need to get out there and listen to people yearning for things."[27]

The growth and potential of this type of collaboration has important implications for communicators. On a tactical level, it suggests that we should enhance co-creation of our communication solutions by involving a wider cross-section of teams and individuals in early brainstorming sessions where ideas are shared, tested and developed. This might be a working group of readers, stakeholders, developers, marketers, mainstream journalists and designers – the more varied and divergent these people are, the better. On a more strategic level, it suggests we should advise our leaders to give the workforce time and space to collaborate – not because it is a fun way to run a business, but because it produces better results. David Weinberger was right to warn that, "hierarchical organisations that rest the pointy end of the pyramid on the back of a single human being are not as resilient as organisations that distribute leadership throughout a connected network".[28]

WHAT MAKES COLLABORATION WORK?

Most commentators agree that for collaboration to work well, various conditions need to be met. After reviewing much that has been written on these conditions, we can cut to the chase – you need a diverse collection of individuals who are both willing and able to give a personal, independent perspective and who are then given the freedom to think within the framework of an overarching goal or mission. Finally, you need an organisational culture that encourages information to be shared widely across internal boundaries.

DIVERSITY

Each person should bring their own, differing perspective and knowledge to the problem. Some may have highly relevant expertise, others may bring worldly wisdom and others may simply be no help at all. What matters is that everyone is not thinking along the same lines. As Scott Page writes in *The Difference*: "The best problem solvers tend to be similar, therefore a collection of the best problem solvers perform little better than anyone individually. A collection of random but intelligent problem solvers tends to be diverse. This diversity allows them to be collectively better."[29] Surowiecki also believes this is the case, explaining that "if you ask a large enough group of diverse, independent people to make a prediction or estimate a probability, and then average those estimates, the errors each of them make in coming up with an answer will cancel themselves out".[30]

Could the lack of diversity at the top of our organisations be doing more than stifling innovation and creativity? Some have argued that too much uniformity has been at least partly responsible for some catastrophic business failures. One of the most homogeneous industries I have encountered over the past 25 years is financial services. At a certain point in the hierarchy, from senior middle management upwards, those individuals who were not white, male and middle-aged were a talking point. The danger for any organisation is not just uniformity – a workforce of similar people thinking similar things – but *con*formity where everyone, whether a member of a majority group or not, feels compelled to follow the party line.

The financial industry has had a difficult recent history, and studies show that the banking crisis may well have been at least exacerbated by its conformist, uniform nature and the lack of diversity and independence among decision-makers. After the standard five-year delay, transcripts were published of the meetings of the Federal Reserve Board in 2006, just before the US economy fell off a cliff and sparked a global economic recession. The minutes show the board had information about the housing bubble but they did not feel overly concerned. But many others were. These were the people living next to neighbours who were refinancing their houses for $250,000 when they had only ever been worth $80,000. Predatory mortgage brokers were spinning a line to lower-middle class families that the housing boom would last forever, but not everyone believed them. Luke Visconti, who pens a regular online column on diversity issues, 'Ask the White Guy', writes that at the time, the Federal Reserve Board of Governors and Federal Reserve Bank presidents were 14 white men and four white women. In his words they displayed a "stunning lack of diversity".[31] Visconti asks what might have happened if the Federal Reserve Board feelers had reached out further into the market. "What if they were supported by a diversity-management structure, chairing their diversity-council meetings, meeting regularly with employee-resource groups and mentoring people who were not from their background?" It is impossible to say whether the crisis could have been avoided no matter who had been in charge at the Federal Reserve, but Visconti's warning is: "Does your organisation have the vulnerability of a limited perspective at the top?"[32]

However, it is too simplistic to say more minority groups at boardroom level would solve the problem. Page writes of the problem of 'lumping', which leads to stereotypes and stigmatisation. "We lump a recent immigrant from Nairobi, Kenya, a grandson of a sharecropper from the Mississippi Delta, and a daughter of a dentist from Barrington, Illinois, into the same category: African Americans."[33] Page argues that people can feel compelled to represent their identity groups when they are underrepresented within the crowd. "Someone might try to act and think as a woman of Asian origin, not as herself."[34] I would argue the opposite could also be true. It is likely that a woman who has risen through the ranks to the highest echelons of the finance industry in today's world would feel the need to behave in a more 'masculine' manner than the men around her. People may feel compelled to represent a demographic group or equally compelled to distance themselves from it. Either way, lumping people into 'categories' is unhelpful. Our ethnic identity and gender do not define us. In searching for true diversity within a group, we should not confine our view to variances in age, race, sex and religion. As Page tells us, the problem in using identity as a crude proxy for cognitive diversity is "employees look different but they may not think differently".[35] Sawyer puts it this way: "Group genius can happen only if the brains in the team don't contain all the same stuff."[36]

For many years, the push for greater diversity in our organisations was an equality issue. It was rooted in ethical and social responsibility. To be a good corporate citizen, organisations needed to be more inclusive and offer an equal opportunity to all. The argument is now shifting. There is wide acknowledgement that a lack of diversity is also commercially damaging because it leads to uninspiring, undifferentiated, 'me-too' products and services that appeal to a group of consumers who are as demographically narrow as the decision-makers who created or approved them. Technology companies wanting to reach out to the growing number of women spending their money on gadgets need to employ more women at a senior, direction-setting level. Accountancy and audit firms wanting to position their services as more rounded and complete 'management solutions' need to stopping hiring people who think like accountants and auditors. There is great comfort in hiring, promoting and training 'people like us', but whoever we are – even if we are one of the most renowned experts in our industries – our knowledge and experience is limited. It is far more powerful to have differing – even opposing – views on the problem. Two different heads are better than one.

INDEPENDENCE

Surowiecki believes an independent spirit is another precondition for effective collaboration. Independence and diversity are mutually reinforcing. Independence allows diversity to have a value, because it makes it easier for these contrasting individuals to say what they really think. For the crowd to be wise, each individual needs to feel willing and able to share their own opinion. This mitigates the need to conform and the consequent danger of the mob mentality, where people simply follow the herd or whoever has the loudest voice. As Surowiecki explains: "Independence doesn't mean isolation, it does mean relative freedom from the influence of others."[37] In short, diversity is of no use if people do not feel able to express their individualism or privately held thoughts. We see this in workshops comprising employees and their managers. In many corporate cultures, employees feel that proffering a differing opinion will get them labelled 'a troublemaker'. This behaviour stems from a culture that does not understand the power of feedback and dialogue. Hansen explains that leaders who want to implement a collaborative style need to "behave in such a way that people feel it is safe to speak up without fear of retribution. Leaders who praise dissent and alternative suggestions (even if they were not followed) help create this safety".[38]

In his 1972 book, *Groupthink*, Yale psychologist Irving Janis explains how panels of experts can make colossal mistakes because they are forever worrying about their personal relevance and effectiveness, and feel that if they deviate too far from the consensus, they will not be taken seriously. As a result, they can self-censor personal doubts about the emerging group consensus in order to conform. Many commentators on collaboration have subsequently agreed with Janis on the dangers of groupthink. Page writes that it "reduces perspective diversity and stifles the collective ability of the group to find good solutions".[39] The reason, as Surowiecki explains, is groups that are too homogeneous are insulated from outside opinions. Information that might challenge conventional wisdom is either excluded or rationalised away and people become stuck in a constantly reinforcing echo chamber. Sawyer describes the result, that "in many organisations, the group ends up being dumber than the individual members".[40]

DECENTRALISATION

A further prerequisite for effective collaboration is decentralisation. People should specialise and draw on local knowledge. Yet, power should not be devolved to local teams and units without a clear, unifying purpose that keeps this local activity aligned to a central goal. In business, the popularity of central control comes and goes. At times, the corporate centre might hold complete sway over its business units – directing and dominating the decision-making process. At other times, head office devolves its power and is keen to be seen as merely a facilitator. It may even change its name to highlight its 'support' function. Effective collaboration requires the independence and experience of local units to be maintained and respected. This encourages people to own their problems. Like Sawyer, Morten Hansen writes of 'decentralised collaboration', describing it as "giving people the freedom to 'own' a chunk of work, to be responsible, to be entrepreneurs building something great, to be close to customers, and to be rewarded for the results".[41]

For employees to own the problem, it has to be one they recognise and can influence. Campbell's article 'The Proactive Employee' suggests "that employees' commitment to unit objectives and responsibility for unit successes are closely tied to their feelings of ownership of the unit, its goals and its processes. Such ownership springs from the belief that their judgement counts, that it is organisationally valued, and that it makes a difference."[42] This is strikingly similar to Elton Mayo's discovery at the Western Electric Company some 70 years earlier. We often see leaders asking employees to rally around a corporate cause they cannot hope to change, own or even influence. In truth, very few employees have the appetite for remote or hypothetical problems, especially if they have their own more immediate problems to worry about. As communicators, we can help by explaining the local consequences and ramifications of a group-level problem, but when asking employees to collaborate, it may be wiser for them to focus on what matters to them.

On the flip side, decentralisation has its weaknesses if no one is aggregating all this local knowledge and activity, and if people are not aligned behind a common, overarching goal. If good practice and horrible failures are all kept buried in silos, the collective wisdom of the organisation is no better or worse than any one operating unit. According to Surowiecki, the answer is a "curious form of centralisation"[43] where valuable information uncovered in one part of the system finds its way through the rest. As Hansen puts it: "Disciplined collaboration requires that organisations be decentralised and yet co-ordinated."[44] This feels like another job for a communicator – helping colleagues identify and share their knowledge and solutions.

A UNIFYING GOAL

A goal or mission that links everyday tasks to something bigger stops people engaging in well-meaning but wasted activity that does not align with their organisation's overall direction. It means local and group-level activity can become mutually reinforcing. The opposite of this is what Hansen sees as 'over-collaboration without purpose', which became a problem at BP. John Leggate, a BP executive, feared that "people always had a good reason for meeting. You're sharing best practices. You're having good conversations with like-minded people. But increasingly, we found that people were flying around the world and simply sharing ideas without always having a strong focus on the bottom line".[45] A balance needs to be struck between local freedom and central direction. Sawyer describes it as 'managing a paradox'. Organisations must establish a goal that provides a focus for the team – "just enough of one so the team members can tell when they move closer to a solution – but one that's open ended enough for problem-finding creativity to emerge."[46]

Steven Shapiro sets out clear rules for effective collaboration, including asking the right challenges in the right way. Just asking for involvement for the sake of it, and without parameters is a waste of time. Communicators and leaders could spend countless hours sifting through irrelevant or entirely impractical suggestion, however well meant. We must pose the right challenges, in the right way, to the right people. "Establishing boundaries does not necessarily put constraints on innovation efforts. In actuality, if done correctly, it has the capacity to dramatically enhance creativity and increase organisational effectiveness."[47]

For collaboration to work well, groups need to be diverse, independently minded and willing to speak openly. They need to own the problem at hand; be given direction but not controlled; and yet be cognisant of the bigger picture – where their organisation is going and why.

According to the urban myth, if you stopped someone cleaning the toilets at NASA during the 1960s space race, and asked what they were doing, they would say they were helping to put a man on the moon. While this may or may not be true, it perfectly illustrates the power of having everyone focused on one unifying – and ideally, emotive – goal. This is another job for leaders and communicators. We need to amplify the organisation's commercial imperative, making it less likely employees will wander off down the wrong path.

A CULTURE OF SHARING

According to Hansen, "collaboration rarely occurs naturally because leaders, often unnaturally, erect barriers that block people from collaborating".[48] Fostering internal competition creates one of the worst impediments, encouraging people to hoard and protect useful information. Many of us have probably witnessed the 'not invented here' syndrome in your own organisation where people resist ideas developed in other parts of the business. Equally damaging, we see people treating their own ideas and expertise as 'proprietary' and keeping them under lock and key. This turns a loose federation of business units into closed fiefdoms. Then there are enterprises where teams may be happy to share but with seemingly insurmountable search problems – information is inaccessible. Hansen goes on to suggest our organisations should develop, and seek out, 'T-shaped managers' who deliver two performances: results in their own job (the vertical part of the T) and results by collaborating across the company (the horizontal part of the T). He argues: "The idea of cultivating T-shaped management puts the whole business of 'the war for talent' in a new light. The idea is not to attract or develop anyone who is a star. It's a misplaced focus. The war for talent should not be about stars of all kinds but about T-shaped stars."[49] Managing collaboration might be counterintuitive for many, as it requires an approach very different to traditional management methods. Sawyer explains: "The manager of a traditional team is responsible for breaking down the task, keeping everyone on schedule, and co-ordinating the team members. But the leader of a collaborative team couldn't be more different; this leader has to establish creative spaces within which group genius is more likely to happen."[50]

ALL THAT GLISTERS…

The conventional view of technology, and especially the web, is that it fosters collaboration by enabling us to connect with each other on a scale never before seen in human history. In previous decades, knowledge workers toiled alone or in small teams. Today's technology – particularly the internet – means knowledge workers can collaborate on a grander scale. According to a report by the Chartered Institute of Personnel and Development, entitled 'Social Media and Employee Voice', "in the same way that machine technology forced the rise of mass production in the industrial revolution, social technology is driving us headlong into the age of mass collaboration and mass transparency."[51]

Before we celebrate too prematurely, it is worth looking more closely at the reality. Technology has not yet liberated knowledge. Information is not flowing freely between individuals and teams, and psychologically very few of us feel part of one large, connected family. Indeed for many, technology actually thwarts our human desire to connect. The most obvious examples are those colleagues who sit within arm's reach of each other but exchange emails rather than have a conversation. The ability to work away from the office has placed a premium on the face-to-face meeting, which despite the advances in virtual meeting software, is still the most powerful and effective way of doing business. The increased isolation of today's knowledge workers – working from home, cafés or airport lounges – hinders an otherwise natural tendency to share and collaborate. Tammy Johns, author of 'The Third Wave of Virtual Work' for the *Harvard Business Review*, writes that remote workers often lack a sense of community and experience far too little unstructured social contact. She adds that even at seemingly collaborative workplaces like IBM, "a sardonic comment started circulating among employees: The company's initials, they said, stood for 'I'm by myself'".[52]

The proliferation of personal devices constantly connected to the net gives the impression we are always on – engaged in one, long and continuous conversation with our colleagues and clients. But although the volume of contact we have with others might be high, the quality still leaves a lot to be desired.

LIMITLESS KNOWLEDGE AND WHOLESALE COLLABORATION

Yet despite technology's limitations we have all, at times, glimpsed a brighter future. When we search the internet, connect with someone on a social network or use a virtual library to store and retrieve information, we experience how technology is changing the nature of knowledge and the mechanics of interaction. I have heard my fellow communicators describe the web as a new printing press – simply another way to disseminate information – but many commentators on the power of the web vehemently disagree. As Tapscott and Williams see it, "the new web is principally about participating rather than about passively receiving information".[53] Weinberger explains that the internet's "massiveness alone gives rise to new possibilities for expertise – that is, for groups of unrelated people to collectively figure something out, or to be a knowledge resource about a topic far too big for any individual expert".[54] He describes the phenomenon of crowdsourcing, and the power of posing questions online: "The internet enables us to gather and interpret information simply because the internet is so damn big that you need only a tiny fraction of people to volunteer".[55] For those who question our human desire to co-operate and interact, the very existence of the web weakens their argument. The web only exists thanks to our desire to connect, share and assist. As academic and political activist Lawrence Lessig writes: "The value of the internet came from no single institution or company, but from the collective innovations of millions of contributors."[56]

The challenge for today's corporations is to harness the combined power of their many online communities. Sawyer explains: "Our success in solving the most critical problems and needs that we face, today and in the future, depends on our ability to tap into the creative power of collaboration".[57] Online technologies enable knowledge workers to share ideas and opinions regardless of structural, geographical or hierarchical boundaries. Tapscott and Williams believe "a tough new business rule is emerging. Harness the collaboration or perish".[58] New technology might help, but alone it cannot make an organisation collaborative. Leaders must model the culture and values they want to see replicated.

As communicators, we must look for opportunities to work differently – to ask the audience. Established enterprises employing many thousands will not transform into collaborative collectives overnight, but pockets of good practice, especially visible ones that start at the very top, have great power to influence and guide others.

SO, WHAT'S THE BIG IDEA?

We are now seeing commercial, social and technological trends converge at the same point. Far-sighted businesses are beginning to recognise the power of a connected enterprise where employee talent is brought together in new ways to co-create solutions. As Weinberger so eloquently writes: "When an expert network is functioning at its best, the smartest person in the room is the room itself."[59] Employees find it motivational to be asked to get involved in problems within their grasp but not necessary within the confines of their role profile. And technology is driving this by enabling interaction on a far grander scale than previous generations would have ever believed possible. Sawyer believes "today's pervasive and high-bandwidth communication and social networks give us the potential to be far more creative than humans have been at any time in history."[60] As a result, organisations with rigid hierarchies, that do not allow ideas and opinions to percolate through their ranks or permeate divisional boundaries, need to think again. Tomorrow's corporate successes will be built on open, fluid ways of working. The winners will be those enterprises that make full use of their human resources. New and ingenious ways will be found to combine diverse talents and skills. Not merely because this will help corporates keep the right people on the payroll, but because this will be the best – and perhaps only – way to truly innovate, particularly in highly established sectors.

If we accept that organisations need to harvest and deploy the collective wisdom of their employees to stay ahead, then communicators have a vital role to play in securing corporate success. We need to help create the right environment for conversation and collaboration to flourish by giving the five generations that now work inside many of today's organisations the inspiration and confidence to speak up. We need to view employees less as an 'audience' and more as thinking, connected and curious partners. We must give them a cause they can rally round. We must not pigeonhole them according to their role profiles. Instead, we must converse with employees as the rounded, diverse human beings they are; ever-mindful of the multi-faceted contribution they are capable of making, especially when they work together.

In conversation with Saskia Jones

Oxfam is a global confederation comprising 17 organisations working together in more than 90 countries around the world, striving to find practical and innovative ways for people to life themselves out of poverty and thrive.

As head of internal communications for Oxfam GB, Saskia Jones brought this passionate workforce of 10,000 employees together across functions, environments and timezones in the organisation's own time of need through a collaborative online platform.

What inspired the project?
In May 2013, Oxfam was severely affected by the economic downturn. Our income was declining but our projects were just as necessary. It was clear we needed to reshape and restructure how the organisation operated, and find new ways to save money.

Because we knew there were difficult times ahead, we wanted to get staff involved from the outset.

Oxfam is a charity and we are obligated to be open and accountable in how we treat people; we are so good at fulfilling this with those we help, and it's crucial to apply the same values and respect to our own staff too.

When change is handled badly, it can be especially damaging. We knew that there might be job cuts, but we couldn't discuss this quite yet.

Instead we wanted get staff thinking about what they would do to change Oxfam to save money if the organisation belonged to them. We wanted to provoke radical cost saving ideas, and prepare them for the period of change that was coming.

What made you pick a crowdsourcing approach?
I'd previously run a successful crowdsourcing initiative at Cancer Research UK. I had seen the power of not just asking people for their ideas, but allowing them to share them and build on the ideas of others. By tapping into the collective wisdom of staff and volunteers, ideas are more well built - and much more likely to be successful.

I wanted to encourage staff to have exciting conversations and work together on this important business priority. We created 'Oxfam Future Shapers' so that everyone could play their part in shaping an Oxfam for the future.

I knew that if we did this as a token gesture it would backfire. It had to be championed from the very top and followed through.

What technology supported the initiative?
Our technological infrastructure for internal communication isn't great and with so many field-based staff it can be challenging to find a common way of engaging everyone.

Rather than use our existing intranet, which has limited functionality, we created a bespoke tool where staff could submit ideas through a website, vote and comment on the ideas of others, and discuss surrounding issues.

Because lots of our employees are working in project countries, with limited access to technology, we also created discussion packs. These meant team leaders could talk about 'Future Shapers' face-to-face. Whole teams could come up with ideas, and only one person needed to log on and submit them.

How did it work?
It was amazing to see people around the world, who would never even normally connect, building on each other's ideas and collaborating on a global scale.

Our staff quickly got on board and we had no shortage of ideas. There were even submissions and comments being posted in the middle of the night – it was a really addictive tool!

The people who work for Oxfam are hugely committed, with high levels of energy and motivation. This tool provided an outlet for them to share their knowledge, experience and expertise.

The site generated a wide range of ideas, from major restructuring to recommendations that we regularly check the tyre pressures of our vehicles to improve fuel efficiency. They were being suggested and honed by people all over the world. An idea would originate in the Philippines, be built on by a team in Uganda, and then reinforced or voted on by people in the UK.

How did senior leaders respond?
Our communication has typically been top down: the leaders of the organisation broadcasting and cascading messages. This was something very different.

There were some worries about tackling such difficult issues openly; it would have been easier to keep silent until we had made all the decisions about the future.

Our chief executive, who had just joined at the time, really understands the value of internal communications and is keen to listen and respond to staff. He quickly got on board with the project. Some of our executives were naturally good at getting involved; others needed a little extra guidance.

It was important to keep the senior leadership team well informed and report on all the good ideas coming from the site. It was vital to have support from the top. Plus I wanted to ensure that we were keeping our promise to staff and ensuring their valuable feedback and ideas were being heard by the Oxfam leadership and used to help inform decision-making.

One of my arguments for using technology like this is that many people are already comfortable with social media. So many of us regularly visit Twitter and Facebook, LinkedIn and other forums or forums, that people almost expect to be communicated to and engaged in this way.

What challenges did you face?
The most challenging thing about this collaborative tool was actually its growth. The more the participation and volume of ideas grew, the greater the amount of work it became to capture everyone's suggestions into clear themes for Oxfam's leadership to read and respond to.

This was mainly a challenge about the time commitment involved for the team, because we were totally committed to acting on these ideas and demonstrating we valued people's input.

Did you encounter any challenges with policing the website?
We generally allowed 'Future Shapers' to police itself, because on collaborative tools for discussion every party has the opportunity to respond.

We didn't create any strict guidelines. All staff agreed to our code of conduct when they joined the organisation, and we would expect them to adhere to the same values and behaviours online as they would in person.

Of course, people do post certain comments and suggestions that are bound to rattle some cages, but I like that odd bit of controversy because it shows people are having honest conversations.

Why do you think Future Shapers was so successful?

Telling staff to do something is not engaging; involving them in the process is far more powerful. The site was fun to use and, while it focused on a business priority, it didn't look corporate or too much like hard work.

There was also an element of competition. Every contributor got points for participation and there was a real-time leaderboard.

There is something for everyone in this process. Employees less driven by this competitive element, or perhaps less confident in their ideas, could still be part of the project by voting or commenting on the ideas of others.

How has this collaboration affected the culture of the workplace?

As time passed, 'Future Shapers' grew and so did our levels of engagement. This began to shape our culture into something new and collaborative, with a flatter structure that involves those who wouldn't usually speak out.

Make no mistake, the main objective of using this tool was always linked to a big business priority – in this case, ideas for saving money – but in reaching out to employees in such a creative way, we got rid of many of the silos people were working in.

We've built a global community now familiar with these tools and how to use them, and since 'Oxfam Future Shapers' we have run even bigger global ideas exchanges with staff across the confederation.

Before we knew it, these global conversations were building brand new networks across the organisation. It's an incredibly useful way of identifying and unearthing people whose valuable ideas might otherwise get lost in the system.

Chapter 4

What does success look like?

WHEN THE RUBBER HITS THE ROAD

There is an old joke that goes: "A consultant is someone who sees something working in practice and wonders if it will work in theory." Whenever I hear someone make this joke, it is always the consultants who laugh loudest. We are at least self-aware of our love of models and concepts. The question often posed by our critics is whether our grand theories work in practice. One of the challenges for me when planning this book was to show what success actually looks like by giving tangible examples of the shift from cascade to conversation inside today's organisations.

"Although many companies talk a good game when it comes to pushing authority away from the top, the truth is that genuine employee involvement remains an unusual phenomenon,"[1] warned James Surowiecki in 2004. Ten years on, this is largely still the case. There are plenty of organisations where far-sighted departments or teams may be using conversation and collaboration to drive innovation and performance. In some cases, this is not an isolated working practice but the start of something bigger – a new way of thinking about employee participation. However, we found only a handful of organisations where a deep and meaningful conversation with employees has become its modus operandi – driving decisions and informing ways of working at all levels. What should we conclude from this? Critics might take it as evidence we are indeed espousing grand but impractical theories. We would argue, while there is still some way to go, the direction is increasingly clear and the first steps are already being taken.

"The only thing we know about the future is that it is going to be different,"[2] said renowned management consultant Peter Drucker. The way we communicate inside organisations *will* change, just as marketing, accounting, regulation, health and safety and technology continue to evolve. Employee communications is a young discipline that has already come a long way in a short time. Today's practitioners are passionate, ambitious and curious – the characteristics of a profession that does not intend to stand still.

This chapter considers specific initiatives we consider best practice, and the companies using them. But it does so in the knowledge that all case studies are essentially lessons from history. Even the mightiest organisations have fallen from grace and they will continue to do so in the future. A company's success, whether brief or long lasting, is rooted in unique conditions and consequently cannot be easily emulated. We question whether a 'search for excellence' has led us to fixate on superstar, inimitable organisations while missing smaller, but more revealing stories of success closer to home. Do we have a tendency to overlook the first signs of success inside our own organisations? We also challenge the traditional definition of success, which in a highly uncertain and turbulent world may mean simply surviving the next wave of change.

We use stories of success to encourage us, reaffirm our values and corroborate our view of how things should be done. But we can also learn from failures, understanding why disasters struck some, and how we might avoid being next. Success will look different for every organisation, and indeed every individual. Each vision will be unique so we seek only to provide some inspiration.

SEEING IS BELIEVING

We have become convinced conversation is the answer – smarter, more productive and rewarding – after seeing first-hand what works inside organisations and what does not. Over 50 years, research with thousands of employees and having the privilege of helping hundreds of bodies – large, small, public and private – with their communications, has taught us much at AB. When you step inside an organisation you can instinctively tell whether you are among people who share a common goal, respect each other's views and feel able to make a difference in their roles. Author Patrick Lencioni tells us "a good way to recognise health is to look for the signs that indicate an organisation has it. These include minimal politics and confusion, high degrees of morale and productivity, and very low turnover among good employees".[3]

Poor communication is not just something you identify through a survey or when something has gone horribly wrong. It is written on the faces of those employees who feel misunderstood, voiceless, uncertain or insecure. You sense the frustration in those who want to give their best but feel unable to do so. You feel the bemusement when what they see and hear is disjointed or, worse, contradictory, and watch the bewilderment of those who feel detached or isolated from the wider group. These are not emotions felt only by those on the frontline. I have met many leaders who felt genuinely misunderstood or disconnected from swathes of their organisation, not just downwards through the chain of command but also within their peer group. As consultants, we have repeatedly seen a sincere exchange of views solve the most intractable problems. It sounds deceptively simple to recommend people participate in a more open, honest exchanges; that they listen harder to each other. But, often the solution is a conversation – or series of them – which until now has been thwarted, marginalised or absent altogether.

Success often means doing things differently. In practice, banishing broadcast looks like organisations doing less telling and more asking; leaders using their ears to run their enterprises and tapping into the collective brain of their organisations to extract knowledge and insight that competitors cannot find or do not have.

BUILT TO LAST…FOR A WHILE

The danger of naming companies as beacons of best practice is that tomorrow their glow fades or is extinguished altogether. In 2004, 10 years after Jim Collins and Jerry Porras wrote business classic *Built to Last*, an article appeared in *Fast Company* magazine asking 'Was "Built to Last" built to last?'. Jennifer Reingold and Ryan Underwood examined the bestseller's 18 visionary companies and concluded almost half had "slipped dramatically in performance and reputation, and their vision currently seems more blurred than clairvoyant".[4] Motorola, Ford, Sony, Disney, Boeing, Nordstrom and Merck all took a stumble in that intervening decade. What this teaches us is that, even for the best in class, success is hard to sustain. A trusting relationship with customers, employees and the public takes time and patience to build but can evaporate quickly. Even companies that know how they *should* behave, sometimes forget to take their own medicine. Despite best-laid plans, markets change and external forces prevail. Many CEOs freely admit a large part of their organisation's success is good luck.

This brings us to the central question of how we define success. For some, it might be superior financial returns. But, as Pixar founder Ed Catmull explains, money "is just one measure of a thriving company and usually not the most meaningful one".[5] For many organisations, it is not what has been achieved so much as how. It is possible to drive short-term returns with sharp practices or by acting in ways that damage relationships. In our view, accomplishments are only truly valuable if they are sustainable. For this chapter, we have looked at those organisations that have built their success by making a fundamental shift from cascade to conversation.

CULTURE FIRST, SECOND AND LAST

Today, the online shoes retailer Zappos receives much attention for its collaborative and transparent culture. Its CEO, Tony Hsieh, says what distinguishes Zappos from its competitors is putting company culture above all else. He believes "by being good to our employees – for instance, by paying for 100 per cent of healthcare premiums, spending heavily on personal development, and giving customer service reps more freedom than at a typical call centre" – Zappos can offer better customer service than their competitors, leading to repeat custom and fast growth. Five years after the company was launched, "amazingly, it all seemed to be working."[6]

However, back in 2009, amid a recession, credit crisis and with a disgruntled board, Hsieh believed the only way to save his company was to sell it to Amazon. True to the company's open culture, anyone can read Hsieh's letter to employees announcing the company's acquisition on its website.[7] The good news for Zappos' employees and those of us on the hunt for the new 'built to last' enterprises is that the story does not end there. A year after the takeover, net sales were up almost 50 per cent and the Zappos workforce had grown by several hundred. "The growth has made Amazon very happy, but it's also creating new challenges," said Hsieh. However, Zappos is fighting hard to prove that "a company doesn't have to lose itself as it grows bigger – or even after it gets acquired."

In 2014, Amazon borrowed an idea from its newly acquired subsidiary – its 'Pay to Quit programme' is based on a Zappos initiative called The Offer. Once a year, fulfilment centre employees are offered a payment to leave the company. The first time it is for $2,000, and this figure increases by $1,000 each year after that up to a maximum of $5,000. "Once a year at Amazon, frontline employees, whose jobs are anything but glamorous, get a chance to sit back, reflect, and choose whether to re-commit to the company and their colleagues. In a sense, Pay to Quit is an annual performance review of the company by its employees: Can I imagine not working in this department, with these people, for this company? It is they who are making the call, they who are choosing not to take the money and run — which creates a deeper sense of engagement and affiliation,"[8] writes Bill Taylor in a blog for the *Harvard Business Review*. The reasoning behind the scheme is perhaps summed up by Simon Sinek: "If you hire people just because they can do a job, they'll work for your money, but if you hire people who believe what you believe, they'll work for you with blood and sweat and tears."[9]

Employment law, trade union relations, the cost of recruitment and inevitable disruption this is likely to cause would make a Pay to Quit scheme unthinkable for many of us. The Zappos approach may be compelling, but this is a young company, founded in 2000, with around a few thousand staff led by a CEO who believes "getting the culture right is the most important thing a company can do".[10] For those working in a multinational organisation, with tens of thousands of employees and a corporate history longer than anyone's memory, can the Zappos story be anything other than an entertaining diversion? Even the companies named in *Built to Last* that remain successful to this day, "haven't all been built to emulate".[11]

Rather than looking for initiatives to copy, we should look deeper at the physiology of these organisations. We should be asking the leaders of these organisations, "what gets you up in the morning? What keeps everyone more committed than ever, more engaged than ever, more excited than ever, even as the competitive environment gets tougher than ever?"[12] says Bill Taylor. He believes it is not just that the most successful innovators think differently from everyone else, rather "they care more than everyone else – about customers, about colleagues, about how the organisation conducts itself in a world with endless opportunities to cut corners and compromise on values". The challenge begins within, you "can't be special, distinctive, compelling in the marketplace unless you've built something special, distinctive, compelling in the workplace".[13]

KNOWING YOUR REASON FOR BEING

Success should not be limited to one stellar performance or dazzling initiative. For many, the ability to adapt and survive might be achievement enough. "The average life span of a corporation is much shorter than its potential life span,"[14] says Arie de Geus, in his *Harvard Business Review* article 'The Living Company'. "It appears that in the corporation we have a species with a maximum life expectancy in the hundreds of years but an average life expectancy of less than 50 years." He asks why so many companies die young, and concludes "mounting evidence suggests that corporations fail because their policies and practices are based too heavily on the thinking and the language of economics. Put another way, companies die because their managers focus exclusively on producing goods and services and forget that the organisation is a community of human beings that is in business – any business – to stay alive".[15] De Geus examined what is different about the world's most successful and oldest companies, including the Swedish company Stora – now Stora Enso – which began life more than 700 years ago. We tend to think of change as a modern day scourge, but this organisation has survived the Middle Ages, Reformation, conflicts of the 1600s, the Industrial Revolution, two world wars and a series of economic booms and busts. Over that time, Stora's business shifted from copper to forest exploitation, iron smelting, hydropower, and eventually paper, wood pulp and chemicals. The histories of entities like Stora "tell me that such companies are willing to scuttle assets in order to survive. To them, assets – and profits – are like oxygen: necessary for life but not the purpose of life. Stora was in copper in order to exist; it did not exist to be in copper. These companies know that assets are just means to earning a living".[16]

Simon Sinek believes asking and explaining 'why' is much more important than 'how' or 'what'. Apple is an example of an organisation that has a reason for being distinct from the product it makes. "We believe in challenging the status quo. We believe in thinking differently. The way we challenge the status quo is by making our products beautifully designed, simple to use, and user friendly. We just happen to make great computers"[17]. Apple could completely change sectors, and begin producing clothes or soft drinks, while remaining true to this ideal of 'challenging the status quo'. Sinek argues that consumers "don't buy what you do; they buy why you do it". If we support the underlying ethos or philosophy of a company like Red Bull, Google or Virgin, then our loyalty will extend beyond a single product or service. By positioning itself as more than a search engine, Google can now extend its brand to mobile phones, glasses or even driverless cars. As customers, we expect a specific Google approach, not a specific Google product.

De Geus believes that in a living company members "are aware that they hold values in common. They know the answer to the definitive question about corporate identity: what do we value?... The sense of belonging pulls together even the most diverse members of the company".[18] He is not the first to tell us that the world's most successful organisations have a profound sense of their own unique identity and place in the world. Why does this purpose and presence matter? "We spend more time working than we do on almost any other activity in our lives. People want all that time to mean something,"[19] says Laszlo Bock, senior vice president of People Operations at Google. Inside successful enterprises, everyone has their sights on one overriding goal, no matter what surprises are thrown at them. "Other companies make similar products, and yet our employees tell us that they are drawn to Google because being here means something more than 'just' searching the internet or linking friends," says Bock. In their article 'Building a collaborative enterprise', authors Adler, Heckscher and Prusack remind us "a shared purpose is not the verbiage on a poster or in a document, and it doesn't come in via charismatic leader's pronouncements. It is multidimensional, practical, and constantly enriched in debates about concrete problems" and, if properly understood, "a shared purpose is a powerful organising principle".[20] It is what attracts the right people, keeps them on track and inspires their advocacy even after their term of employment ends.

The John Lewis Partnership has enjoyed 150 years of success even as many of its competitors have struggled. Its overarching 'Principle One', which has nothing to do with groceries or retail of any kind, is enshrined in the 'constitution' of the company: "The Partnership's ultimate purpose is the happiness of all its members, through their worthwhile and satisfying employment in a successful business."[21] John Lewis admits "not many companies have a written constitution".[22] Although the original constitution has been revised over the years, the latest edition – published in 2014 – "is a direct connection to his original inspiration – it defines what we are".[23] For conversation to work and organisations to flourish, there needs to be a deep and clear sense of why the company exists. Some might argue that for John Lewis, where every employee is a part owner in the business, the commitment to fundamental goals is easier to achieve, but is also all the more vital. If your owners do not know what you stand for, how will your customers?

Marvin Bower, a founder of McKinsey, reminds us "even without planning or specific effort, any company will gradually develop a philosophy as people observe and learn through trial and error 'the way we do things around here'". For Bower, a company's philosophy is guided by "informal, unwritten guidelines on how people should perform and conduct themselves".[24] You can let this philosophy or culture emerge, or you can direct, shape and promote it.

FROM AUTOCRACY TO DEMOCRACY

Success for many smart, collaborative companies looks like a genuine devolution of power; one that renders traditional power cliques increasingly obsolete. The phrase we hear often is 'freedom within a framework'. This is not a free-for-all where people do as they please, but neither is it automatons in straitjackets doing only what is asked of them. Governance, controls and accountability are not weakened in such environments, but strengthened. Rules and responsibilities are followed not out of fear or mere obedience – *I have to do it this way* – but because the rationale for them is clear, understood and respected – *I want to do it this way*. Ori Brofman and Rod Beckstrom, authors of *The Starfish and the Spider: The Unstoppable Power of Leaderless Organisations*, argue a strong culture has self-enforced values and 'norms' in place of stringent corporate regulation. Moreover, "norms can be even more powerful than rules. Rules are someone else's idea of what you should do. If you break a rule, just don't get caught and you'll be ok. But with norms, it's about what you as a member have signed up for, and what you've created".[25]

A much-quoted example of power sharing in action is Semco, which began as a manufacturer of centrifuges for the vegetable oils industry. Today it has grown into a diverse portfolio of enterprises – from real estate and inventory services to industrial equipment. Keith Sawyer, author of *Group Genius*, describes Semco as "a knowledge-age company in an industrial-age business. It may be the world's largest collaborative organisation".[26] Many companies say they believe in empowering their employees through participation, writes Sawyer, "but most of them don't look like Semco". Too often, participation is little more than a tactic to increase employee job satisfaction or to get their buy-in for the latest senior management decisions. "Semco is what real participatory management looks like: collaboration, improvisational, emerging from the bottom up. It's a radical rethinking of the organisation, and most companies aren't willing to go there yet. But as innovation becomes ever more important, there won't be any other choice".[27]

The Semco story is all the more compelling because it is not about knowledge workers or the dotcom services sector where collaboration is often considered easier. The man at the helm of Semco, Ricardo Semler, describes his approach to management – or more accurately, self-management – in a *Harvard Business Review* article entitled 'Managing without managers'.If you are on the hunt for a portrait of success that moves and inspires, my advice is to read every word. One of many recurring themes we see inside more participatory organisations is the principle that, in Semler's words, "we hire adults, and then we treat them like adults".[28] At the time he was writing, Semco had 800 employees who set their own working hours and had access to the company books – a balance sheet, a profit-and-loss analysis, and a cashflow statement for his or her division. They attended classes to learn how to read and understand them. This was not just to increase their awareness of business performance: "It's up to them to see the connection between productivity and profit and to act on it."[29] In terms of the strategy, the majority are asked to vote on many important corporate decisions. "Outside the factory, workers are men and women who elect governments, serve in the army, lead community projects, raise and educate families...but the moment they walk into the factory, the company transforms them into adolescents. They have to wear badges and name tags, arrive at a certain time, stand in line to punch the clock or each their lunch, get permission to go the bathroom...and follow instructions without asking a lot of questions."[30]

Success for many is the abolition of meaningless, frustrating and patronising rules that tell employees they are not trusted, valued or respected. No one at Semco is required to sign off expenses. As Semler explains: "If we're afraid to let people decide in which section of the plane to sit on, or how many stars their hotel should have, we shouldn't be sending them abroad to do business in our name, should we?"[31]

There is logic to giving employees the freedom to exercise their own judgment and address local frustrations. To move from cascade to conversation, employees need not only to have a voice but also believe in its power to make a difference. If I cannot get the kettle fixed in the staff kitchen or use my initiative to make a process more effective, am I able or willing to contribute to the organisation's wider goals? In our research into engagement and, in particular, what motivates employees to put in discretionary effort, we always hear people talk of having a degree of control. This echoes the work of Daniel Pink into workplace motivation, driven by 'autonomy, mastery and purpose'.[32] "In an immense production unit, people feel tiny, nameless, and incapable of exerting influence on the way work is done or on the final profit made. This sense of helplessness is underlined by managers who, jealous of their power and prerogatives, refuse to let subordinates make any decisions for themselves – sometimes even about going to the bathroom,"[33] says Semler. If we leave our employees feeling impotent, we cannot hope to get the best from them.

The communicator is often well placed to help identify those rules and norms that send the wrong signals. At the Big Yak 'unconference' in 2014, in a session on the shift from cascade to conversation, practitioners shared their experiences of helping employees tackle those 'minor frustrations'. The message this sends is a powerful one – if together we can fix the small things, sorting the bigger ones is only a problem of scale.

SMALL CIRCLES NOT BIG PYRAMIDS

Throughout this book we take regular and unapologetic swipes at traditional management hierarchies that put everyone in their place. David Weinberger says: "Modern business almost universally has chosen a particular type of togetherness: a hierarchy. There are two distinguishing marks of a hierarchy: it has a top and a bottom, and the top is narrower than the bottom. Power flows from the top and there are fewer and fewer people as you move up the food chain."[34] Yet time and time again in researching this book, we have found, like Warren Bennis and Patricia Ward Biederman, authors of *Organising Genius*, "great groups tend to be non-hierarchical. Members make contributions based on talent, not on role".[35] The rigidity and lack of expectation characteristic of the conventional management pyramid stifles participation and involvement, and as a consequence, the ingenuity and freedom that breeds innovation. "Both the internet and Linux are powerful demonstrations of pure market conversation at work. They show what can happen when people are able to communicate without either the constraints of command-and-control management, or the straitjacket of one-message-fits-all"[36] write Weinberger and co-author Doc Searls.

Speaking about how Pixar fosters creativity, co-founder Ed Catmull says: "Everyone must have the freedom to communicate with anyone. This means recognising that the decision-making hierarchy and communication structure in organisations are two different things. Members of any department should be able to approach anyone in another department to solve problems without having to go through 'proper' channels."[37] Catmull admits that escaping an ingrained hierarchy is difficult. At Pixar, he found that the physical environment could enforce boundaries and restrict the flow of conversations. He describes how creative meetings took place around a long boardroom table with designated seating. Senior executives sat in the middle, where they could hear everything and easily contribute, forcing more junior members of staff to the ends of the table, struggling to keep up, let alone participate. It was not until an accident forced the meeting into a different room that leaders recognised the impact of the table. People were being effectively excluded from contributing, limiting the conversation and consequently the creativity in the room.

Christopher Locke, one of the authors of *The Cluetrain Manifesto*, believes "top-down command-and-control management has become dysfunctional and counterproductive".[38] In his view, employees need more power in organisations, "not to lord it over others, but to make intelligent decisions on the fly and not see them overturned two days later by managers who don't know the territory."

Semler puts it more dramatically: "The organisational pyramid is the cause of much corporate evil because the tip is too far from the base. Pyramids emphasise power, promote insecurity, distort communications, hobble interaction, and make it very difficult for the people who plan and the people who execute to move in the same direction."[39] Inside smarter, more conversational organisations, the 'hierarchy' is not sacrosanct; indeed it is little more than a reference document showing the latest structure chart. It is largely ignored in favour of seeking out those best placed to help get the job done. There is a respect for knowledge and skills that characterises these enterprises, plus a genuine desire to elicit the views of others.

A STREAM OF FEEDBACK

A characteristic of successful conversational organisations is the effort made to maintain a continuous dialogue with the workforce. This is not an annual exercise but an everyday activity. "We try to have as many channels for expression as we can, recognising that different people, and different ideas, will percolate up in different ways,"[40] says Google's Laszlo Bock. At Semco there is a similar drive for dialogue from the front-line to learn more about the potential obstacles and opportunities within the business. "Twice a year, subordinates evaluate managers. Also twice a year, everyone in the company anonymously fills out a questionnaire about company credibility and top management competence. Among others things, we ask our employees what it would take to make them quit or go on strike,"[41] says Semler.

Before asking for feedback and opinion, the organisation – and leaders in particular – need to prepare themselves. What they hear may be uncomfortable, disappointing and will almost certainly highlight problems not previously on their to-do lists. There will be some who shudder at the thought of this constant commentary from employees, thinking it sounds like a heady mix of chaos and anarchy. We do not advocate building a consensus around every decision, turning every piece of communication into a discussion or having a system without controls or accountability. If leaders prove to be transparent and open, they will gain the trust of their workforce. Consequently, when difficult unilateral decisions need to be made, with no room for consultation, they will face less resistance.

DEFAULT TO OPEN

Both our research and experience tell us that a successful shift from cascade to conversation is based on an exceptional degree of transparency. "When we speak of 'transparency', we mean much more than the standard business definition of the term – full disclosure of financial information to investors," write James O'Toole and Warren Bennis in their article 'A Culture of Candour'. "While such honesty is obviously necessary, that narrow interpretation produces an unhealthy focus on legal compliance to the exclusion of equally important ethical concerns, and on the needs of shareholders to the exclusion of the needs of other constituencies."[42] The authors believe there is a 'blinkered assumption' companies can be transparent to shareholders without first being transparent with their people, when, in fact, "no organisation can be honest with the public if it's not honest with itself".[43]

Our Investor Relations colleagues will be quick to remind us there are Stock Exchange rules governing what can be announced and when both to employees and the wider world. While not contravening these regulations, some organisations successfully prioritise informing staff about company news, ensuring they do not have to hear it from external media sources. When Justin King resigned after 10 years as Sainsbury's CEO, every member of staff working that day was given a face-to-face briefing. As the walls of our organisations become more permeable, the gulf that once existed between internal and external communication is narrowing. We are seeing some organisations using this to their advantage by making internal announcements publicly available, sending a strong subliminal message that they have nothing to hide. "We sometimes post our CEO's employee letters on his Facebook page to make sure that the outside world hears Siemens news directly from leaders. This creates not only transparency, but it also helps build trust with employees who see that what we're saying to them isn't different from what we're saying externally,"[44] says James Whaley, SVP of communications and marketing at Siemens.

"We've argued for more transparency for a long time – but the truth is, we haven't seen much progress," admit O'Toole and Bennis. In the 50 years they have been studying organisa-tions, "the most common metaphor we've heard managers use to describe their own cultures is 'a mushroom farm' – as in, 'people around here are kept in the dark and fed manure'".[45] We have heard the same from employees at all levels – but they tend to use a different word for 'manure'. Our research shows employees have a keen interest in the performance of their organisations, in comparisons with competitors, sector trends and the views of commentators and analysts. It is too easy to assume employees know more than they do. Inside head office, we are dealing with facts and figures about our organisation every day. We can easily forget ours is a privileged position that gives us insight others further from the corporate centre do not have. Successful enterprises understand and feed this appetite for 'hard news' among their employees, creating a workforce that can converse with confidence and passion about their organisation. To drive change at Home Depot, director Ram Charan says metrics were used to drive behavioural change. "By making various aspects of Home Depot's performance transparent to all employees, managers could clearly see – in cold, hard facts – the broader financial impact of their own decisions. This prompted candid discussions about how to improve that performance and focused employees' vaunted commitment on taking the needed actions".[46]

In an 'always-on and super-enabled environment', this need to create a truly informed workforce is becoming more critical. That is the conclusion of Weber Shandwick's report 'Employees Rising: Seizing the Opportunity in Employee Activism', which states we are moving beyond employee ambassadors or champions to a new era of 'employee activism'. "Employers will increasingly need a band of employees who can take action by spreading the right messages for them, helping them recruit the best of the best or defending their position when they are under scrutiny." To successfully cultivate these internal activists, organisations will need to move quickly as "employees are already taking matters into their own hands and, left unattended for too long, will define their employers' brands and reputations on their own. Social media enhances this risk, but also the opportunities."[47]

We must create well-informed employees able to converse about their organisation inside and outside its walls. Successful leaders cultivate an environment where people feel able to speak up, alerting others to problems that, if left to fester, could spell disaster. O'Toole and Bennis examined the results of "an intriguing, relatively obscure study from the 1980s" by organisational theorists Robert Blake and Jane Mouton, who had examined NASA's findings on the human factors involved in airline accidents. Cockpit crews – pilot, co-pilot and navigator – were placed in flight simulators and tested to see how they

responded during the crucial 30 to 45 seconds before a potential accident. "The stereotypical take-charge 'flyboy' pilots,
who acted immediately on their gut instincts, made the wrong
decisions far more often than the more open, inclusive pilots
who said to their crews, in effect, 'We've got a problem. How
do you read it?' before choosing a course of action."[48] They
claim that, like the pilots, leaders are more likely to make mistakes when acting on too little information rather than waiting
to learn more. But, say Bennis and O'Toole, the research shows
something deeper – those pilots who made the right choices
"routinely had open exchanges with their crew members".
Moreover, crew members who regularly worked with the more
'decisive' pilots were unwilling to intervene – even when they
had information that might save the plane. This lesson for
business leaders and communicators is silence does not always
equal agreement or even compliance; and silence born of fear,
apathy or 'groupthink' can result in disaster. Edgar Schein
argues "in the NASA Challenger and Columbia [space shuttle]
disasters, and in the British Petroleum gulf spill, a common
finding is that lower-ranking employees had information that
would have prevented or lessened the consequences of the accident, but either it was not passed up to higher levels, or it was
ignored, or it was overridden".[49] Successful leaders demonstrate
they are open to hearing bad news – speaking up is not a rare
act of bravery or whistle-blowing; it is the way problems are
identified and resolved.

LEARNING FROM FAILURE

While success can be inspiring, failure can be just as instructive.
In 'Roads to Ruin', a report by Cass Business School, a series
of substantial, well-known corporate crises are examined. In
all, 21 organisations' pre-crisis assets – totalling more than
$6 trillion – were studied, including those of Shell, BP, Cadbury

Schweppes, Northern Rock, Enron, Railtrack and the UK Passport Agency. These were crises of significant proportions: six of the firms subsequently collapsed and "most suffered large, uninsurable losses and their reputations were damaged, sometimes severely".[50] The report aimed to identify the causes of these crises and found seven risk areas "beyond the scope of insurance and mainly beyond the reach of traditional risk analysis and management techniques". Three of these areas relate to communication, in particular the "inability of risk management and internal audit teams to report to and discuss, with both the 'C-Suite' (leaders such as the chief executive, chief operating officer and chief financial officer) and non-executive directors, the risks emanating from higher levels of their organisation's hierarchy, including risks from ethos, behaviour, strategy and perceptions".[51] The report concludes there needs to be a free flow of information so that "things that are known within the organisation, but not to its leaders and their proxies,"[52] are not left to flourish hidden from leaders' sight.

However, it is not only during tough times that leaders and communicators need to listen to the wisdom of their crowds. "When things are going well, there is a tendency to ask fewer questions than when things are changing or going wrong, which is a mistake".[53] The report references Nassim Nicholas Taleb, and his work *Fooled by Randomness*. Taleb believes successful leaders can be fooled into thinking their success is due to skill rather than good luck. Enron's board, for example, "should have questioned how their companies were producing exceptionally – and consistently – good results." Not only might this have uncovered wrong doing more quickly, but also knowing that the executive team was equally likely to question success "would have acted as a deterrent, at least, to fraudulent activities".[54]

ACKNOWLEDGE THE SMALL WINS

Success is rarely achieved in one momentous step. "Don't view transformation – even something as cataclysmic as the central-isation of purchasing – as a one-time event or a point to be reached. Rather, view it as a work in progress that will con-stantly need to be modified,"[55] says Ram Charan, writing about Home Depot's culture change in 2009. Even with the benefit of hindsight, it can be hard to spot those moments in the life of an organisation when it made a significant step forward. I was reminded of this when reading 'The power of Jam', a blog post by internal communications practitioner Helen Deverell.[56] Her organisation, leading business and financial advisory firm Grant Thornton UK LLP, launched Jam, its Jive platform, in March 2014. Although 65 per cent of its workforce had signed up, "we felt people were still struggling to see the value, espe-cially as our partners hadn't engaged with it," writes Deverell. A partner conference presented an opportunity to demonstrate its information sharing and collaboration potential. As well as using Jam in the run-up to the conference, "eight of us went along to the conference, set up at the back and furiously typed, took photos, wrote status updates, set up polls, replied to com-ments and invited questions that would be put to the partners". The team also set up stalls in coffee areas to talk to partners about Jam and social media more generally, providing a guide on maximising people's LinkedIn profiles, for example.

A poll that ran at the end of the first day of the confer-ence asked people what they thought of Jam's output from the event. While the response was positive, people wanted to see partners contributing to the conversation. Then, that evening "something amazing happened. We all went back to our rooms before the drinks reception in the evening and comments from partners started to appear. For the first time, people at all levels across the business were having their voices heard by the most senior people. And it has carried on throughout the weekend as partners have taken the time to write thoughtful and considered answers to people's questions." In those two days, which Deverell describes as "truly exciting, exhausting and rewarding", the firm made progress "breaking down barriers and demonstrating how we can use Jam to collaborate with colleagues at all levels and that everyone's opinion or idea is as equally important as the next".

Success is often a series of steps that may have seemed small or even inconsequential at the time. According to a Chinese proverb, 'it is better to take many small steps in the right direction than to make a great leap forward only to stumble backward'. It may be beneficial to deliberately include a series of small, attainable successes in a communication plan, which can be celebrated and shared. Success is about maintaining momentum, which demands we are continually re-energised to remain focused on and committed to the goal.

A CLOSE RELATIVE OF SUCCESS

"Success is to be measured not so much by the position that one has reached in life as by the obstacles which he has overcome,"[57] said the US educator Booker T Washington. In other words, success is relative. For organisations only broadcasting to employees, who in turn feel unable or unwilling to speak up openly, a frank conversation about a sensitive subject might be an achievement. For others, capturing the authentic voice of employees in channels that, until now, have been pumping out internal PR, might be a huge step forward. The mere act of asking the workforce for help, to overcome an obstacle or suggest improvements, might be a turning point. The moment a leader ceases to be a remote figure of authority but a human being with frailties like us, trust in them might deepen. Success may be as small as ensuring 'communication' is at the bottom of the agenda at every meeting, ensuring that at least people consider their duty to share discussions and decisions with others. Inside some organisations, the simple recognition that change is necessary may be a mighty step forward.

KEEPING THE FAITH

So far we have explored corporate rather than personal success because our private achievements are often tied to the fortunes of our organisations. However, for some, maintaining resilience and persistence is a significant achievement. Communicators often find themselves in the vanguard of change; forcing uncomfortable truths into the open that have hitherto been ignored, sidelined or misunderstood. Our solutions often push the limits of how open and interactive organisations wish to be. It is not unusual for practitioners to feel frustrated, even downtrodden, by our seeming inability to effect change. Success can be keeping the faith; still being determined to do better. Success might be learning why an initiative failed and adopting a different approach. It might be maintaining your curiosity and a desire to question and learn. The organisation's view of employee communications is not just formed by what it sees and who. Your attitude and approach to work – not just your output – tell others what they can expect from employee communications. Success is being well informed about our organisation – its performance, marketplace and strategic challenges – and at the forefront of good communications practice. Success is developing and using your professional network to share learning and ideas. Unsurprisingly, our profession loves to write, blog, tweet and talk – success may be as simple as knowing you are never alone.

While it can be educational to look at the successes and failures of others, there is plenty our own companies have to teach us. In 'Roads to Ruin', we are reminded that "organisations often have difficulty in learning from experience, whether it is their own or that of others".[58] As a communicator, there will be much to learn from the pockets of good and bad practice that undoubtedly exists inside your own organisation today. We need both cautionary tales and sources of inspiration to drive change, and when they come from closer to home, their power is greater. One way to kick-start the conversation might be to ask colleagues to share their personal stories of communication successes. This helps ensure the organisation truly 'knows what it knows' and demonstrates the simple power of asking a question and listening to the answer.

In conversation with Caroline Thomas

Operational Design and Talent Manager Caroline Thomas joined DIY giant B&Q in 2011.

She was brought in as a HR specialist in organisational design and change management to assist in rebuilding the business's head office from the ground up.

Every one of the company's 1,400 employees had a say in the new shape, structure and role of its head office.

Caroline speaks candidly about bringing change to a company that had attempted to restructure many times since its launch in 1969, but never quite succeeded.

How did the structure of B&Q's head office need to change, and why?
As an organisation, we had been constantly evolving ever since Richard Block and David Quayle opened their first store, introducing many new teams and departments, but we'd never really stopped to think about the overall structure of the company as it changed, and how all of these new components worked together.

I think everyone recognised there was a simpler way of

doing things. We operated with convoluted methods that had a way of isolating teams and there was a real lack of internal communication.

Teams and departments had developed their own ways of operating. In some cases, these methods led to a repetition of practices because we were not keeping everyone in the loop.

Identifying the need to make changes is a big step, but how did you start the process?

Before we could build a new structure, it was important for us to create a plan of how the change process would work. I worked with 50 functional experts to help formulate a plan.

We knew a different structure could mean role changes and job losses, so we wanted to be as open as we possibly could be in order to help everyone through it. We wanted every employee to feel like they could speak openly and honestly about the future.

From the beginning a number of phrases kept cropping up, like 'adult-to-adult conversations', 'creative' and 'diverse'. We knew that our new structure had to reflect a culture based on these values.

You can easily think you've got the design of a company 100 per cent right when sitting in a closed room. But a structure on paper is worthless if it doesn't work in practice. Involving employees throughout the process of a redesign is vital.

What did the process entail?

It was something we called Co-Build. In simple terms: we had our employees building the structure of the company without anyone in it. We needed a structure defined around roles and activities rather than individuals, because people can move on.

First we defined the role of our board, and then presented every employee with the opportunity to give their opinions and ideas. All of this was carried out with complete impartiality and honesty; hierarchy wasn't important. We didn't have a solution waiting in a drawer, it was genuinely a blank canvas that everyone had the chance to help complete.

I think it probably took a fortnight or so for people to actually believe we were serious about the Co-Build principle. We knew we were never going to get the buy-in of our employees by making decisions behind closed doors. Candidness and honesty breeds trust in a workforce and that's the type of culture we wanted to create.

How did you gather ideas and begin to shape the new structure?
We hosted regular workshops with all levels in the company. Everyone was entitled to their view, irrespective of their position in the current hierarchy. The views of all our employees are just as important as those of our managers.

These weren't just a free-for-all; there were limits on the number of people involved in each to encourage conversation, and a general theme or topic for discussion.

Of course, not everyone is comfortable with airing their views in public. We had a shed in the atrium of our head office where people could go in and share their views to a camera, as well as offering one-on-one sessions. We didn't want to force people to talk, but it was essential that everyone had the opportunity.

Through these conversations we identified around 170 processes that were cumbersome and impractical.

When we started the workshops, people were understandably hesitant to raise certain points, especially if they had a suggestion that would have implications for someone else in the room, like removing a role to streamline a process. Soon though, those involved came to appreciate that the workshops were to help everyone, and that their purpose was for all participants to work as one for the good of the company.

One workshop containing 40 people sticks out as a particularly good example. A director, some managers and functional specialists were discussing the process of getting a new product to store. The consensus was there should be fewer stages in the process, allowing employees to see things through from start to finish. Once the discussion was over, the director present actually stood up and said: "There isn't a role for me or my team in this new process, but I completely agree with it."

Objectivity and impartiality was crucial to the process, but so was remaining human. The emotion of those candid workshops wouldn't have been possible to get across on a piece of paper or through a cascaded message.

How did you keep people informed?

The workshops weren't minuted. Instead we had rough designs on flipcharts and Post-its, with ideas, examples and scenarios flying around. There were never briefing notes or instructions on how they should be conducted so people spoke could speak freely about all issues.

Everything that came about as a result of the workshops was pulled together into workshop summaries, emailed to the attendees and then communicated to employees regularly. Martin Philips, our CEO at the time, would pull people together in the atrium to tell people where we were at, building trust and maintaining momentum.

I met with the board every week to ensure progress was clearly outlined and key decisions were fully explained and explored.

After about three months we had come up with a framework of the new structure.

It would be fair to say the board were uncomfortable at

times in the process. However, because so many people were involved and the development of the structure was so fruitful, I was able to show them clear and consistent progress.

Once you had a framework designed from the ground up, what was the next step?

It was time to place our people into the structure. We spent a month working through it, fitting our existing individuals into the new roles. Improving some processes did mean that some positions as we originally knew them had become defunct.

In total, the final structure of our head office required 220 redundancies. However, these employees could apply for new vacancies in other teams or departments that had been created. Thanks to the communication through the process, the news didn't come as a shock to anyone.

How did it all go down with employees?

The real test of how successful the Co-Build approach had been came when the redundancies were publicly announced in October 2012, along with the new roles, and a consultation on the entire structure opened.

All employees had another opportunity to have their say, and it soon became clear that everyone in the company believed in what we were doing. There was no bad press, no sense of doom. Because people had invested so much in putting this new structure together themselves, they had genuine desire to make it a success.

Do you consider the process finished now?

It's not a case of the change being done and dusted. We will always find things that need to improve; we are a market leader, which means change is inevitable, but the working environment we've created is now so transparent that our employees feel comfortable voicing suggestions.

In retrospect, involving our store network more in the restructuring of our head office is something we could have done more of, but that's why we're keen to keep evolving. We'll never say never to more change, as long as we stay true to the founding principles of the organisation.

What has been the biggest benefit of the restructure?
The most rewarding part for the whole business was the process itself.

Early on we thought the finished product would be what fixed everything, but it turned out to be how we designed the structure and engaged our staff that had the biggest effect. The constant face-to-face conversations broke down silos and built new bridges.

For an organisation to say all 1,400 people in its head office are going in one direction is very powerful.

I remember when I first asked each board member who it was who owned key activities such as sales or stock. There was either a reluctance to claim accountability or multiple people all claiming it rested with them. I know that they found the process difficult, but ultimately they could clearly see we had succeeded in creating a better working environment, with clear accountability and ownership at all levels.

What advice would you give to other organisations about the problems and the process?
First off, just because you have a board with knowledge and experience, it doesn't mean they have all the answers. Employees all have views about their roles and what it is they do. Conversation is a very powerful tool that shouldn't be underestimated.

Unlocking the potential that already exists within an organisation is far more powerful than most of us realise.

Chapter 5

Preparing organisations for conversation

IT WILL NEVER WORK HERE

As consultants, we often present a client with what we think is a brilliant idea to be told: "That sounds great but it'll never work here." The client foresees structural, financial or cultural obstacles standing in the way. In our experience, the greatest negativity comes from those clients who recognise their problems stem from the last on the list – culture. They fear a set of collective and deep-rooted beliefs and behaviours will impede the initiative or stop it dead.

Two organisations of a similar size, with a comparable history, in the same sector, will never face exactly the same cultural challenge. Every enterprise is a collection of individuals, and the strengths and weaknesses of each one is as unique and fascinating as the people that constitute it. Organisations do not change, but people do. Trying something new can be difficult because as individuals our habits and attitudes are ingrained and altering them is challenging even when we *know* change is necessary. In fact, we are even more likely to revert to type when we feel threatened or under pressure. As Steven Van Belleghem, author of *The Conversation Company* explains "cultural change is the single most difficult thing to achieve in a corporation that is hardwired to resist, bypass and obfuscate".[1]

The enablers and barriers to transformation inside a business may be well known internally – people are generally self-aware. The response 'it'll never work here' is rarely from someone who cannot articulate what the obstacle is or why it exists. This chapter explores some of the many cultural hurdles that leaders and communication practitioners are likely to face, and considers how best to address them. It is not a 'how to…' guide to change management, but a broader consideration of how communicators might lay the groundwork for transparent, unrestricted dialogue between people regardless of where they sit in the organisational structure. We consider whether every organisation is capable of engaging its workforce in a more open, productive dialogue. We have heard it said that some workforces, or at least tranches of them, simply want to perform a task, get paid and go home. But, as we shall see, leaders and communicators should not reject these groups as unreachable. Rather, they need to consider the immense commercial benefit of unlocking the local knowledge and opinions of even the most intransigent employees.

PUSHING WATER UPHILL WITH A FORK

Your organisation may already be primed for conversation. The CEO might have bought into the idea, his or her executive team might be largely supportive and employees at all levels might have demonstrated an ability and willingness to get involved. In which case, feel free to skip this chapter. For those others working in organisations not yet using conversation as a tool to improve operational performance, or only just beginning to, the first obstacle to overcome may be the belief that change is even needed. Leaders in organisations with a long history of broadcasting messages from the executive may insist that all they need to get through to employees is a louder megaphone. Research by Andrew Pettigrew, professor of strategy and organisation at Oxford University, found that "companies often hold on to flagrantly faulty assumptions about their world for as long as a decade, despite overwhelming evidence that that world has changed and they probably should too".[2]

Having been part of a programme of major strategic and cultural change in a 350-year-old financial services organisation in the early 2000s, I witnessed this denial first-hand. The greatest lesson I learned was that a few visionary or harebrained individuals (depending on your point of view) can try their utmost to convince others to change, but it is often not until there is a 'burning platform' – a tangible and immediate threat posed by not changing – that the opinion of this small minority will gain traction. In every business, large or small, a tipping point is often reached when both internal and external conditions force even the most complacent to re-evaluate their position. Following the near collapse of the banking sector in 2007, all eyes were on the survivors to see how quickly and extensively they were able to reform. After replacing CEO Bob Diamond, Anthony Jenkins launched the 'Transform Programme' at Barclays, demonstrating a clear desire to change. However, doubts remain, not least among Barclays' own employees, over the bank's ability to do so. After the bank's subsequent Libor scandal, it commissioned a report for which 600 employees were interviewed. The report's author, Anthony Salz, found that 70 per cent of respondents had a high degree of scepticism about Jenkins' proposed changes to culture, values and strategy.[3]

It is not human nature to make fundamental reassessments of our situation in an instant, particularly when our behaviours have long been embedded and reinforced. It may take months or even years before enough – and the right – people reach a consensus: that there is a pressing need for change and an agreed way to achieve it. History is littered with companies that were just a little too late in doing so. Ironically, too much success can often be an organisation's ultimate downfall. *If it is working well, why would we change?*

MAKING THE CASE FOR CHANGE

If you want to help your organisation change its communications, the first step is to join the dots for those who have not yet decided change is necessary. Whether leaders choose to see it or not, their organisation's performance metrics (market share, profitability, operating income, customer service and so on) all tell a story about employees. The Engage for Success taskforce sprung from a government sponsored project looking at the impact of employee engagement. In 2012 the group published 'Nailing the Evidence' a report which uses existing research to demonstrate clear connections between employee engagement and organisational productivity, customer satisfaction, low absence rates, high retention, and better health and safety records.[4] Across your business, behaviours, beliefs and outlook, will be underpinning performances good, bad or indifferent. Moreover, a collaborative and engaged workforce has become more crucial in today's innovation-driven economy. As Silicon Valley venture capitalist John Doerr puts it: "In the world today there's plenty of technology, plenty of entrepreneurs, plenty of money, plenty of venture capital. What's in short supply is great teams."[5]

Unfortunately, you cannot create a high performing team simply by flicking a switch; the Hawthorne experiments demonstrated that nearly a century ago. As Tom Peters asserted some years later, it is "attention to employees, not work conditions per se, that has the dominant impact on productivity"[6] Paying attention to employees cannot be left to the Human Resources or Communications functions alone. If leadership teams believe that engaging with their people is solely a job for one or two central teams, however capable, they are missing the point – and the first spark that will light their burning platform. Our advice to communicators is not to go it alone, but to build a like-minded team around you – seek supporters from Finance, Strategy, Human Resources, Operations and Marketing. Use your influence and insight to help others see what you are seeing, and keep yourself connected.

An external perspective can help. Independent research on the power of collaboration might convince the undecided how interesting and innovative practices in other organisations could be successfully copied. We witnessed one international client use a well-known book on business management to drive a change initiative. Leaders across this multinational business were encouraged to read it and adopt its methodology. An outsider's view can be more persuasive than suggestions from within. As consultants, clients tell us, 'I've said this before but if you say it, they might listen'. Leaders need to trust the advice they are given and feel that a recommendation to do things differently is not a criticism of their previous actions. They may be more comfortable sharing problems and conceding mistakes to an outsider. External objectivity can provide greater clarity to identify issues, and the confidence to challenge the status quo.

Many organisations require a formal project-initiation document (PID), or similar, before a project can proceed. While there is nothing inherently wrong with compiling a PID, one must be wary: in my experience, the less an organisation believes in an initiative, the more forcefully it demands evidence of a return on investment. We address the issue of proving our worth in chapter 10, but as Charlene Li asks in the insightful *Open Leadership*, "what's the ROI of a handshake?" Li believes, and we quite agree, "it's hard to quantify the value of a relationship, because we can tap into that value in so many different ways".[7] More than hard, it shows an inherent misconception of human relationships. We should not be striving to assign specific financial value to interaction. If you are spending valuable time trying to convince colleagues of the blindingly obvious, this is a sign. A tipping point has yet to be reached and yours is likely to continue to be a lone voice. I have worked in organisations where change was remarkably slow or seemingly impossible. As defeatist as this may sound, the best advice for innovative practitioners in this situation might be to move on – other organisations will need and value you more.

START AT THE TOP

As a leader of a small business, my heart sinks when I have to inform leaders of far larger organisations they need to do more to listen, inspire and involve their people. I know that in truth very few leaders seek to do anything other than engage and motivate their staff. If they fall short, it is because working life for most CEOs, vice presidents and managing directors is an endless round of back-to-back meetings, trying to solve their organisation's most intractable problems, which weigh heavy on their shoulders day and night. However well compensated leaders might be for their sleepless nights, providing inspirational leadership is a constant, personal challenge that should not be underestimated. Communicating in a way that builds trust and connects with others cannot be faked or forced. For a leader's message to be truly believed, he or she must believe it first – a leader needs to feel inspired to inspire others.

As complex and demanding as your leader's role may already be, you cannot ignore his or her pivotal role in promoting change. As Morten Hansen writes in *Collaboration*, "the very job of leaders is to unite people to pursue a common goal".[8] Luckily, the predominant advice is not for leaders to work harder, but better. It is about adopting a more discursive and inclusive leadership style that, unlike more traditional management approaches, is blind to people's position in the hierarchy and looks only at the value of their involvement. James Surowiecki, author of *The Wisdom of Crowds*, explains "the real cost of a top-down approach to decision-making [is that] it confers the illusion of perfectibility upon the decision-makers and encourages everyone else simply to play along".[9] This way of working cuts conversation short as leaders' opinions are accepted without debate. It also means the execution of a decision can become perfunctory 'playing along' rather than wholehearted support.

The aversion to a traditional management hierarchy and command-and-control mentality is a recurring theme among today's management gurus and communication advisers. Shel Holtz, author of *Corporate Conversations*, believes that "the hierarchical org chart is a relic of the industrial economy", harking back to a militaristic concept of business popularised following the Second World War.[10] The authors of *The Cluetrain Manifesto* are equally disparaging of such business environments, arguing they are "usually based on intimidation, coercion and threats of reprisal".[11] In contrast, they advocate creating an atmosphere of free and open exchange where genuine conversation can flourish. The challenge for leaders is not to push messages more forcefully down through the tiers of their organisation, but to adopt a more egalitarian management style. "Today, the organisation chart is hyperlinked, not hierarchical. Respect for hands-on knowledge wins over respect for abstract authority."[12]

We have met many leaders who look at us with a mixture of incredulity and irritation when they hear us suggest a more consensus-driven culture where issues are open for debate. They explain to us that not everything can be up for discussion; in factories, depots, laboratories, chemical plants, power stations and the like, rules and directives are necessary to ensure operations run safely and efficiently. We accept there are occasions when a discussion is entirely inappropriate. In some cases, this is because the reason is blindingly obvious – having to wear a hard hat on a building site. However, there are many occasions when a discussion *is* necessary. If instructions or orders have been issued, we are more likely to comply if the reason for them is clear and our concerns or queries have been answered. It is true that not every communication can be – or needs to be – a free and open exchange, but if employees are not following simple instructions, a conversation – or series of them – might be the best way to change that.

A 2012 Accenture study, 'Leadership Ensembles', argues that in an increasingly globalised world "the paradigm for effective leadership is changing. Companies can no longer rely on single individuals at the top to handle the complexity and uncertainty of the global environment". Instead, the study argues for "an agile, future-focused and intelligent 'leadership ensemble' at the top".[13] This ensemble approach is focused around leadership teams rather than individuals, who are able to manage and make decisions with greater fluidity and agility.

Today, leadership demands a more inclusive communication style throughout an organisation. It means making better use of the combined knowledge and experience that sits within an enterprise; issuing fewer instructions and asking for more input and ideas. Leaders need to acknowledge that they do not have all the answers and are only as good as the people who advise and support them. In some ways, the traditional pyramid structure must be turned upside down, placing the emphasis on the majority – the frontline – to innovate and drive performance.

For leaders who like to issue edicts from an ivory tower, this participatory approach is unlikely to appeal, at least initially. As communicators, we need to help executives overcome their reticence and appreciate the potential gains.

TALKING THE TALK

Once signed up to fostering a conversational company, leaders may find it challenging to take even the first step. Appointment notices for senior executives rarely list 'superior listening skills' as a must-have, so while some leaders will have a naturally open, conversational style, others may be required to learn a new set of skills. Leaders are often given 'media training', but this is designed to deal with print, radio and television journalists, not with speaking to colleagues or soliciting input and taking advice. Indeed, such training will more than likely promote and inculcate a broadcast approach to delivering messages and avoiding awkward questions. In a company that converses rather than cascades, it is important for leaders to develop more rounded communication skills. Daniel Goleman, author of *Working with Emotional Intelligence*, believes that "interpersonal ineptitude in leaders lowers everyone's performance: it wastes time, creates acrimony, corrodes motivation and commitment, builds hostility and apathy".[14] As professional communicators, our job is to help leaders acquire and improve these interpersonal skills.

In some cases, this will mean some formal training. Our advice to communications practitioners is to experience such training first-hand before recommending it to others. Everyone in our agency attended a one-day workshop with The Craft of Communication, a UK training company founded by John Abulafia that uses theatre-based techniques to help individuals develop their communication skills. Abulafia and his team help executives develop a greater awareness of their body and voice, to understand how others see them, and how changes to one's voice and body can alter other people's perceptions. The coaches put us through exercises to explore body language, articulation, impact and gravitas. Whatever coaching you choose, it should not be designed to turn people into false, or less authentic, versions of themselves. Despite a theatrical background Abulafia explains that the goal is to present each of us as "the very best version of you possible". Pretending to be something we are not destroys rather than builds trust.

CLARITY OF PURPOSE

For any change to succeed, decision-makers need to unite around a clear and common purpose that supports whatever change is required. The Accenture report 'Leadership Ensembles' admits "the need to be aligned to a single goal or task might seem like awfully basic advice". However, in its research with leaders of global enterprises, Accenture found that: "It is not uncommon to encounter standing groups and committees in organisations that have been around so long that no one questions their raison d'être. Why do they exist? The answer is usually a variant on 'they exist because they always have'."[15] The reasoning behind a more conversational approach cannot be because it is nice to do, or because we think we should. These arguments will be all too easy to ignore or overlook, especially when times get tough. Morten Hansen makes clear in his work on the topic, *Collaboration: How Leaders Avoid the Traps, Create Unity and Reap Big Results*, that the "goal of collaboration is not collaboration, but better results".[16] This will look different for different organisations. It might mean the easier flow of information, leading to greater efficiencies and savings; it might mean better interaction between diverse groups, leading to greater innovation; the goal may be a more human conversational business approach that aids better customer interaction. Or, ideally, it might mean all of these things.

As well as a meaningful reason for introducing a more conversational approach, you need a specific task for your leadership team to tackle. Be wary of catch-all terms such as 'sponsoring change'. This can mean anything from saying a few kind words to wholeheartedly embracing a radically different way of working. If open, honest dialogue is the goal – particularly in organisations where this is a break from tradition – be prescriptive about what leaders need to start doing and, crucially, *stop* doing.

A good rule, for any leader, is to demonstrate the behaviours they want others to emulate. As Hansen makes clear: "Leaders who implement disciplined collaboration successfully also walk the walk – they exemplify a collaborative leadership style."[17] There is no better way to instil a behavioural change than have it showcased by a team of respected and charismatic leaders. But behaviours must not be demonstrated only at carefully choreographed events. They must become the default mode for your leadership team, especially in challenging times. Ram Charan, writing in the *Harvard Business Review,* tells readers: "By using each encounter with his or her employees to model open, honest and decisive dialogue, the leader sets the tone for the entire organisation."[18] It must be remembered that a single false step will be highly influential; employees need just one example of leadership failing to practise what they preach to have an excuse to break the rules and revert to type themselves.

DON'T BOTHER HERE

Getting leaders on board is just the beginning. The rest of the organisation will also need to be convinced, and an ensemble-minded manager will need resilience and fortitude to kick-start and sustain a genuinely open dialogue with those around them. This is especially true if previous experiences have made people sceptical of change or if employees seem to have no desire to get involved with anything other than those duties strictly related to their job function. A lack of discretionary effort is usually a direct outcome of mistrust and low engagement.

We often hear clients doubt whether collaboration will ever take hold in their organisation because, in their view, too many employees see their work as purely transactional. These workers do not want to give any more of themselves than what is strictly necessary to complete the task at hand. It would be wrong to assume that it is only blue-collar workers who feel this way. Plenty of office employees seek to do only what is required of them. What motivates them is getting paid and leaving on time. However, we urge against ruling out these groups. It may be that their transactional approach has developed in response to leaders who never asked for – or even allowed – greater involvement. Offer these employees the opportunity to speak up and you may be surprised by the result.

We advise asking workers to discuss what they know best – their interactions with customers, the operation of plant machinery or quality control. Do not ask broad or abstract questions about the company's marketing strategy, but instead ask them what products sell well during heavy snow, whether a new layout for the stockroom would allow them to access products more quickly or if a new ordering process could help hit sales targets.

The danger for an organisation with a workforce that simply turns up, gets the job done and goes home, is if its competitors have more employees prepared to go the extra mile. We live in rapidly changing times; most businesses face a continual challenge to stay ahead of the competition, customers' expectations and technological advances. Those with employees who are working to rule and sharing none

of their experiential expertise face a significant operational
risk. The dynamism and flexibility to succeed will be severely
curtailed, and what could be an enormous pool of ideas and
fresh thinking will go untapped. It will be harder to strike up
a conversation with an intransigent, disengaged minority, but
they are a unique and valuable resource – however hard to
unlock – and therefore worth the extra effort.

MACRO ISSUES AND MICRO IRRITATIONS
It can take patience and perseverance to start a conversation
with certain people. We spoke to communications specialist
and academic Kevin Ruck about his time working at BT. He
described an initiative that put senior managers in a room with
frontline staff to encourage open debate, break down hierarchical restrictions and generate strategic insight from experienced staff. He told us that in one of the first meetings his
heart sank, as frontline staff only wanted to talk about holiday
allowances and canteen prices; he worried that the senior
manager would feel he was wasting his time. As consultants,
we have had similar experiences, trying to engage employees
about strategic issues only to be told – at length – about their
windowless office or how some people are given better leaving
parties than others. Seemingly trivial issues can have a dispro-
portionate impact. However, it pays to listen to the smallest
issue, to acknowledge its importance and, if possible, tackle it
quickly. By showing a caring, responsive attitude to the petty
annoyances, employees will be much more forthcoming about
larger obstacles.

Carol Bernick, former executive chairman and CEO of
Alberto Culver, producers of haircare products like VO5 and
TRESemmé, splits issues up for discussion into macros and
irritations. When the company first asked employees for their
opinions and suggestions, they received lots of irritations –

"our lack of personal days, direct deposit capabilities, and – I'm not kidding here – Post-it notes" – but very few macros. However, as they began to tackle the irritations, most of which could be overcome with relatively quick fixes, they began to get more strategic input. Bernick believes that "you have to remove immediate annoyances before people can focus past them".[19]

Before rushing headlong into a new communication initiative, therefore, it may be worth taking a moment to check that your organisation is getting the basics right. For internal communicators, when we talk of 'basics', we mean operational communication – *the things I need to know to do my job*. We often find it helpful to make this distinction between operational and strategic communication. While there is an overlap between the two – aspects of how organisations operate have strategic importance – there is a level of procedural information employees need, or at least expect, to perform their roles each day. This is different from communication that gives context, background and meaning to their work. Operational information is usually communicated through a line manager, supervisor or, in the case of mobile and remote employees, sent directly to them. In our experience, if operational messages are ineffective, there is little point in trying to implement more innovative communications solutions. Our advice would not be to launch a crowdsourcing initiative, for example, if employees do not have an up-to-date telephone directory, or are missing information about when their shift starts or their sales targets. You cannot expect employees to participate in productive conversations about topics beyond their primary function if the conversations they *need* to have each day – with a line manager, supervisor or other teams – are not working.

CULTIVATING FERTILE GROUND

Even if you have support for a more conversational approach

to communication, your initiative can stumble. Things might start well, with an imaginative launch campaign and plenty of executive involvement, but for all the excitement, your initiative fails to get off the ground. Instead, it disappears as quickly as it arrived, consigned to the corporate memory as a quirky attempt to try something new.

Even great ideas need the right environment to flourish. In the McKinsey study 'The Social Economy', we are reminded that improved productivity through conversation "will require both a successful implementation and the appropriate tools, and, more important, climbing a steep organisational learning curve: changes in processes, organisation mind-sets, and behaviours will be needed to build up habits of open communication and information sharing, particularly when ideas and knowledge must flow across functional silos".[20] In other words, we cannot expect a bright, shiny new tool and an imaginative campaign to prompt our employees to simultaneously erupt into productive and meaningful conversation, especially if no one has ever asked for their opinion and, crucially, *listened* to it, in the past. Pierre Goad, Global Head of Communications for HSBC, told us about the organisation's HSBC Exchange programme, an initiative that encourages open communication across its hierarchy. He was honest about the fact that in the beginning managers faced 'tumbleweed moments' in meetings where employees were reluctant to contribute. It has taken patience and commitment to create a 'speak up' culture. Goad is keen to stress that this initiative is still in its infancy although the benefits are already being felt.

According to Chade-Meng Tan, Google engineer and author of *Search Inside Yourself*[21], research shows we need three positive experiences to outweigh one negative one. A negative experience cuts deeper. This explains why organisations can launch a grand, well-designed initiative only to receive a lukewarm response. We had one client do just this, and when we held focus groups with employees, we discovered the initiative was held back by wariness and mistrust stemming from badly handled experiences three years previously. Because the organisation had never confronted and acknowledged these mistakes, the frustration and scepticism of colleagues had just continued to fester. However great the new offering appeared, employees just did not believe it, having been let down in the past. As listening expert and hostage negotiator Richard Mullender told us, trust is crucial; "lose this and you've lost everything".

A PLACE OF SAFETY

Employees are unlikely to speak up if they do not feel it is safe to do so. If confidentiality has been broken in the past, this can cast a long shadow over subsequent attempts to engage them in open dialogue. Morten Hansen feels there is a need to create an environment of 'psychological safety' where leaders "behave in such a way that people feel safe to speak up without fear of retribution. Leaders who praise dissent and alternative suggestions (even if they were not followed) help create this safety".[22]

Face-to-face, low-key events are a great place to start, as we discuss further in chapter 9. Some of these initial sessions may well feel awkward, even uncomfortable, as they were for Kevin Ruck and Pierre Goad, but maintain the momentum because over time these sessions will be thought-provoking and enlightening for all those involved. The topics people choose to raise, the language they use and their frame of reference will be gold-dust to anyone interested in moving the organisation forward.

If your CEO would rather cut off his arm than converse without notes or an agenda to a group of employees, do not despair. Before you rush off to find a new job, is there anyone on the management team who might take up the mantle? Your mission is to get one executive doing this well, gaining great feedback from employees and using his or her new-found knowledge from these sessions to demonstrably improve their understanding of how your organisation works. If you can achieve that, others will want to follow suit. The McKinsey report 'The Social Economy' tells us that in the future "managers will need to reward employees for the information which they share, rather than the information they hoard".[23] Smart leaders – and the communicators who support them – value feedback even when the news is bad.

The IPA and Tomorrow's Company report 'Releasing Voice' includes a case study from Unipart, the manufacturing, logistics and consultancy group, where there is a 'no blame culture'; employees are encouraged to take ownership of their work, get involved and speak up. This is reinforced by the belief that 'no problem is a problem'. In Unipart, there is acknowledgement that rather than avoiding problems, they should be actively sought out as opportunities for improvement. The company's internal channels are therefore "designed to elicit [employee's] knowledge"[24] and expertise, so potential problems might not only be quickly uncovered, but also addressed and overcome.

Of course, encouraging people to highlight problems is not always easy. The McKinsey Institute recognises that it requires "courage to hear honest feedback from individuals".[25] In the first few days of becoming managing director of AB, a colleague came into my office, closed the door and explained how I needed to improve my communication to the company. I had barely got my feet under the table, so my instinctive reaction was to defend my behaviour and close down the conversation as quickly as possible. Luckily, I took a moment to consider my response. In the future, I would need people around me who were willing to speak up. I would never have enough eyes and ears to fully understand how people were feeling on my own. So, I thanked my colleague and asked her to carry on giving me honest feedback, good or bad.

MAINTAINING MOMENTUM

Running a pilot is often the starting point for an organisation wary of making a wholesale change. By starting with a discrete exercise, limited in its scope, the cost, impact and risk are contained, making it easier to secure high-level buy-in. Of course, the pilot must be a success for it to be extended and adopted elsewhere, but for all those involved – even its most ardent supporters – starting with a pilot might mean fewer sleepless nights.

Of course, initiatives and pilots can only be coined a success when they cease to be projects and become 'the way we do things around here'. As soon as something is working well – if conversation is successfully being nurtured in one part of your organisation – your job as a leader or communicator is to replicate it elsewhere. The first step to making this happen is talking about it. Promote the value and highlight the benefits reaped by a conversational approach, acknowledge its champions and encourage others to appreciate and reproduce this success. Use the often-privileged position of the internal communications department to your advantage – we can have contacts and influence far beyond the boundaries of our team. Do not think purely in terms of creating an 'internal communications' initiative. All projects and programmes – wherever they originate – need to be communicated. Speak to the leader of the next IT transformation programme, department restructuring or new manufacturing process about the benefits of open dialogue and collaboration.

You will no doubt have heard the maxim 'what gets measured gets done'. To maintain momentum for conversation then, it may be necessary to ensure performance metrics for managers include a more conversational approach to communication and decision-making. Stephen Shapiro's white paper, '10X innovation ROI on your internal collaboration', urges executives to "define what your organisation values and then reward it". He makes it clear precisely what a leadership team can do to broadly promote conversational initiatives: "If you want to encourage open innovation of cross-business unit collaboration, then recognise people for that. If you want employees to take risks, make a big deal out of employees who do that. If you want to let people know that failure is ok – when done the right way – then promote situations where something didn't work as planned yet powerful lessons were learned and risk was mitigated."[26]

If the organisation is serious about this shift towards capturing and using the employee voice, potential new recruits to your organisation need to demonstrate their ability to stimulate and maintain productive conversations. Internal promotions should be given to those who demonstrate the appropriate behaviours, and those who prevent or avoid an open exchange of views need to be called to account. In one organisation, I witnessed a long-serving senior executive who was openly hostile to a particular change initiative moved sideways to an offshore division. This was a symbolic act. It told us all that the leadership team had made a decision: this is the future – get on board or get out. Cultural change is about the 'r' policies – reward, recognition, retention and recruitment. All must reflect the right behaviours and traits so that, over time, the DNA of an organisation evolves.

PATIENCE IS A VIRTUE

Fruitful conversation is unlikely to blossom inside any organisation unless the cultural conditions are right – unless there is mutual trust, a feeling of security and a belief people's voices will be heard. Effective conversations need meaning and purpose; if the subject under discussion is too abstract or wide-ranging, they lose their way. Equally, if the topic is tangential to daily business, the conversation will be considered a distraction from 'real' work and people are likely to participate only under sufferance. When cultural change is necessary for conversation to flourish, the road ahead will be challenging. Behaviour, whether individual or collective, is often deeply ingrained. Even when we know we must change – when change is necessary for our very survival – doing things differently takes effort. We start with good intentions but all too quickly slip back to our old ways. People who were assured of change feel let down. Future commitments or intentions to change fall on deaf or sceptical ears. An unfilled promise of change is worse than no promise at all.

The answer lies in not promising too much – setting realistic expectations and introducing small interventions or pilots to get the organisation talking. Conversations should have a commercial imperative and should not be squeezed into already packed diaries. Rather, they should be integrated into existing processes, procedures and exchanges. Unproductive meetings need to be eradicated, no matter how formal or long-standing. Even when change is afoot, it needs to be sustained. If new behaviours are associated with only one or two executives, what happens if they leave?

Leaders need fair warning that fostering and sustaining productive conversation is difficult. "Organisations should recognise that proactive employees are not always an unmitigated benefit. They have associated costs, and require a shift in mind-set from the firm," writes Donald Campbell, in 'The Proactive Employee'. It takes patience, resilience and tolerance to engage in a genuinely open debate. But Campbell explains "for firms successfully achieving this shift, the benefits can be substantial: increased competitive advantage in complex, competitive environments."[27] In accomplishing this worthwhile goal, the groundwork is inescapable.

In conversation with Wendy Jordan

Wendy Jordan is group communications officer and intranet manager for Wheatley Group, Scotland's leading housing, care and community regeneration group. Comprising four social landlords, a care organisation and two commercial subsidiaries, the group spans 12 local authority areas across central Scotland.

The driving force behind the Group's brand new intranet, Wendy is passionate in her pursuit of employee engagement, going to remarkable lengths to build a collaborative, open working environment with her remote workforce.

How do you build relationships with the workforce of Wheatley Group and its different entities?
Our organisation has seen a lot of change over recent years. With a workforce of around 2,400, we aren't massive, but we do have a wide geographical spread.

The number of our subsidiaries has increased, bringing in new people with different roles and ways of working.

Since 2009, I've been shadowing new employees for the day. I use the opportunity to find out what they really do and how

I should be communicating with them.

Building these kinds of relationships is crucial.

Are these relationships confined to the office?

Not at all. When it comes to fundraising, for example, I won't promote anything I would not do myself. I've zip-lined from the roof of our offices, abseiled down one of our buildings, walked on fire with someone and will be competing in 2014's Tough Mudder challenge. If I can't take part, I'll make sure I'm out there supporting those involved. Doing this makes things more personal, breaks down barriers and builds bridges.

Understanding employees as people also helps me build a network to gather content. For employees with families, I have bought admission tickets for the Glasgow Science Centre and re-sold them at a discounted price before the school half-term holidays. It's a way of reaching out to people who might not otherwise speak to me. And once I've done them a favour, I know I can call on them in future.

What is it that makes you so passionate about internal communication?

In 2005, I finished a trip around the world with £60 in my pocket and a degree in film, media and politics. I actually joined Wheatley as a temp assistant in the finance department. Things grew and I stuck around, but it wasn't until 2009 that I found my niche in internal communication.

I read all of the books on the profession available at the time, completed all the Chartered Institute of Public Relations courses, attended industry conferences and did everything I could to feed my desire to master internal communication. The reality is that the industry is still quite a closed shop.

It was astonishing how much I loved the role and its purpose. Very few people I've met are aware of the internal communication profession and I often find myself explaining it.

Really successful communicators tend to share a passion for people, words and building understanding.

As far as I'm concerned, I work for the staff, not the management. It's my job to help the frontline do its job.

The workforce hasn't always been as engaged as it is now though. Much of what we have achieved is down to the success of our intranet, Holmes.

Why is Holmes so important?
Wheatley Group has a policy of engaging customers in a trusting, honest environment, and Holmes – now two years old – gives its employees an online environment that reflects this ethos internally.

It is widely embraced by our employees and has been since it was first introduced.

Our old intranet had more than 10,000 documents on it. Most of these were pointless, useless or out of date. This made them inaccurate, and it is crucially important that our people have the right tools to do their jobs.

Before Holmes was introduced, we surveyed intranet users and found people were spending upwards of half an hour searching through records for what they wanted. Staff should have the answers they need at their fingertips. They needed an intranet that fits with the way they work.

How did you build an intranet that suited your employees?
The first thing we did was involve them. We chose not to migrate anything from the old system and start with a blank slate.

We surveyed our people at the outset. This meant the very foundations of Holmes were built on the feedback of our employees.

We also held 100 meetings across Wheatley Group, questioning people in different departments at different levels. We had one set of questions for everyone:

- What functions do you use on the intranet?
- What do you create on there that other people use?
- What do you use that other people have created?
- What do you need the intranet to do?

The answers became our plan of attack. I looked at a lot of other organisation's intranets, but if I'm honest, I was underwhelmed by what's out there.

It seems many people take the path of least resistance when it comes to creating an intranet, meaning that many are not as useful as they should be.

Because I had spoken to our staff, I understood what the intranet needed to do.

I kept going back to our users to find out what processes we could slim down, rework, add or eliminate. There was such an enthusiasm for it throughout because they were a part of it.

Getting that buy-in from staff right at the start helped keep them on board during the development. They chose everything, down to the name.

Was it all plain sailing?
We did hit a snag right before we were about to sign the contract for development. Our IT department put the red light on the whole thing.

The first they saw of Holmes was a fully formed plan and they found it difficult to see how it would integrate with our business because it was completely new. At the time, people were demanding a lot of IT, with lots of departments trying to introduce new applications that didn't integrate with the existing intranet easily. They thought Holmes would only complicate things.

Fortunately, I was able to show that developing Holmes could be a front door for applications.

Obviously we won the IT department over, and I think it was very important not to let them get in our way. You can't allow something for all employees to be limited by IT fears.

Did Holmes make an immediate impact?
Our old intranet had a flat, lifeless homepage with no opportunity for engagement, very few channels for feedback and no analytics.

When Holmes launched, it had video and blogs on the homepage, completely new elements to Wheatley Group. The visual impact was huge.

There was a real sense of anticipation and excitement for the launch. We had a great comms plan in place to build up momentum and on the day Holmes went live, a remarkable 80 per cent of our workforce signed up to it.

The IT department took more than 200 calls from our grass cutters who hadn't previously used the intranet, but wanted to generate a password in order to log on and see the new site. Even they had heard the buzz about it, and we couldn't have generated that without involving our people in the site's creation.

We now have 94 per cent of our workforce registered and using Holmes. The entire construction of it cost less than £60,000 and it has been such a good investment.

How has it helped improve dialogue with staff?
Holmes is stuffed with news and blogs that represent the voice of the people in the organisation. We have extra pages

on there focusing on timely things like the 2014 Glasgow Commonwealth Games.

The blog function allows us to put a human voice behind the processes and events. The comments section on our blogs is now a crucial part of how we communicate too.

People may have been able to email the chief executive, but they are far more likely to comment on his blogs. It makes him more accessible.

We had one senior manager blog about a problem with rent collection. In it he openly admitted he had reached the limits of his understanding on the subject and asked for advice from staff. There were reams of comments with people telling him what to do and it opened a door to a real conversation.

Now managers are always asking for suggestions and inviting comment.

With so many new features to get used to, how did you encourage engagement with users?
We trained an army of young apprentices to use Holmes before it launched.

They had grown up with liking, blogging and commenting, so we just trained them to be experts in what we'd created. They went back to their respective offices, departments or environments as intranet experts.

It was useful because it gave these youngsters new responsibilities and exploited their skills as a generation more familiar with technology.

Some of them are now my content managers. They were champions from the outset, getting all of our people on board and changing the way we work. There are fewer silos now because everyone is connected through Holmes.

Holmes is such a resounding success for Wheatley Group, what could larger organisations learn from your experience?
You have to start with what your people want, rather than what technology might be able to provide.

The technology we've used to construct Holmes is brilliant, but wasn't the first step.

So much of internal communication is about respecting and listening to your people. I consider myself very lucky to work with the people I do. I'm constantly aware of my responsibility to the frontline and work hard to make their jobs as easy as possible.

Chapter 6

From the corporate to the employee voice

MIND THE GAP

If you are one of the three million people who use London Underground every day, you will be painfully familiar with the announcements made over the tannoy. We are told to 'mind the gap' or 'stand back as this train is ready to depart'. The messages wash over us weary commuters; they may reach our ears, but rarely our brains. However, very occasionally Transport for London employees will inject some personality. On a busy morning at Aldgate East, one passenger reported hearing: "Please use all available doors. There are some really good ones at the front of the train." Then there was the announcement heard during an extremely hot rush hour on the Central line: "Step right this way for the sauna, ladies and gentleman...unfortunately towels are not provided."[1] These rare personal broadcasts have a magical effect. Travellers who would never have dreamt of making eye contact exchange a smile or even a few words. With just a touch of humour, warmth and personality, these announcements break a spell; suddenly we are no longer sleepwalking through our journey, alone in a crowd of faceless strangers, we have connected with the message and each other through a shared experience.

Now consider your workplace. While you would hope that employees are somewhat more alert than an army of zombie commuters, they are still more than capable of filtering out a message that fails to interest or inspire them. We are bombarded with so much messaging and so many announcements that we have become skilled at, and accustomed to, sifting information as soon as we receive it. This is bad news for a corporate world where too many messages blandly warn staff to 'mind the gap', rather than give voice to the many personalities within its walls.

TRYING TO PLEASE EVERYONE

I have heard it said we should blame the grey-suited corporate communicators for the monotone nature of much internal communication because passionate communicators with style, flair and personality are simply not attracted to corporate roles. If only it were that simple. In my experience, the individuals working in corporate communications are full of life, character and opinions. If anything, they are some of the most challenging and nonconformist people in central function roles. It is too simplistic to blame those that broadcast – or even create – these messages. Instead, we must look at the culture that underpins how and why communication decisions are made. Sadly, for many corporates, collective behaviour is driven in part by fear. Most organisations have numerous constituencies they need to please, or keep on side: employees, trade unions, shareholders, institutional investors, lobby groups and the media. All of these combine to help shape public and consumer opinion and influence the share price. The amendment and approval process for all broadcasts, whether internal or external, is, in effect, a test; will this communication offend one of our many stakeholders? To err on the side of caution, the message is honed to be as safe and sterile as possible, but while this results in a message that is unlikely to offend, it is equally unlikely to engage. Trying to please everyone results in pleasing no one.

ONCE MORE, WITH FEELING

Of course, some would argue that certain announcements are meant to be clear and unambiguous, the facts represented plainly, without commentary or opinion; and certainly without sentiment. Newsreaders, at least those in the traditional mould, are particularly adept at this – keeping emotion and personal disposition in check, at most allowing themselves a raised eyebrow or an extra two-second pause before moving on. However, when their façade slips and genuine emotion is revealed – even for a moment – our connection to the broadcaster and the story shifts; suddenly it is not just the facts, but also the meaning behind them that is being conveyed.

Of all the news broadcasts announcing President Kennedy's assassination in 1963, one is replayed over and over. Walter Cronkite, by then already a veteran broadcaster, was the CBS news anchor that day. During one of his many bulletins on that Friday afternoon, he was handed a sheet of paper. Cronkite stopped speaking, put on his glasses, looked at the bulletin sheet. He read: "From Dallas, Texas, the flash, apparently official, President Kennedy died at 1pm Central Standard Time." He took off his glasses and glanced up at the clock on the wall. "Two o'clock Eastern Standard Time, some 38 minutes ago." Clearly choked with emotion, Cronkite paused, taking a moment to put his glasses back on. With an audible croak in his voice, he resumed, telling viewers that Lyndon Johnson would become the 36th president of the United States. It is not the degree of Cronkite's emotion that touches us – it is the momentary slip of a consummate professional – but more that, for a moment, Cronkite was not merely announcing the news, he was feeling it.[2] Similarly, when covering the moon landings in July 1969, Cronkite could not hide his boyish enthusiasm at the events unfolding before him.[3]

By allowing enough of his personality to shine through, Cronkite became more than just a mouthpiece for announcements. He was, as President Obama said at his 2009 memorial service, "a familiar and welcome voice that spoke to each and every one of us personally".[4] Cronkite put just enough of himself into his broadcasts for his audience to feel not just informed but emotionally connected to the story. It is hard to fake emotion; politicians and bad actors remind us of this regularly. Phony emotion feels deceitful to the onlooker, whereas a display of genuine feeling builds trust. In 1972, the US polling company Oliver Quayle asked Americans which public figure they most trusted; Cronkite topped the poll.[5]

Corporations are experts at drafting news announcements. These factual, impersonal statements have often been amended and approved by a committee. They are not so good at allowing enough personality to shine through to make an emotional connection with their staff. Take your company's name off the header of your most recent communication, replace it with that of your biggest competitor and ask yourself if the language or tone would feel incongruous? Probably not. There is a generic character to most of these announcements – clear, confident, often unequivocal and sterile. It is a tone that typifies not just press announcements but also the raft of communication that organisations disseminate both internally and externally. In this chapter we examine the contrast between the corporate and human voice – with all its frailties and foibles. We explore why the life is often squeezed from corporate communication and argue that a shift towards more human language and expression would take corporate communication to a new level of effectiveness, not least by engendering greater trust. In the eminently quotable *The Cluetrain Manifesto,* we are told "in just a few more years, the current 'homogenised' voice of business – the sound of mission statements and brochures – will seem as contrived and artificial as the language of the 18th century French court".[6] The authors argue, "natural, human conversation is the true language of commerce".[7] We have a truly global communications network, we should restore "the banter that came with the bazaar…tear down power structures and senseless bureaucracies and put everyone in touch with everyone".[8]

AUDIENCE IS KING

The danger when crafting any communication – from a speech to a news article – is losing sight of your audience. Effective communication is built around the needs, values and expectations of the recipient. It should speak to them about their interests and in their language. The more specific you can be about the recipient, the more detailed portrait you can paint, the more tailored and powerful your communication. In their essay 'The Audience is Dead; Long Live the Audience!', Deborah Jermyn and Su Holmes argue that "as we settle into the 21st century, this perception, and the concomitant notion of a 'mass' audience, has become increasingly fragile and problematic".[9]

Just as they can often water down the content of announcements, organisations have a tendency to do the same with their audience; they standardise and dehumanise recipients, viewing them as 'stakeholders' or 'interested parties' rather than people. In a productive audience-speaker relationship, a speaker must recognise his or her audience as more than a crowd of passive onlookers; they are an active and integral part of the communication process.

When clients ask us to develop more differentiating and

engaging communications, we start by asking 'who are you?' and 'who is your audience?' because a clear understanding of both has often been lost or forgotten. These can be surprisingly difficult questions to answer. They require profound self-analysis, raising questions about an organisation's past and future, and its definition of success. Getting people to agree on such things without producing insipid, bland statements is challenging. The question 'who is your audience?' might appear easy to answer, but too often we find organisations know surprisingly little about their audience, even when it is on the payroll. Sadly, too many rely on their all-staff engagement survey to judge the mood of employees when these blunt, quantitative surveys cannot do much more than check the temperature of the patient. They rarely, if ever, diagnose an underlying condition. Knowing your audience means talking to them. It means asking open questions that enable you to find the root cause of both positive and negative feelings. Identifying the personal values of your audience, and understanding the language and terminology they use, helps craft communication that feels relevant and meaningful. Effective communicators know this already; audience analysis is not new, and in the external world of marketing is always a matter of course.

WHAT THEY PAY TO READ

As readers, we feel a familiarity and fondness for our favourite newsstand or online titles; they know us and speak directly to us about our concerns and interests. Your employees no doubt have their preferred titles – those they feel speak to and about them. That is why, when creating content for employees, our first question is 'what are they paying to read?' That is where we set the bar. Employees too rarely have the option to unsub-scribe to their company's communication – but they can ignore it. They may not be spending their own money on this content, but it is competing with the titles and channels they *are* paying for.

The pessimists will say that internal communicators' budgets do not stretch to those of the news corporations, so we cannot hope to compete with mainstream media for readers' attention. However, as internal communicators, we do have one significant advantage over traditional outlets. We really know our readers – or at least we should do. Certainly, if you are not sure what your employees are paying to read today, you can simply ask them. Indeed, we would argue that you should be researching the employee base as thoroughly as your marketing team researches your organisation's most profitable customers. This means moving beyond traditional demographic or HR information and moving to a more rounded analysis of employees' social and economic habits inside and outside work. How do they spend their money? Where do they go on holiday? What TV programmes do they watch? What newspapers do they read? What smart devices do they own? What are their favourite apps? Mainstream media finds these insights invaluable when making editorial decisions about content, approach, tone, personality and humour – employee media must do the same.

The internet has served to raise audience expectations of specialised and targeted content – and online it almost always comes free. As Charles Leadbeater explains in *We-Think*, "the web provides many more niches for people to start a conversation on something about which they feel passionately. The old, industrial media, newspapers and television, do not have enough room to cater for all the majority interests of their readers and listeners".[10] For internal communicators, the key lies in the appropriate use of channels. An all-employee publication is unlikely to be a suitable place for an in-depth discussion or debate on the intricacies of a new process or product, but it may be possible to provide an online forum for those who want to engage with the topic. We would suggest creating such a space, or, even better, allowing employees the freedom to create one for themselves. By doing this, a communicator not only ensures employees have an outlet for these specialised interests, but also demonstrates a recognition of their needs as an audience.

BETTER BROADCAST

Having a genuine conversation with readers about proposed content through an editorial panel or network of champions can help keep broadcast channels relevant to readers. If you ask, employees will tell you exactly what they want to know more (and less) about. They will explain what would make a piece of communication credible and interesting, and equally what feels like propaganda or marketing hype. It would be wrong to assume your employees have no appetite for corporate strategy and that you have to force-feed them this information by dressing it up to be something it is not. Tailoring information, and speaking in a human voice, does not stop you talking business. For some clients, our internal communication is about helping to develop thought leaders within the industry. Internal content should not be limited to long service awards, product launches and project updates.

This mistaken assumption that "there is no great demand for information about corporate-level decisions that do not immediately impact on the employee's local work area"[11] may stem in part from the vastly successful *Communicating Change*, written by TJ and Sandar Larkin in 1994. With chapters such as 'Your employees don't care about the company', they preached that it was line managers and local work areas that held all the power. However, not only was their book focused on change management, it was based on research conducted by IABC and Towers Perrin in the 1980s that was fatally flawed. Rather than have respondents rank preferred sources, they were asked to pick *one* source for *all* their information. Measurement consultant Angela Sinickas has long argued that these were the wrong questions, based on an illogical premise. "We all prefer different sources for different types of information."[12] It is the job of the communicator to identify the right source, time and tone for each message.

American academic Tom Davenport believes "there is no such thing as information overload because as an information hungry society, we can stand all the information we can lay our hands on – about the stuff we're interested in. It is only when we are forced to slog through material we do not care about that we experience overload".[13] Our research supports such a claim. Year after year, employees can list a range of subjects they would be keen to learn more about: the performance of the company against its targets, what the competition is up to, a sneak preview of the company's future plans, bright ideas they can borrow. When people feel overwhelmed by the volume of communication they receive, it is because far too much of it is too long, badly written, poorly signposted, mistimed and prob-ably irrelevant.

Newsstand titles use a range of research methods and ana-lytics to monitor reader habits and opinions. Advertisers often demand this to justify the return on their advertising spend. Every aspect of reader behaviour is assessed and tracked to paint a picture of what people are reading, when, for how long, where and, most crucially, why. These insights are used to make editorial, design and platform decisions; it is why (whether readers can see it or not) their favourite title is constantly evolving. For communicators then, having grabbed the atten-tion of the internal audience, how do we keep it? It requires a strong editorial vision based on what interests and excites the audience, followed by close monitoring of the readership. Are they still engaged? If not, why? A paying readership will vote with their wallets, so any decline will be painfully apparent. For internal communicators, a decline may be less obvious, so regular measurement is vital to check that a message is still engaging its audience.

It is also worth remembering the level of openness and honesty that is needed with employees. Organisational change expert Gary F Grates believes "companies make a mistake when they use a marketing lens of a marketing approach in dealing with employee communication... you can sell to customers because they don't see what's behind the curtain. They just see the end product, and they base their relationship with a brand on what that end product does or doesn't do. When you're an employee, you see the warts. You see under the rug".[14] There is no point proclaiming particular values in the hope of winning over employees if this same group can see full well that such values are all talk and go undemonstrated in their working life.

ENCOURAGING 'STIRRING PERFORMANCES'
Those looking after a company's purse strings might justifiably ask why money is being spent providing the workforce with communication that echoes commercial publications and websites. Surely we are employing people to work, why should they need to be entertained? Investing in high-quality communication is not about providing a benefit; it is about exploiting untapped commercial advantage. As Douglas McGregor explained: "The blunt fact is that we are a long way from realising the potential represented by the human resources we now recruit into industry."[15] It is not an employer's duty to provide the self-respect or self-fulfilment that leads to discretionary effort or, as William Kahn puts

it, "more stirring performances". However, McGregor does believe it is their duty to create the conditions that allow individuals to find this for themselves, not least because "people deprived of opportunities to satisfy at work the needs which are now important to them behave exactly as we might predict – with indolence, passivity, unwillingness to accept responsibility, resistance to change, willingness to follow and demagogue, unreasonable demands for economic benefits".[16] As communicators and leaders, we see disengagement manifest itself in these behaviours regularly, and it is clear that such passivity has financial implications.

Clearly, a printed or online title, however carefully crafted, is not capable of driving employee engagement by itself. This is true for all communication because words are never enough. Personal experience must support stated intentions. The role of any official internal channel is to reflect and support the corporation's strategy. If this is to motivate, engage and collaborate, the communication that emanates from within the walls of the corporate structure must support this objective. Conversely, corporate channels cannot be used to mask faults and imperfections. When a problem exists, a clear, frank explanation is needed of what is wrong and why is more effective than a contrived or clipped response. Equally, if not all sides agree, an acknowledgement of this is more effective than simply turning up the volume on the megaphone. To have content that truly engages with employees, organisations need to become comfortable with being honest and transparent.

MAKING IT PLAIN

Plain language is the foundation of any honest conversation. Throughout this book, we have seen how a culture of trust is necessary for individuals and groups to share their thoughts openly. Opaque or confusing communication strikes at the heart of a trusting relationship. A lack of clarity suggests a deliberate attempt to misinform even though it may simply be a bad choice of words.

Research from employees and subpostmasters said the Post Office's tone across all its communication was bureaucratic and patronising – a hangover over from its civil service roots. So we helped it embark on a tone of voice progamme. Led by the internal communications team, employees from Finance, HR and Marketing attended workshops to explore why this tone persisted, why it needed to change and how to tackle it. While the Post Office acknowledged it needed to adopt a tone more in keeping with its values and strategy, change would not be easy. During the workshops, those responsible for crafting and sending material to employees identified a number of obstacles.

Legal language – *we have to say it like this*
Complexity – *there's no easy way to explain it*
Tradition – *this is how people expect to receive it*
Lack of time – *we don't have time to re write it*
Fear – *we can't be that bold and direct*

We addressed each of these concerns. One of the most difficult was working with legal and regulatory teams to find ways to make their language more accessible. Step-by-step plain language guidelines were developed. People were encouraged to submit examples of poor communication to be rewritten, and by taking a 'train the trainer' approach, the programme spread. Over time, the organisation started to 'speak' in a voice that echoed the relationship it wanted to develop with its internal audiences, which also better reflected its external marketing.

When the telecoms giant BT embarked on a similar process of changing the tone and style of its internal communication, it became clear that it was a full-time job for an expert. This led to the appointment of Jon Hawkins, BT's head of brand language. Speaking at the Institute of Internal Communication's conference in 2014, Jon explained that the company carried "an awful lot of baggage from our previous background as a Government department. The civil service had a particular writing style, which is old-fashioned and stuffy. We're also a technical company so we get wrapped up in technical jargon." Jon's role is to help present a more human, consistent and distinctive face to the world. BT's language programme has been running for five years. It started with writing workshops for people involved in communications and spread wider as managers asked for their teams to be trained. Around 8,000 people across BT have attended a writing workshop, including employees in China, Australia and the US. Jon reinforces the view that the programme does more than introduce plain language; it also captures the distinctive personality of BT in all communications to its 87,000 employees.

Plain language does more than build trust; it saves money – sometimes significant sums. Forms are more likely to be completed correctly, fewer queries arise and instructions are more likely to be understood and followed. A study involving naval officers tested the effect of two business memos, one written in plain language and another in a bureaucratic style. Those who read the easy version understood it better, took between 17 per cent and 23 per cent less time to read it and felt less need to read it again. The projected cost saving if all naval personnel, not just officers, were given plain language documents was estimated to be between $250 and $350 million a year[17]. In 2010, the promotion of plain language was given a boost when President Obama signed the Plain Writing Act, ushering in a law requiring federal agencies to use "clear Government communication that the public can understand and use".[18]

Of course, sometimes inaccessible or jargon-laden language

is deliberate. Writer Steven Poole calls this 'unspeak', language engineered to make simple ideas more complicated, direct or deflect blame and make unpalatable truths more agreeable. One of his many examples is the difference between 'climate change' and 'global warming' – the first sounding far less concerning than the second.[19] The manipulation of language to shape opinion is nothing new. The worry for communicators is that some corporate voices hinder rather than help conversation. During an average working day, what do the messages employees encounter say about their employer? An interesting exercise might be to gather communications from a typical day at work – from the signage we see walking though reception, the poster next to the coffee machine, the notice on the back of the toilet door and the forest of emails cluttering our inbox. If your corporate voice were personified, how would you describe this individual? Would you welcome a conversation with him or her; or would you be more likely to cross the room to avoid them? As BT tone of voice expert Jon Hawkins says, this is about more than accessible language and a friendly tone. It is about conveying a distinctive personality based on a set of values or principles. Brand experts tell us that from the consumers' perspective, every 'touch point' with the organisation must reaffirm these differentiating beliefs. Does your employer brand – the totality of people's experience internally – stack up? Do the recruitment ad, induction pack, intranet, weekly team briefings and messages on payslips all tell the same story? Or are there glaring discrepancies that undermine how the organisation aspires to communicate? If so, you may need to instigate a programme to identify and address this.

REALLY HEARING THE EMPLOYEE VOICE

The shift from the corporate to the employee voice is not simply about replacing one style with another, moving from cool detachment to a warmer, personal tone. Equally it is not solely about paying more consideration to the requirements and desires of employees; it is about viewing internal communication in an entirely new way. The IPA and Tomorrow's People 2012 report on employee communication, 'Releasing Voice', states that "effective employee voice demands a new mind-set, a paradigm shift".[20] In the past we saw internal communication as a transaction between sender and receiver. Now we must see it as a collaborative effort between those who originate, reshape, like and share information. This puts traditional roles – those of 'audience', 'editor' and 'broadcaster' – under threat and means we must rethink the tactics we once employed to gather, write and disseminate content. Published content is now the start of a conversation. Readers can rate or 'like' an article, make a comment, raise a question or share it with others. It is not unusual to find the comments made by readers at the end of a story more interesting than the story itself. This has implications for the internal communicator, some of whom will not feel ready to have their content openly reviewed and judged by the audience.

In all aspects of our life, the way we create, consume and interact with content has altered. We are now far more active participants in its generation and development. This shift has been felt keenly even in television broadcasting where the audience was once clearly defined, quantifiable and confined purely to the role of spectator. Audiences are granted new degrees of power as we now schedule our own programmes. Pay-to-view, view on demand, record and download options mean we choose when, where and how we view content. The programmes themselves – reality and talent shows such as *I'm a Celebrity, Get me Out of Here!*, *Big Brother*, *The Voice* and *The X Factor* – depend on audience participation, while their sister shows such as *Big Brother's Little Brother* rely on the "constant solicitation of viewer opinion".[21] Deborah Jermyn and Su Holmes argue that while the traditional concept of a merely passive audience may have been exaggerated in the past, there is no doubt that today the audience is being asked more directly and often for their feedback and comment. This is shaping content across the spectrum, from reality shows to news programming. In short, the audience has far greater self-awareness and is increasingly comfortable in a more participatory role.

Nowhere is the collaborative spirit between those who produce and consume content more apparent than on the web, as Weinberger explains: "Every blogger is a broadcaster, and every reader is an editor."[22] Accordingly, when organisations do take steps to embrace an open, more participative conversation with their employees, it is typically around online content on social intranets. Here employees are increasingly invited to comment on, rate, share and 'like' what they read. This is a welcome step, but too many organisations still have someone standing at the gate, deciding which comments to let through. This desire to 'control the message' is both antiquated and counterproductive. People love to talk, especially about subjects they care about. Many companies paying good money for customer insight restrict and inhibit employee feedback when this is both free and easily attainable. Plus, because employees see under the hood, their insights are more likely to be grounded in the operational realities of your business than those of your customers.

UNLEASHING ANARCHY

Boris Groysberg and Michael Slind believe organisations need to move on from "giving employees a say behind closed doors to giving them a say in an open forum".[23] The benefits are clear: more varied organisational content and a boost in engagement, as "employees become active producers (rather than passive consumers) of content".[24] However, their research shows the reluctance within many organisations to embrace this 'open forum'. Despite the existence of European Works Councils and similar bodies, most still feel reticent about handing over the megaphone. When Groysberg and Slind surveyed participants in an Executive Education programme at Harvard Business School in 2012, 51 per cent said the goal of "encouraging employee voice" had no priority or low priority at their company.

They asked participants whether employees throughout their company "are able to publish original content (such as blog posts) on internal channels". Nearly half of them said no. They also asked whether employees "are able to participate freely and openly in intranet-based discussion forums", and again 51 per cent said no.[25] In the same year, the IPA found that one of the main barriers to accessing the 'employee voice' cited by business leaders, HR professional and managers was employees themselves. The most common barrier was "cynicism from staff" highlighted by 54 per cent of employees, while 44 per cent cited "getting buy-in from staff" and 39 per cent the "lack of response to initiatives".[26]

Be honest, what would be the more insightful read – your corporate strategy or the comments from staff on it? We still meet clients who are nervous of giving their employees an unrestricted voice. Most have internal naysayers and those who, for whatever reason, seek to cause trouble, but companies that allow a truly unrestricted dialogue to flow find they do not need to appoint guardians of the conversation, as Larry Solomon at AT&T explains: "What happens over time is that the community self-polices."[27] Just like on the internet, trolls and troublemakers are quickly identified, and if their complaints are unreflective of the group feeling at large, they are dismissed, ignored or actively rebutted. Our clients who are already allowing open conversations among staff have told us of the power of having complaints about the organisation being refuted and attacked by frontline employees, as opposed to by a corporate response from head office. Of course, it may be that negative sentiments are more broadly expressed than an organisation would like, but if this is the case then by allowing for such a discussion, managers can uncover issues and act to solve them before they fester and lead to resentment and disengagement.

Asking employees to rate and review content can also help to combat the constant challenge of ensuring internal communication stays credible and involving. If it is hard for an internal communication team, with a small budget, to constantly research audience views in order to create tailored, meaningful content, why not let the audience do much of the work for you? In *Crowdsourcing: How the Power of the Crowd is Driving the Future of Business*, journalist Jeff Howe considers the power of the audience when it comes to voting on content. He looks at businesses such as Threadless.com that rely on the opinions of their consumers to dictate their production practices, ensuring they have customers ready to buy before they even print a T-shirt. *American Idol*, Howe tells us, "isn't a television show; it's the largest focus group in history".[28] Imagine the power of knowing that you have buy-in from employees before you launch an initiative, or how they like to be communicated with in a crisis.

In chapter 8, we explore ways practitioners can use the power of collaboration and conversation to create more effective screen-based communication. However, we should not imagine that the ability to comment on and interact with content is limited to digital content alone. The inclusion of a letters page (with genuine employee questions and honest responses) can work wonders to ensure a printed publication stays connected to its audience.

CONTENT NOT COMMENT

As we have seen online, audience participation rarely remains restricted to simply responding; audiences soon take content *creation* into their own hands. Not so long ago, gathering and disseminating news and information was the preserve of a handful of commercial and governmental institutions; it could not be done without money or power; usually both. Today, individuals around the world, empowered by digital technologies, are contributing to and creating their own news. From the 'Arab Spring' uprisings to the effect of severe weather events, people are making the news in a literal sense.

Governments still try to control the agenda by issuing carefully worded and timed statements, but it only takes one eyewitness with a smartphone to destroy any semblance of control. *The Economist* report 'Social media: The People Formerly Known as the Audience' recounts how Sohaib Athar, a computer consultant living in Abbottabad, the Pakistani village where Osama bin Laden had been hiding, unwittingly described the operation to kill bin Laden as it happened. A series of tweets: "Helicopter hovering above Abbottabad at 1AM (is a rare event)"[29], "A huge window-shaking bang here in Abbottabad…I hope it's not the start of something nasty :-S"[30] gave an on-the-ground perspective to an event that journalists simply did not have. *The Economist* report tells us that the rise of social media means reporters no longer act alone, gathering the news. Instead, news "emerges from an ecosystem in which journalists, sources, readers and viewers exchange information".[31] This change, it argues, began in 1999 when blogging tools first became widely available. Jay Rosen, professor of journalism at New York University, believes that this resulted in "the shift of the tools of production to the people formerly known as the audience".[32]

Dan Gillmor, seasoned journalist with *The San Jose Mercury News*, also believes that today's web tools have given rise to what he and many others call 'participatory journalism'. The reaction to his blog about technology in Silicon Valley made him realise a significant fact: "My readers know more than I do." This is the reality for every journalist, no matter what his or her beat, according to Gillmor. He relishes this as an opportunity rather than a threat, because when readers share their knowledge "we can all benefit. If modern American journalism has been a lecture, it's evolving into something that incorporates a conversation and seminar".[33]

The suggestion that an 'amateur' readership can improve on the work of well-established journalists, forced to adhere to standards of fact-checking and accuracy all-too often ignored by Twitter users, is not unchallenged. Andrew Keen, for one, is furiously against the idea of distinguished *New York Times* reporters being dropped in favour of the work of "millions and millions of exuberant monkeys – many with no more talent in the creative arts than our primate cousins" who, rather than pumping out Shakespeare on their typewriters, are "creating an endless digital forest of mediocrity".[34] Keen may be right to argue that a bored student's commentary on the Syrian situation be paid less heed than that of an experienced conflict journalist, but he fails to deal with the argument that a Syrian citizen may offer even greater insight. He may be outraged that the crowd allows such frivolity as 'grumpy cat' to have its time in the spotlight, but he is wrong to dismiss the invaluable contributions of an amateur audience when it came to the frontline reporting and collaborative aid efforts after events such as Hurricane Katrina.

Just as Andrew Keen is worried that the journalistic and

intellectual elite is losing its privileged position as gatekeepers of culture, there are communication professionals who fear losing control of the corporate messages, which they have until this point diligently produced for employee consumption. The role of internal communicators in producing high quality broadcast material should not be disparaged. Undoubtedly, a specialised and professional approach has worked well for many years, keeping employees informed and feeling involved. However, the time has come to surrender some of this control – to be less of a mouthpiece for those above and more of a facilitator, enabling meaningful conversations from every corner of the organisation.

There are many ways employees create content – through user-generated content, discussion forums, chat rooms, blogs, collaborative publishing, grassroots reporting or old-fashioned letters to the editor. All of these make company communication richer, more complete and credible. There is a good chance ideas will surface that may never have been shared at all, or that an issue will be raised and resolved rather than left to fester. Alan Rusbridger, editor of *The Guardian*, calls the process of audience involvement in the gathering, filtering and dissemination of information, the "mutualisation" of news. He believes: "If you are open to contributions from others, you generally end up with richer, better, more diverse and expert content than if you try to do it alone."[35]

Groysberg and Slind give an example from EMC Corporation, one of the world's largest computer-storage providers. In 2009, EMC used employee-generated content to kickstart a conversation about gender inclusion. In the run-up to International Women's Day, the company encouraged a group of employees who were also mothers to produce content about 'the working mother experience'. The contributions it received resulted in a traditional printed book — a coffee-table tome of more than 200 pages entitled *The Working Mother Experience*. In total, 96 EMC women from 15 countries wrote a contribution dealing with the highs and lows of being both a successful employee and mother. Frank Hauck, EVP of Global Marketing and Customer Quality and executive sponsor of the project, believes that "taken as a whole and as individual stories the book presents a new view of EMC – from the inside".[36] This globally collaborative project could only have come from within, from the individuals themselves, and is infinitely more powerful because it speaks of their experiences in their voices.

EMPLOYEES DRIVING THE AGENDA

Currently, the corporate centre drives the communication calendar and 'messaging', which may be planned months in advance. A shift from cascade to conversation demands a revolutionary approach. Instead of starting with the key messages and strategy of a senior few and tailoring these to fit the interests of the many, we should do the opposite. Let us start with the ideas, thoughts and issues of the many and make these the corporate agenda. Vineet Nayar, former CEO of HCL Technologies and author of *Employees First, Customers Second*, says: "Bosses genuinely believe that by virtue of their position at the top of the pyramid, they have a better view of the landscape and are the best situated to make decisions that will benefit the entire organisation."[37] Nayar believes the opposite. Most employees "know very well what is wrong with a company, sometimes even before management does or at least before management is willing to admit it".[38]

At this point, we must acknowledge that for many senior executives, the thought of the 'rank and file' driving the communications agenda will sound absurd and frightening. We can imagine their concerns: *If the crowd governs communication, surely anarchy will reign? Won't an unfettered conversation raise difficult, if not unanswerable, questions? Won't this create greater uncertainty and, in the end, do more harm than good?* These anxieties are understandable because for many years, before the internet and social media, executives had the appearance of control over the communications agenda. In organisations with highly unionised workforces, low employee engagement and trust, or those with employees seemingly resistant to change, the tendency of the corporate centre was to 'package' information in a carefully controlled and edited manner. Bad news was not delivered until absolutely necessary, no matter how wild the rumour mill. The ever-present threat of industrial action meant communicators operated with heightened sensitivity and care, often repeating the same message over and over again, no matter how tired or unbelievable it had become. If the corporate centre has ears, now is the time to whisper in them: 'This approach doesn't work and never has'. Limiting internal communications to one-way corporate platitudes or bland announcements over the tannoy destroys trust, understanding and limits commercial success. Few workforces are perfect in every respect, but change and transformation is not achieved by issuing edicts. As Groysberg and Slind explain: "One-way, top-down communication between leaders and their employees is no longer useful or even realistic."[39]

In conversation with Neil Taylor

A founding member of language consultancy The Writer, managing director Neil Taylor openly confesses to an obsession with good language.

With a degree in linguistics and three books under his belt, Neil is on a mission is to rid the world of corporate jargon, humanising the way we write at work.

Why does improving the way we communicate matter?
Language is rarely seen as something that needs fixing by next week, like a problem with a product or service, but it lies beneath everything. It's the tool for doing business, which means everyone is using it regardless of his or her job.

As writers, we should care whether people read what we've written, but we lose sight of that. We feel we're taking an enormous risk by saying something in a different, more personal way. I think there is a huge risk in the opposite – keeping it generic and having no one read it.

We all recognise business jargon, and in focus groups people have no trouble identifying those offending terms and phrases common to their organisations. But what happens when you ask why, knowing it's jargon, they all use this language. Often people simply want to comply with the norm – they don't want to stand out from the crowd.

What breeds this complicity?

One of the main reasons much corporate language is unnecessarily long, complex and robotic is fear.

Some mimic the language around them because they think it must be right. Others become so immersed in the linguistic style of the organisation they unquestioningly adopt the same style through a process of osmosis.

There is widespread fear of challenging legal language in particular, although in reality legal teams are more approachable on this subject than their reputation suggests. The problem is that they are often used to getting their way. To stand up to the legal team and negotiate a change in language takes guts. That brings us to a crucial trait in the fight for better language at work – confidence.

When people are experts in their field or confident about a specialist subject, why do they lack confidence when it comes to writing?

It's scary to say what you really mean because then you have to live up to it. You are no longer hiding behind reams of corporate mumbo-jumbo.

It's no coincidence that people usually end up writing less as a result of the work we do with them.

We find that employees typically have a simple version of something they need to write in their heads, but have a nagging fear of how they will be perceived if they write with simplicity. As a result, they spend much of their time translating a simple message into something more complex and generic, making it fit what they see around them.

A study by psychologist Daniel Oppenheimer found that the simpler you write, the more intelligent people think you are. It takes intelligence to understand and present something complex in a simple way.

An important part of our work is finding that one important sentence from a forest of PowerPoint slides crammed with information.

Is simplicity the route to success?

Far from it. Good and simple should not be confused. You can write something that is easy to understand, but if it doesn't reflect any personality, then it will be as dull as ditch water. The tone should represent the distinctive culture of the workplace and the personality of the writer. That is what makes communication human and differentiates one organisation from another.

When you are helping people write more effectively, is there a sudden lightbulb moment?

For some people with confident personalities, it can just be a case of flipping a switch. But there are many people out there who have to work at it over months and years, because they have these fears and behaviours I've mentioned ingrained in them.

Others are just so wired into the corporate world that it can be a long journey, and that's understandable. Our challenge is helping them find what makes them human and using it in work. Setting a task as simple as rewriting a sentence in a way that makes it feel like it's your organisation's voice or culture can be a real challenge for people.

All of those fancy flowcharts, phrases and graphics might seem impressive, but the most effective parts of a presentation are those that actually reflect what the company and its culture are like.

It's important to acknowledge that good language might already exist in an organisation's language, but it could just be buried. That's why it's just as essential to look at the parts people already perceive as well written.

The penny can drop when someone has written something new, or found what they should be shouting about deep inside what's already there. The correlation is feeling personally engaged with the language.

Does the moment of realisation trigger a change?

It depends on the person and context. As I mentioned before, it's a case of getting people to go with their instinct and allow themselves to communicate what they think in the first place, rather than complicating it.

Practice is key though. When The Writer was in its early days, we thought that awareness of the right language was the problem and persuading people to use it was the challenge, but actually, most people realise the value of what we offer.

The hard bit is making it stick, because this stuff is so ingrained that people need to keep plugging away at it to prevent slipping back into old habits. The change has to become a part of the culture and be something regularly acknowledged, discussed or refreshed.

What does success look like?

Our field is actually more measurable than you might think. Maybe it's saving money through reduced call times, an increase in consumer satisfaction or even employees reading more email news because whoever is sending it out now recognises that they don't need to bombard people – there are definitive ways to see change as a result of the work we do.

How many times have you ever thought you wanted a work-related piece of writing to be longer and full of more complex language when you read it? For some reason, putting a pen in someone's hand blinds them to their own sense. Success is getting them to think clearly again.

Who is to blame for the prevalence of bad writing?
It's very rarely the fault of any one person or even any organisation.

For example, we had a client in a highly regulated industry and coincidentally worked with their regulating body at the same time. In our view, the client's reports and appeals were overly lengthy and complex. The language made it difficult to truly understand what they were trying to say. They believed being more direct would be inappropriate because the regulator spoke in the same language.

When the regulator presented us with a response they planned to send to our client some weeks later, their language was indeed the same. The regulator's reasoning was the same too; they were just trying to reflect the client's language.

We can all get trapped in this stand-off where no one can remember who told who to speak in this dehumanised, generic way, and no one is willing to make the first move to change it.

How do we get out of this rut?
Again, it comes back to confidence. Someone has to be bold in breaking the norm.

Just think about a CV. It's the most competitive piece of writing anyone will ever do; so why do so many people insist on making their CV look exactly like everyone else's? There is a fear of exposure and stepping outside the bubble of language everyone else is using.

Part of the problem is the way job adverts are written. We see the same generic copy in job adverts and therefore the same replies to them. We work hard to convey our personality in person, so why wouldn't we do this in an email?

We did some work with a county council team responding to complaints about social workers. The people writing these letters were often extremely angry. To be on the receiving end of these complaints is difficult. Typically, replies would be written formally, keeping an emotional distance from the recipient. Employees didn't want to tackle the pain and anger felt by the complainant, but a genuine compassion in their replies actually improved relations and helped solve issues faster.

Is there a parallel between an organisation's leaders speaking in more open language and its workforce following suit?
Sometimes, but often it's more complicated than that. Acceptance has more to do with a broader culture than the approach of a small number of leaders. There are many leaders who don't talk in a bland, corporate style, but their workforces do. This raises an interesting question: Does the authority that comes with being at the top mean you don't have to talk 'corporate' any more, or has this person reached the top because they embrace a more human language?

Look at the behaviour and language of your organisation's social media team – they are often getting it right. It's their job to humanise the company and they're working with tools useful to this approach.

Is the brevity imposed by social media an important weapon in the battle to change language?
Limiting how much people can write forces them to work in a different way. Twitter and its 140 characters is the best example of this today, but people have been constraining themselves by writing on Post-it notes and sticking them in places for upwards of 40 years.

The problem has been not recognising that this process of constraint can be applied to a different context, like the workplace, with the same results.

Has the approach to plain language within the workplace changed over time?

When we started The Writer in 1999, it could take up to 18 months to make real tracks within an organisation. Our challenge then was getting people to understand and make more natural language a part of what they did. In 2014, the perception of language as integral to business success is steadily increasing. Addressing the problem is becoming a common task on many communicators' to-do lists.

This is a blessing and a curse. It makes businesses much more willing to approach us, but it's a challenge to really change the way people use language in the long term if it is merely a tick-box exercise. There has to be a genuine underlying desire to communicate better.

It sounds pretentious, but I believe what we do is good for the world. We're not here just to exercise our linguistic superpowers; we want to help give people the confidence to speak normally.

People spend so much time at work that if we can make their interactions more human and fulfilling there, this can have a dramatic impact on their lives.

Chapter 7

Why paper isn't dead

LIVE NEWS, 24/7

The home of 'all the news that's fit to print', *The New York Times*, sent a report to its staff in 2014, warning of an urgent need for reform. The full report was quickly leaked and reproduced in full on rival websites. It painted a remarkable picture of the 150-year-old institution. Entitled 'Innovation', it told staff: "In the coming years, *The New York Times* needs to accelerate its transition from a newspaper that also produces a rich and impressive digital report to a digital publication that also produces a rich and impressive newspaper. This is not a matter of semantics. It is a critical, difficult, at times painful transformation that will require us to rethink much of what we do every day."[1]

It is not just print behemoths like *The New York Times* that are struggling; there is a global decline in newspaper circulation. The website newspaperdeathwatch.com keeps a running list of the many American metropolitan dailies forced to close since 2007, and the many others that have had to adopt a predominantly or wholly online model. In the UK, where national, rather than local, papers dominate, there have been fewer closures but almost every title has seen a steep decline in readership. The average circulation of daily paid-for newspapers fell from 53.8 million (123.6 per cent of households) in 1950 to just 43.4 million in 2010, or 36 per cent of households.[2] *The Sun* saw its readership decline by almost 10 per cent from 2013 to 2014 alone.[3] Yet at the same time, these newspapers have an ever-growing online presence, with screen views often exceeding printed sales. New titles are typically screen only, such as *The Huffington Post*, which was launched in May 2005 and now receives more than 43 million unique visits a month, or Buzzfeed, which announced in November 2013 that it was receiving 130 million monthly unique visitors, a 350 per cent increase year-on-year.[4]

For many, a daily printed newspaper with its early and late editions is irrelevant when breaking news can be constantly updated and viewed on smartphones. The BBC news website records around 40 million unique users a week, and updates its content 24 hours a day. The same is increasingly true for company news. Why would employees wait for news to be delivered in monthly, weekly or even daily publications, when it can be constantly fed to them through a screen in words, images and films?

Before we too race to stop the presses, we should acknowledge and appreciate the long and impressive history of employee newspapers and magazines as the backbone of internal communication efforts since the beginning of mass literacy. Elinor Hayes, writing about employee publications in 1922, said: "The recognition of the importance both of good spirit and of information among the employees, rising to a height during the war, was reflected by the initiation at that time of a large proportion of the magazines which more than 500 companies have published at some time during the last five years."[5]

Hayes was commenting on the United States, but the trend was echoed in Britain, with the John Lewis Partnership introducing *The Gazette* in 1918. *Lyons Mail*, a monthly magazine for the employees of J. Lyons & Co. was launched in 1922 and was still going strong 70 years later when AB was writing and designing it. Hayes' broader explanation for the introduction of such channels was as a replacement "to meet the loss in personal contact between employer and employee".[6] Even in today's digital age, when paper no longer breaks the news, a regular printed publication can create that sense of connection and community.

TO HAVE AND TO HOLD

Internal print media survives for a variety of good reasons. There are still many workforces that are not desk-based, do not have easy access to a PC or laptop and are not provided with smart mobile devices. *Courier* newspaper has been delivered to the homes of the nation's postmen and women since 1966, keeping them abreast of news and developments at Royal Mail. Almost 50 years later, it proved a vital way of informing staff about the privatisation of the organisation, used alongside printed 'news flash' announcements that were handed directly to employees at work or posted to them at home. Paper remains the ultimate mobile communication device. There is no need to worry about firewalls, login details, screen settings or novice IT users. We find many overestimate their audience's access to, appetite for and knowledge of IT when based in a well-equipped corporate head office.

Ironically, the dominance of screen-based communication can make a paper title more valued and noteworthy. We have clients who produce a printed version of their magazine because readers receive too much information through a screen. A digital publication might get lost in such a cluttered marketplace. One of the best ways to grab the attention of these employees is to give them something physical. Regardless of new technologies, our love affair with the printed page continues. I met one head of internal communications working for a British clothing manufacturer who was expected, like her colleagues, to work without paper. She admitted to hiding a notepad inside the case of her iPad, surreptitiously taking notes the old-fashioned way when no one was looking because she felt she worked better with a pen and paper. For some tasks we still prefer the physical sensation of writing or reading, and the tactile nature of a page in our hand.

Editorial directors of the UK's Slow Journalism Company, Marcus Webb and Rob Orchard, firmly believe in the permanence and lasting value of print. "For all the wily charms of the digital world and its tweets, feeds, blogs and apps, there is nothing like the pleasure created by ink and paper,"[7] they explain. Slow Journalism, according to the company's website, "measures news in months not minutes, returning to stories after the dust has settled". It offers an antidote to "throwaway media and makes a virtue of being the last to breaking news".[8] Webb and Orchard's quarterly magazine – *Delayed Gratification* – is designed to be treasured by readers and end its days "making the bookshelf, coffee table or toilet just a little bit prettier and more civilised".[9]

AB's head of creative, Joel O'Connor, believes all paper publications should have this collectable quality: "Readers should want to keep them, at least for a while, due to the quality of their content and design." The time, expense and effort – whether real or perceived – in creating something that is printed, bound and delivered is a statement in itself, which is why when something important or complex needs to be communicated, many organisations still want to deliver it on paper. This is especially true for commemorative publications celebrating a company milestone or specific project. Often intended as a thank you to reward and celebrate the efforts of employees, these publications would struggle to have the same impact in a digital form.

Abigail Sellen, co-author of *The Myth of the Paperless Office,* researches the differences between reading on page and on screen. She argues it is easier to develop a sense of ownership for a printed product. In research she has found people "think of using an e-book, not owning an e-book".[10] When we really enjoy a work on the screen, many of us then go out and purchase a hard copy.

Print is no longer the place for breaking news. Lead times – even on a daily newspaper – mean news is broken far more effectively electronically. Here fresh content can be posted throughout the day. The same is true for employee publications. Although, even before the internet, the rumour mill was likely to scoop any 'exclusives' in our monthly titles. Now, more than ever, printed publications need to get behind the headlines, offering insight and more considered content. The printed page suits the longer read better than a screen. Research consistently shows that people across the generational divide do not like reading long passages of text on screen – with 83 per cent of 18 to 24-year-olds stating such a preference to IPSOS and Two Sides in 2011.[11]

If we agree paper still has a role in the communications mix, how do we use it to stimulate conversation? After all, the printed word appears to be the epitome of broadcast communication – one way, fixed and finite. In this chapter, we investigate the two-way potential of the page, both in formal employee publications and the vast amount of ad hoc printed material given to staff. It takes determined communicators and careful crafting, but even on paper employee voices can be brought to life and a genuine conversation ensue.

NOT WORTH THE PAPER THEY'RE PRINTED ON

The last 50 years of reading and producing internal communications has taught us too many employees regard their in-house journals as 'propaganda'. Readers say these vehicles exist to peddle the company line, not the reality of working life inside their organisations. Too often they fail to accurately reflect the issues and debates happening around the water cooler or on the factory floor. They dodge difficult or sensitive subjects; they lack personality, wit and the attention-grabbing style of consumer titles. Consequently, they go ignored.

Publications like this, which undoubtedly still exist, have led some, like TJ and Sandar Larkin, to condemn the company newspaper altogether. Writing in 1994, the Larkins claimed "the company newspaper has done enormous damage...[and] has absolved managers from the responsibility of designing real communication".[12] For them, "publications are irrelevant to the communication problems threatening performance".[13] It must be acknowledged that the Larkins' comments are focused specifically on the communication of large-scale organisational change and 20 years have passed since their book, *Communicating Change,* was released. While their argument that the page is not the place for announcing significant changes still holds weight, it is no longer the case – if it ever was – that "your employees don't care about the company".[14] There is a clear desire for information and insight about the broader organisation from the new generation of workers – particularly, but not exclusively, among today's knowledge workers. For these employees, internal publications can and should do more than communicate "information about managers to other managers".[15]

In commercial publishing what finally gets printed is the result of the machinations of large teams: different perspectives all striving to produce something that will truly appeal to readers. If not, sales fall and the title goes to the wall. With in-house publications, there is far less debate or creative tension and sometimes none at all. It is all too easy for a management team to control the content, tone and personality of a company title. It is too tempting for leaders to see these journals as theirs. After all, it is the corporation, not the employees, funding them. Newsstand publishing must contend with reporters, editors, sub-editors, managing editors, shareholders and even advertisers, all pushing back on anything they think will disengage the audience. Employee titles often suffer the opposite problem and are the product of a single decision-making body, which frequently fails to focus on what the audience really wants to read. If asked, many employees say their company magazine lacks credibility and is not an honest, respectful or sincere reflection of company life.

THE POWER OF THE PRESS

The long heritage of newspaper journalism highlights the contrast between investigative, hard-hitting content in newsstand titles and the broadcasting of corporate announcements in their internal counterparts. The grandfather of traditional print journalism, Sir Harold Evans, who edited *The Sunday Times* from 1967 to 1981, believed great journalism is 'peeling the onion'. It is "the vital stuff of placing things on the record, of challenging the official account…Not in a partisan way – just let's find out what the bloody facts are!"[16] Internal communicators face difficult challenges living up to this ideal. But while we must serve our paymasters, it is vital we remind ourselves of our duty to the audience. Communications cannot be a partisan function, acting solely as a mouthpiece for management. While it is everyone's responsibility to communicate effectively, our role is to amplify the voices and reflect the views of those who rarely get heard. It is to ensure what finally gets printed is credible and worthy. This means taking a stand when necessary and insisting on a level of journalistic integrity.

Using the services of an external editorial team can help

maintain journalistic standards as agencies tend to be staffed by editors, writers and designers with a media background. It can be easier for agencies to position themselves as working for the organisation – the workforce as a whole – rather than a senior communications director or the executive team. This degree of independence can help when talking to employees who may feel safer talking to an outsider. The same independence helps when challenging the decisions of the senior team; it is easier to take a fresh perspective unfettered by office politics. External resource must work as an extension to the in-house team with a well-developed understanding of the organisation's goals. Ultimately, whether or not an organisation uses external support, there is much to be gleaned from our journalistic heritage.

Our profession has come a long way from merely producing a monthly or weekly title, yet traditional publishing skills remain surprisingly relevant. The ability to interview anyone, from a truck driver to the CEO, and a passion for roving reporting are vital: it is hard to unearth fascinating stories and get the best quotes if you are stuck in the office. Communicators need to get out and about across their organisations to ensure they really understand the needs and desires of employees. It is easy to spot practitioners who do this; they are the ones who understand what their employees do each day and how they talk about it. They understand call centre employees will never have time to read a three-page editorial and instead write snippets that can be read in 30 seconds; and they are prepared to get out of bed at 2am to have a chat with a tube driver at the end of his shift. Vital to staying connected is developing a network of local champions and correspondents – what national newspapers call 'stringers' – to help keep the editorial team's ear to the ground. Internal communications professional Deborah Brambill remembers while at KPMG, "we drew very heavily on our own personal networks at first when we launched our magazine".

Until a title gains sufficient profile and credibility with the workforce, calling in a few favours may be the only way to gather great stories.

Paper is criticised as being difficult to personalise for specific audiences. With a single print-run, it is not possible to tailor content so that certain items come first for specific readers (a highly appreciated advantage of digital news). This is equally true for the company newspaper. While some run multiple regional covers or inserts for certain units, by and large it is the same content for all readers. This means being careful and cautious about what makes the cut. If a director wants you to run a step-by-step guide to an incoming process that only 20 per cent of the workforce will ever carry out, then however much he or she might insist, you need to be confident about saying no, this is not the right channel. Content must be broad enough to be relevant to all. We can use print's uniformity to our advantage. It provides an opportunity to ensure the same story reaches everyone. As a common source of news, an internal publication can be a great place for breaking down silos and improving cross-departmental understanding. So long as it is a good story, with 'national' implications, employees will be happy to read about events and achievements in less well-known parts of the organisation.

BRAVE EDITORIAL DECISIONS

It is one thing to write a difficult and insightful story, but quite another to print it. As internal communicators, we tend not to have a 'publish and be damned' mentality. We cannot simply print an apology in the next morning's edition. We are ever mindful of the damage we could do to our organisation's brand, reputation, trade union relations and employee morale. Consequently, we are inherently conservative and careful. Readers do not pay our wages and we are only funded by a budget set from above. For that budget to continue or grow, those holding the purse strings need to believe our work is money well spent – that it is helping to advance commercial goals. To satisfy their concerns, we sometimes have to yield to their influence and seek their approval. In some cases this means executives read every word before going to print and retain the power to change any or all of them. Readers can spot the influence of a senior executive a mile away. In one focus group we ran, an employee read aloud – with more than a hint of derision – a quote reportedly from another employee in a similar role at a different site. "He would never have said that. He wouldn't have even used any of those words – it's entirely made up." The employee was right. It was just one line among 24 pages, but in his view the damage was done. Why should he trust anything else he read?

The opposite is also true. Brave editorial decisions that challenge assumptions and demonstrate a respect for readership pay off. We witnessed one editorial team tackle the complex and sensitive issue of depression. In-depth, face-to-face interviews with two senior colleagues resulted in an absorbing and moving personal perspective on a problem that is too often considered taboo, particularly within the competitive corporate world. A month later, I facilitated focus groups in regional offices across the UK, asking colleagues about the magazine. In more than 20 years of creating employee communications, I have never heard such positive feedback. They told me that it stood apart from every other document, email or report that they received. This was their magazine – an honest, engaging reflection of the community to which they belonged. It celebrated their highs and lows with wit and sincerity. They took it home for members of their family to read and showed it to clients as "the best reflection of who we really are". Through the magazine they learned about their peers as people – their work, interests and personal challenges. To achieve this the editorial team has had to fight hard, striving to maintain independence and retain control. The battle becomes harder as the success of a title grows. Your publication will be increasingly attractive as a potential mouthpiece for broadcasting management messages, but used in this way, your readers will quickly abandon it.

What is commercial benefit in a company magazine that does not overtly communicate strategy? Are these magazines doing any more than making employees feel warm and fuzzy about the community to which they belong? We discuss measuring the impact of communications in chapter 10, but our research has showed even when a publication is not essential in supporting people's daily work – they could function without it – it can fulfil a strategic objective. This was summed up neatly by an employee who said: "Our senior partner has told us that the firm values diversity and its people; the very fact this magazine exists proves to me that this is the case." If your organisation's strategic goals have an important people element – the desire to celebrate success, respect diversity, share knowledge or break down internal silos – then a regular publication can be much more than a 'nice-to-have'. It can become one of the best ways of bringing this aspect of company strategy to life. But a publication that is driven by a senior few with little regard for reader opinion and involvement will backfire. Internal magazines and newspapers should never be a regurgitation of the business plan with headlines, standfirsts and pictures. Internal communicators must treat print as a conversational medium, and transform this traditionally broadcast channel into something more interactive.

BY THE PEOPLE, FOR THE PEOPLE
We live in an era when we delight in having our say. Whether

we are reading newspapers or magazines, listening to the radio or watching TV, we like to share our opinions. We are no longer passive recipients of a broadcast message. This desire to speak up – and share our views – does not change when we get to work. The company message is one of many we receive throughout the day. As Deborah Brambill told us: "People have so many sources of information that they like to be able to make their own judgement. We don't like to just get told this is how something is." Healthy debate may not be happening in the internal magazine but, rest assured, it is happening. In an era of open debate and dialogue, the employee magazine cannot be a one-way channel for corporate monologues. Those that are feel like relics from an era when executives thought they could control the message.

It is possible for a printed title to reflect how employees think and feel about their organisation, to capture the essence of their daily discussions and spark new conversations and debates. This can be done in various ways but must be based on a genuine desire to relinquish some editorial control and allow the audience to shape content. Such an approach is not exclusive to printed titles – all employee communication benefits from audience involvement. However, certain feedback initiatives fit well with the regular production schedule of a magazine or newspaper where content is limited by a fixed pagination.

It can be helpful to invite a cross-section of readers to a meeting – either face-to-face or remotely – to guide future editorial decisions and review previous editions. If it is not possible to get a group of readers to advise, an alternative is to enlist the help of a single member of staff for each edition. Too often such a 'guest editor' role is rather superficial – limited to providing a 250-word editorial. We prefer to see guest editors spend the day with the editorial, design and production teams, learning about the entire process of creating the title and sharing knowledge of their business with everyone involved.

The formal page of 'letters to the editor' might seem anachronistic in today's live feedback culture where anyone can post a comment on anything, any time. But it is precisely because not everyone's letter can appear in print that makes each one noteworthy. If you get the page right, and if it openly addresses readers' concerns and becomes a place of true debate, our research shows it will become one of the most read sections of your company magazine. A letters page tells us much about a publication's readers, their anxieties and interests. How a title chooses to respond to questions and criticism is equally revealing.

Printing controversial or critical letters with a response from the appropriate individual can instantly boost the credibility of an internal publication and signal a new, more transparent approach to communication. Although in cases where this kind of honesty is embryonic, the first few letters may have to be cajoled from readers. Even in 1922, Elinor Hayes appreciated the potential of a letters page that tackled tricky issues, believing that "such discussion is much more easily controlled when caught in the plant paper where the light of facts can be brought to play on it, than when it flits about surreptitiously from group to group of workers".[17] If the paper is receiving letters about an issue, then it is likely the workforce is also discussing the same problem. A large tranche of your readership might appreciate an honest response. But it must be just that. Communicators cannot allow evasive 'politicians' answers' and should include follow-up responses and questions when submitted by readers. For an organisation wary of addressing sensitive issues in a public forum, a letters page is a controlled, safe first step. An editor remains in charge throughout, and decision-makers have time to consider their response.

NEVER-ENDING STORY

The perception that the printed word is the end of the story must change. Print may be the place for an authoritative account, but an article should not be the last word on an issue.

The New York Times' 'Innovation' report includes a critical quote from Paul Berry, a founder of *The Huffington Post*: "At *The New York Times*, far too often for writers and editors the story is done when you hit publish. At *Huffington Post*, the article begins its life when you hit publish".[18] If print is the channel for thought-provoking articles rather than breaking news, it should be inspiring debates. Do not be afraid to direct people from your company magazine to an online space where they can share their thoughts. Even when we are reading the printed page, our smartphones are often close at hand. Then, print becomes the ideal place to collate and document the discussion that ensues. Research shows us that even children of the digital age feel differently seeing their name and work in print than on screen. We still consider it a greater validation and compliment to have our views aired in a palpable format than on the intangible web. Printing the words and opinions of employees shows that you are taking them seriously and consider them worthy of reproduction.

Readers should be asked to contribute to existing stories and write their own. All publications should include easy ways to get in touch with as many options as possible – tweet, text, phone or instant message. For a less tech-savvy workforce, provide a Freepost address. People are far more likely to make contact with a smiling face, so avoid anonymous mailboxes in favour of photos of the editorial team and personal contact details.

Rather than supplant print, new technologies can be used to enhance its power. Tools like QR codes and augmented reality make the page more interactive. In 2009, *Esquire* enabled its readers to bring their cover star Robert Downey Jr to life with a flash of their smartphone. Royal Mail did something similar with its Olympic stamps *Courier* cover in 2012. As such technology continues to improve, interaction will become easier and more affordable. Audiences are now demanding content in a whole range of formats, and while a great deal still appreciate the considered, in-depth printed feature, they may also like the chance to watch a short video about the same issue on their smartphone, or view extra related photos on an intranet. Many commercial publications now have Twitter feeds and Facebook pages, as well as dedicated websites. If your company publication has a clear brand and identity then there is no reason this cannot stretch across a range of channels. *Wow*, designed for Post Office Crown branch employees, is both a magazine and a website (www.wow-mag.co.uk). Its strong visual identity and the focused nature of its stories mean employees know what to expect from both print and digital versions. They appreciate the extra content and interactivity online, but like the portability and ease of reading the printed product.

LESS IS MORE

Regular printed publications are often the first to be questioned when budgets come under scrutiny. They are a highly visible expense with a value that can be hard to quantify. Printed titles not only appear costly but also inflexible, old-fashioned and less environmentally friendly, so it is little wonder so many now only appear on the screen. Readers themselves are questioning the green credentials and expense of print, particularly when it appears lavish or ostentatious. Using paper from sustainable sources helps combat some of these concerns, but not as effectively as not printing the materials in the first place.

Ariel, the BBC employee magazine, which began life in 1936, is just one example of this trend. The director-general who oversaw the change from print to digital, Mark Thompson, said: "*Ariel* newspaper has been an important part of the BBC's history for more than 75 years and, like many of you, I will be sad the paper version has to close as part of [cost] savings. However, I am pleased that it will live online, reflecting the lives, issues and challenges that we face every day."[19] Titles like *Ariel* that migrate from paper to screen must be adapted to suit their new format. Simply replicating what was once on paper is rarely an effective solution. Whether sent as an attachment or link, they become yet another unsolicited email clogging up our inboxes. It is also a cruel waste of the potential of the technology available. The best digital magazines take advantage of advanced functionality, encouraging readers to participate in the creation, review, rating and sharing of content to a degree much harder to achieve in print. The content itself must adapt as well – longer reads must give way to video, audio and animation. If your digital publication could be read just as well on paper then it has failed.

Just as digital publications need careful attention, so too does a print magazine. In fact, given the financial investment is often greater, we must be especially mindful when producing anything for paper. In the same way that staff can drown in a flood of emails, so it is possible for them to get lost in a wealth of printed brochures, reports, letters and booklets. If you believe employees will question your decision to print a bound copy of the company's strategy or continue with the printed version of the company magazine, ask them to request a copy on subscription. Less print not only addresses people's environmental concerns, it keeps it special and distinct; more likely to command the attention and respect of readers.

NOT OLD, MATURING

Our penchant for reading on paper persists, not despite the

growth of screen-based communication, but often because of it. The more we read and watch on screen, the more unique the printed page becomes. True, print is no longer the place for breaking news about world events, but if a story requires a considered, longer read then print remains our preferred medium. It is portable, accessible and more permanent than words on a screen. We value it more, taking 25 minutes on average to read a printed magazine while giving the average website only a 60-second scan. "Print is one of the best discovery mediums; it's easy to turn a page,"[20] says Larry Kramer, publisher of *USA Today*. We linger with print longer because of its presumed authority. We believe higher journalistic standards have been applied and give weight to every word, image, full stop and comma, assuming each must be correct. If we find they are not, we are less tolerant than if we see the same mistake on screen.

When it comes to print, it has to be done right. As an industry it remains largely in the hands of professionals – we expect a degree of amateurism online, which we do not in print. If we seek to emulate what our employees see outside of the organisation then we have our work cut out. Some of our clients' employee magazines have no commissioning budget, which makes sourcing great imagery or expert columnists a real challenge. Other publications are produced entirely in-house, and on occasion on the side of a very busy desk and alongside numerous other responsibilities. Engaging print is far from dead and still occupies a special place in the communicator's toolkit. But all those things that make it powerful – a sense of authority, permanence and value – mean that bad print is especially damaging. Kramer says print offers advertisers 'a big tableau' to hawk their wares.[21] This larger canvas can either undermine the credibility of an organisation and its leaders or capture our imaginations and get us talking.

In conversation with Carol Miller

Carol Miller has more than 35 years of experience as a journalist, having reported on some of the biggest UK news in the 1980s with internationally renowned agency, the Press Association.

She now works as editor of *The Waitrose Chronicle*, a weekly news magazine for the supermarket's 57,000 staff at its 320 sites.

The *Chronicle* is run by a team of dedicated, trained journalists that works independently of other communication channels and HR. Its integrity reflects a wider culture at the John Lewis Partnership, of which Waitrose is a part, where every employee is a co-owner. She offered her personal insight into the importance of her printed publication.

The structure of Waitrose and John Lewis Partnership is rare in the modern workplace. What effect does this have on you as an employee?
As co-owners, we enjoy both respect and responsibility, and are made aware of that from the minute we start.

The advancement of the business is in everyone's interests.

Waitrose is based on a clear set of principles that determine how we work, our presence in the community and our treatment of employees.

Our first principle informs everything we do:
"The Partnership's ultimate purpose is the happiness of all its members, through their worthwhile and satisfying employment in a successful business. Because the Partnership is owned in trust for its members, they share the responsibilities of ownership as well as its rewards – profit, knowledge and power."

How is this openness reflected in the *Chronicle*?
Employees in every organisation should have the opportunity not just to voice their opinions and questions, but also to get answers from their leaders and directors. This is even more important at Waitrose, because our people are partners. We build the *Chronicle* from the back; letters from readers are the key part of the publication.

We are obliged to print every letter we receive unless it is libellous, malicious or detrimental to the business. The pagination of the *Chronicle* either expands to fit every letter or content is cut from elsewhere to accommodate them all. We've made a promise to answer every question, so we have to do this to maintain the publication's integrity.

Each letter is sent to a relevant director. It is their responsibility to reply within three weeks.

The *Chronicle* has always been one of the most important channels we provide for partners. Employees have a right to know what's happening in the business, have their say and receive a reply.

Letters and their right of reply are a great foundation for the publication, but how do you replicate this objectivity elsewhere?
We run the *Chronicle* like a traditional newspaper. I have

reporters, sub-editors, an online reporter and a designer, as well as a pool of freelancers.

Our reporters are always out meeting employees and engaging with them on the frontline. We have regular champions across the business we can rely on for sourcing ideas and comments.

As a trained journalist, I look for the newsworthy angle in all the articles I'm writing, but as an internal communication journalist, it's also my job to make coverage as easy to digest as possible for busy colleagues.

I look for the human interest element in any story, as well as a news angle. Content in the *Chronicle* is brought to life by the voice of the frontline. Corporate information is tight and concise, and detail often tends to come towards the end of the copy – just as it would be in a newsstand title.

We can't paint a rosy picture of everything either. It's not our role as communicators to pass judgement and declare something fantastic; it's employees who have to decide that, which is why we are comfortable about interviewees sharing their concerns in print.

How do you maintain that journalistic integrity in a corporate environment?
Rather than being in the internal communication or HR department, the *Chronicle* team sits within a department called Registry. It's like an ombudsman, there to be an objective representative of partners' interests.

Working for the partners doesn't mean working against the management team. Everyone is working for the good of the business due to our common interest in seeing Waitrose succeed.

The honest, open connection with our employees is extremely valuable, especially when it's between a frontline

partner in one of our smallest stores and a senior leader. We
will always try to make sure our reporters are there to capture
those moments.

How has the strength of your external brand affected the magazine?

I think it's fair to say people adore Waitrose products and services. There is no shortage of internal ambassadors praising
the brand, as well as long lists of applicants for every Waitrose
position. This means the organisation is able to hire only those
people it believes will care about the Partnership.

Filling an organisation with people who care means there
are important commonalities among our staff. The *Chronicle*
reflects this with plenty of coverage on the environment, health
and wellbeing, food and nutrition.

Where does something like the *Chronicle* sit within the rest of the partnerships channels?

It's supported by online activity on the cross-partnership
intranet, which has enabled me to introduce video,
adding a live aspect to our editorial and giving a fresh
perspective on content with greater partner involvement.

The aim of expanding online was always to ensure that
coverage complemented rather than duplicated that of the
printed *Chronicle*.

As communicators, it's our responsibility to extend our
reach to as wide an audience as possible. While our digital
tools have grown, it is important not to forget that print is a
fundamental part of the mix, and has been since 1937.

How has the *Chronicle* evolved as a printed publication?

The *Chronicle* we see today is a far cry from the parish news-
letter it used to be in the 1930s. Then, Waitrose had just

10 grocery shops in London. It has adapted to the shifts in dynamics and size of both the business and the Partnership.

When I joined as a deputy editor, there was no networking done across the business for the *Chronicle*, no archiving, or databases of contacts or research. It was a very haphazardly produced publication.

They hired me as a professional communicator because they lacked that journalistic knowledge and experience.

I identified three key areas for improvement: assessing and organising the resources within the publication; building its profile across the business; and setting a clear editorial direction.

Up until this point, the *Chronicle* had always been popular, but mainly for its job adverts and the trading figures. It needed to be a publication employees wanted to read for more than this.

Does the *Chronicle* do more that just promote a sense of community?
I believe the *Chronicle* has a tangible effect on the growth of the business.

Every week it gives staff our trading figures. Our rivals might be surprised by our transparency, but we believe staff have a right to know.

The *Chronicle* has also helped with specific problems. One example was with 'dark stores', a colloquial term for the depots that supply our waitrose.com side of the business. We were struggling to recruit people for this area, due to misconceptions about the environment they would be working in.

The recruiters wanted to advertise in the *Chronicle*, and also needed to reassure potential applicants they would still be partners with the same principles, benefits and ethos as everyone else in the business.

Our dark stores are one of the fastest growing areas of the business and very exciting – not dark at all! We did our best to convey this in a full editorial feature in the *Chronicle*, rather than just an advert. The recruiters had an overwhelming response as a result.

The *Chronicle* has a significant impact on Waitrose and its power comes from the open and honest ethos inspired by Principle One.

Chapter 8

Conversations via a screen

LOSING TOUCH?

The software development company Collective Idea devised an app for a game that many of us are already playing. Called Downside, its premise is simple, as founder Daniel Morrison explains. "Most of us are used to staring at our phones instead of talking to the people in the room. Downside makes a game out of keeping your hands off your phone." Any group around a table can make use of the app by flipping their phone face down and trying to resist the temptation to pick it up again. As soon as someone does, they lose and it is their turn to buy the drinks. It's also being used in other ways: "Families are getting their kids to pay attention around the dinner table. There's even been talk about using it in business meetings to focus on the task at hand," says Morrison[1].

The mere existence of the game highlights the pervasiveness of mobile communication. This is also a trend noted by Sherry Turkle, author of *Alone Together: Why We Expect More from Technology and Less from Each Other*. She says: "My students tell me about an important new skill: it involves maintaining eye contact with someone while you text someone else; it's hard, but it can be done."[2]

The ability to have multiple conversations with people across time and space is alluring. How often have you seen couples dining in silence but absorbed in any number of virtual conversations through their mobiles? Thirty years ago Microsoft's vision of 'a computer on every desk and in every home' seemed an impossible dream, an aspirational goal that would take many lifetimes to achieve. Now, most of those living in the developed world have computers not only at home and work but also in the palms of their hands. The spread of technology has infiltrated every part of our lives and had a profound impact on the way we communicate.

Despite its incredible reach, this technology has its limitations. Susan Tardanico, CEO of the Authentic Leadership Alliance, doubts the capability of screens to accurately convey our emotions. "Anyone can hide behind the text, the email, the Facebook post or the tweet, projecting any image they want and creating an illusion of their choosing. They can be whoever they want to be. And without the ability to receive nonverbal cues, their audiences are none the wiser."[3] Face-to-face communication might initially seem more time-consuming, but using more than just words – or emoticons – to get our message across makes our communication vastly more powerful and ultimately boosts our efficiency.

It is not only the constraints of technology and remote communication that can hamper genuine understanding. The sheer deluge of messages we receive on our personal and professional devices every day can inhibit effective communication. The speed and ease of sending messages using a screen increases the temptation to send employees countless messages at all hours. As a result, employees tell us that they are missing important information because it is impossible to filter everything they receive. Many hit the delete button in defeat.

Problems associated with the quantity of communication are worsened by organisations' blunt, inflexible or archaic information technology, which leaves employees having to be panhandlers, searching for nuggets of gold in a stream of irrelevant, old or badly categorised information.

Some believe our increasing reliance on the internet to connect with others is resulting in terabytes of superficial, fragmented or downright dumb information flying virtually around the globe. Others believe the web is a powerful, participative tool that is transforming our ability to create and share knowledge. As is often the case, the truth lies somewhere in between. The web is a tool for disseminating information – good, bad and indifferent. How businesses use it, is a reflection of their culture and priorities. If they are to be productive and the source of greater revenue, they must be managed appropriately. Email, intranets, and enterprise social networks (ESNs) are common workplace tools, but they do not manage themselves. Without planned, considered implementation and support, they can cause frustration, confusion and stress.

Screen-based communication has come a long way in a very short time. We've moved from the birth of email, the introduction of intranets and the growth of ESNs, to a point where communicators are thinking digital first. This chapter is not a comparison of one social media tool over another. We have not interviewed software coders or developers to write it. Rather, we spoke to communicators who are tackling the deeper issues of sparking and sustaining meaningful, engaging conversations with employees through a screen.

A BRIGHTER OUTLOOK

It is estimated that by the end of 2017, 132 billion business emails will be sent and received every day[4] – several hundred million messages every minute. Email is an incredible tool for communicating at a distance, sharing documents and creating a physical record of conversations. It is so ubiquitous that when French technology company Atos announced its intention to become 'zero email', it was met with incredulity. The mere possibility of an organisation operating without email seems absurd. We find similar reluctance when we suggest clients consider just one monthly 'no email day'. They tell us it would be impossible, that nothing would get done. Despite hearing endless complaints of overloaded inboxes, when we ask employees how they get their most valuable information, email generally comes second only to word-of-mouth. While some, like Hootsuite CEO Ryan Holmes, attack email as "the biggest time killer in the modern workplace"[5] and consider the tool to be outdated and ineffective, consultant and founder of worldwide 'No Email Day' Paul Lancaster blames users rather than the technology. In his manifesto urging employees to switch off, just for a day, he proclaims that email "is a vital and important part of our daily life and one of the greatest inventions known to man. However, it's been overused and abused and hijacked by the spammers and time wasters over the years to the detriment of the human race".[6]

Few of us are taught good email etiquette or how to make optimal use of our email software. As a result, misunderstandings and differing approaches can cause unintended offence. In one focus group with a large manufacturing and sales company, we heard office staff from a factory location complain about the rude messages sent from a senior manager that read just 'FYI', without a 'Dear Sandra' or a 'Kind regards'. The manager clearly meant no offence. He was probably sending hundreds of emails just like this between meetings from a mobile device every day. However, those on the receiving end of his messages only felt a cold, terse tone. Some of them rarely saw him in person, making this rare contact all the more meaningful. Good email practice should start with those emails from the internal communications team. Employees tell us when sending them large amounts of information it is better to summarise this in an email and include hyperlinks for further content; regular scheduled news round-ups are better than an unplanned scattergun approach, and email titles should be as informative and succinct as possible. Mark Hurst, in his book on dealing with overload in the digital age, suggests content creators consider the fact "every time you send an email…you're adding drops into an ocean that's plenty deep enough. Are you sure that your message is important enough to add?"[7]

Further to Hurst's point, does your message need to be in every single inbox it is destined for? Distribution lists should be reviewed regularly to avoid employees being informed about bake sales at a site they left months, or even years, before. Maintaining up-to-date lists might feel trivial and mundane, but it is hard to sell-in something more exciting until you get these basics right. Ideally, we believe recipients should be able to unsubscribe if they decide that certain content is irrelevant. As consultants, we once differentiated between 'push' and 'pull' communication – information employees were *required* to receive (even if no one could guarantee they would actually read or understand it) and information they were permitted to seek out for themselves. This classification now seems outdated. A more desirable culture is surely one where employees are trusted to sign up for the information they need. There will always be some messages we need everyone to read, but we should not be bombarding employees with everything from the lunch menu to notifications about the power outage in the Falkirk office.

Training, guidelines and the ability to opt in and out may lessen the volume and increase the quality of email we receive, but as a tool for conversing via a screen on any kind of scale, email is not the solution. As individuals, we may be able to converse, in some sense of the word, through the exchange of emails, but the messages sent en masse to staff by leaders and communications teams are all too often classic broadcasts: a response is not expected, required or on occasion even possible.

A SLIGHT IMPROVEMENT ON PING-PONG

Intranets promised so much in their early days. These were to be highly collaborative, social platforms and the backbone of all business operations. If you wanted to book a meeting room, spark a discussion or find a colleague with a niche skill, the intranet would be where you turned. Many organisations made their intranet home page the default setting on all employees' PCs and laptops, such was its perceived importance. Internet gurus like David Weinberger and Doc Searls praised the rise of internet and intranet in the same breath in their forward-thinking *The Cluetrain Manifesto*. They proclaimed: "When corporate intranets are not constrained by fear and legalistic rules, the type of conversation they encourage sounds remarkably like the conversation of networked marketplaces."[8] Yet despite such possibilities, in 2012 Prescient Digital Media found that only around 20 per cent of organisations rate their overall satisfaction with their intranet tools as good or very good.[9] Few intranets heralded a new dawn in communication.

"Prior to the emergence of the intranet, [digital] collaboration took the form of document ping-pong and occupational spamming – multiple email strings with numerous people copied. Both of these activities resulted in information being lost, files being stored on individual computers, version control issues and problems with timelines," writes the director of Webtrends, Jeff Seacrist, in a white paper on 'Using analytics to measure your intranet'. In his view, such tactics were counterintuitive to collaboration and caused frustration, although they still remain common practice. Seacrist believes "intranets emerged to provide organisations with a platform for collaboration. However, years later, intranets often suffer from low adoption, a lack of collaboration, and bad practices still prevail".[10]

Back in 1996, Steven Tellsen said that an intranet offered "new options for more effective coordination of organisational activities in a distributed decision-making environment". However, his guide to clear 'IntraNet' management structure came with a warning; to effectively use this new infrastructure, we need to become "as proficient at managing content and coordinating our actions on our intranets as we are at managing content and coordinating our actions using paper today".[11] In the years that followed, such warnings went unheeded. Instead the first few pages of most intranets were carefully managed – perhaps overly managed by a small central team – but behind the home page, most of these sites descended into labyrinthine libraries of old, forgotten content. Part of the blame must be laid at the feet of internal communicators, many of whom left important questions relating to system architecture, technical infrastructure and publishing rights to those without a background in communication. Although, in their defence, few practitioners were given the remit or budget to take the wheel.

Tellsen believed that alongside the formal content created by intranet managers, 'informal information' would quickly start to appear "when authors and users discover how easy it is to publish within the existing infrastructure".[12] He hoped that personal folders and directories would serve as repositories for white papers, notes and concepts that could be shared with others in the enterprise to further common interests and fill the unfilled needs of the system. This informal information could then "become a powerful stimulus for the collaborative development of new concepts and ideas".[13] In reality this kind of informal, spontaneous, employee-generated collaborative content was hard to find. Few employees were given the permissions or training to take any ownership of their intranets. Instead these sites became yet another centrally controlled broadcast mechanism. Perhaps leadership teams feared what they would hear if employees began posting in an open unrestricted way. Today's executives are slowly realising that providing space to hear employees' opinions – good and bad – inside the organisation on an internal site is better than closing down the conversation and pushing it outwards to the worldwide web, where permission to post is unnecessary and anyone can listen in.

Just as Tellsen emphasises the value of 'informal content' created by users, so Christopher Locke believes that "great intranets come from corporate basements, not boardrooms".[14] Locke writes that just as the internet invites participation from all of its users, so intranets must do the same. This kind of mass involvement is even more vital in work environments where "people at the bottommost tiers of the organisation often have far more valuable knowledge than managers and corporate control freaks".[15] Like so many others, Locke believes "top-down command-and-control management has become dysfunctional and counterproductive".[16] When it comes to managing complex content-heavy tools like intranets, a single owner has proved utterly insufficient. Sites consume limitless time and resource, demanding more regular updates and amends than it is possible for most communications teams to deliver. When intranet homepages are competing for employees' attention with sites like BBC News, updated constantly with interactive content, managed by a staff of hundreds, it is little wonder that corporate intranets rarely hold our attention.

Using an intranet as a static repository of information is a cruel waste of what the web can do for us. The idea of total quality management, which gained traction in the late 1980s, promoted the benefits of greater discourse within companies. "People were encouraged to share what they knew with each other, with other departments and divisions, and within the company as a whole".[17] The *Cluetrain* authors hoped that intranets would play their part in this learning and development. Yet Euan Semple believes "the trouble with much corporate training is that it is very focused around delivering 'content' to people who then 'consume' it rather than about informed conversations between people learning from each other and passing on the latest knowledge".[18] Semple's 2012 book, *Organisations Don't Tweet, People Do* argues that the web is a vital, but unexploited tool for learning. "If you are trying to keep up with the latest information, the answers you are looking for may well not be in books or manuals yet. They may only be in the heads of other people. The best way to get access to that knowledge is through online conversations with the people themselves."[19] Despite long-standing hopes, most intranets have remained broadcast channels rather than dynamic, knowledge-sharing environments. There are some exceptions – sites that are living up to the dream, such as the Wheatley Group's Holmes or BT's extensive site, which intranet manager Richard Dennison discusses as the end of this chapter.

Commentators are now talking about social intranets, as organisations finally begin to recognise the need for more inclusive online spaces – where employees can post, comment, vote and contribute freely. Yet, many of these interactive sites are being introduced alongside, rather than in place of, existing static intranets. This has left many internal communications teams grappling with a suite of multiple channels with overlapping purposes, and leaving employees confused. Andrew Lord, VP of Transformation and Efficiency at a global specialist in energy management, has seen this first hand. "For

many of our employees, it is not completely clear what platforms and channels to use for what tasks."

TWEETING, YAMMERING AND POSTING ON WALLS

The growth of online social networking has been swift
and widespread. Facebook hit 500 million users in
2010, just six years after Mark Zuckerberg unleashed
it. If it were a country, Facebook would be the third
most populous nation in the world after China and
India. Social networking has had a huge impact on society;
playing a pivotal role in collective mobilisations, protest
movements and fundraising efforts. It continues to rewire our
social lives and have a transformative effect on knowledge and
understanding.

It is little wonder that the revolution has now made its
way into the workplace. Instant messaging, blogs, forums and
wikis are now common business tools within organisations.
According to research conducted by Prescient Digital Media,
at least one social media tool is now present in 71 per cent
of organisations.[20] As corporate intranets themselves become
more 'social', there is further expectation that such interactivity will spread, along with growing use of video content
and vlogs. Semple believes such growth is inevitable as new
generations enter the workforce. "People who have grown up
with the web and use social tools are frankly not going to work
for organisations that won't let them continue to use these tools
as work."[21] This is good news for conversationalists. Communication that takes place through social networks is generally
discursive, open and personal; all the things corporate broadcasts are not. Rules around using social media outside work
are forcing organisations to follow them internally. Externally everyone is equally entitled to have their say; individuals
are only as valuable as their contributions; and any hint of

insincerity instantly destroys reputations. Naturally we increasingly expect the same at work.

Yet, as we saw in chapter 5, investing in social technology and publicising it to employees will never be enough. Andrew Lord knows full well that "successful deployment does not guarantee immediate efficiencies. For that you need behavioural change". Meaningful social exchanges that add value to the company will not spontaneously erupt across a workforce unless the conditions are right. An absence of trust, from either side, can make a workforce wary of speaking up and leadership appear wilfully incapable of hearing even if they do. The chatter on your centrally created social media channel might be non-existent, but informal conversations will be taking place across your organisation in corridors, the canteen, in the pub after work and even on social media channels outside the walls of the enterprise on sites such as glassdoor.com. Type 'unofficial' and your organisation's name into Google and see what comes up.

Throughout this book we have argued that it is better to have the conversation with employees and customers in-house – to proactively encourage it no matter how harsh the criticism you might hear – than have the debate happen next door. Rick Levine writes in *The Cluetrain Manifesto* that "not conversing, participating, is not an option. If we don't engage people inside and outside our organisation in conversation, someone else will. Start talking".[22]

ORGANISATIONAL GATEKEEPERS

At this point we should give a nod to those readers charged with protecting the external reputation of their organisation. All walls have ears and it would be naïve to suggest that a controversial or newsworthy internal debate would not leak. The live tweeting of a mass firing of HMV employees in

January 2013 is just one of many examples of internal events going viral, much to the despair of internal communicators and marketing teams.[23] This is true regardless of how actively you pursue a social media strategy. There will always be those who, for whatever reasons, share a little too much with the outside world. It is not only social networks that leak. Sensitive information can be, and has been, hacked or emailed mistakenly. "The bottom line on security is if you don't want someone to read what you have written, don't write it on a computer,"[24] advises Semple in *Organisations Don't Tweet, People Do*.

A conversation that takes place on the fringes of your organisation is far more likely to include more detractors than advocates. If you allow most of your employees to debate and comment openly, your online community is more likely to self-police. When we know our comments will be visible for all to see, they tend to be more considered. If you feel that guidance is necessary for employees, it should be drafted in the spirit of trusting employees to use their personal judgement – just as we might give advice on how to use a telephone or have a face-to-face conversation. The former chief talent officer at Netflix, Patty McCord, writes convincingly of adopting this approach: "Hire, reward and tolerate only fully formed adults."[25] Take this step and you do not need to rely on strict policies to make people behave as you wish. The company's expenses policy, for example, is just five words: 'Act in Netflix's best interests'. Similarly, IBM's social media policy, after being reviewed and amended by several meetings and committees was distilled into just 'be professional'. When Jonathan Schwartz, CEO of Sun Microsystems, allowed employees to blog, there were just three simple rules: "Don't do anything stupid, write about something you know, make it interesting".[26] Strict guidelines on how to behave should be unnecessary and if they are not, you must ask why. When I see organisations burden their social networks with onerous terms and conditions, it suggests a bigger issue needs to be addressed before an adult-to-adult conversation can take place. In these cases the preparatory phase is not yet complete and the organisation is probably not ready for social tools at all.

Enterprise social networks still seem threatening because they promotes peer-to-peer conversations that are indifferent to hierarchy. There is no 'we' or 'they'. We are all participants, whether we lurk in the background reading and commenting to ourselves, or share our every thought with the world. The audience is far less concerned with your position in the organogram and far more influenced by how interesting you are. Try to pull rank on a forum, presenting your ideas as indisputable rules and "the conversation is really a lecture".[27] These are sites for conversations, which, according to Levine in *The Cluetrain Manifesto*, "overcome the class structure of business, suspending the organisation chart, at least for a little while".[28] Such equality is not without its detractors. Andrew Keen's *Cult of the Amateur* rages about the dangers of a "web where everyone has an equal voice [and], the words of wise man count for no more than the mutterings of a fool".[29] Keen seems to give little credit to the wisdom of the crowd. We would argue that employees are entirely able to distinguish foolish mutterings from insightful comments.

SOCIAL IS NOT A TOOL

We have met many clients over the years baffled by the deafening silence of their employees on a bright new social tool. The problem is, social is a behaviour not a tool, as Euan Semple reminds us. If your new social media channel is eerily quiet, ask yourself 'how social is my organisation?' Are debate, discussion and particularly dissent openly welcomed and encouraged? Does your leadership participate in open, informal debates, whether online or in person? Do leaders listen and, just as importantly, do they show they are listening by acknowledging and acting on the feedback they hear? If no one else is commenting on your chief executive's blog, is he or she commenting on anyone else's? Moreover, is your CEO being truly social and sharing a genuinely personal view that exposes his or her true self?

There is an immediacy and informality to online exchanges that means what they can lack in substance they need to make up for in authenticity. If your CEO is unable to blog then it is worth considering alternatives. Why not post regular videos or interviews instead? Or search out another senior leader more comfortable with the process. With social networking, the more you give the more you get. If leaders refuse to communicate with feeling, they are likely to end up disappointed with the response.

Millions might hang on your every word if you are Barack Obama, but most chief executives and senior leaders will need to give employees a good reason to read, follow or comment on their posts. We spoke with senior communications practitioner Deborah Brambill, whose 25 years' experience in the industry has shown her that deference is on the decline. People are no longer willing to sit mutely and have content fed to them; instead "employees are now a lot more critical and discerning". With so many sources of information available to them, outside the office as well as within, content has to compete in terms of interest and accessibility if it is to achieve any cut-through with employees.

Semple explains the difference between conversations and broadcasting. He believes it stems avoiding an attitude of 'us and them'. "If one of them is the boss and acts like it, this is not a conversation – it is a broadcast. If the other is too scared to be open and say what they think – it is not a conversation. If one is aware of being superior in any way and is not interested in really listening – it is not a conversation. If one is a corporation and one is an individual – it is not a conversation."[30] As Weinberger puts it: "Conversations can only take place between equals."[31] Senior leaders need to get used to treating their employees as equals, but also being treated as equals by these same employees. With declining deference, and the permission for interaction that social media provides, leaders may be taken aback to find themselves openly questioned and criticised. Criticisms levied in public at least allow for a response. Those same frustrations, had they remained private, may have grown and festered. Social communication is personal, transparent and immediate. For those reasons alone, it is a powerful internal tool. However, it cannot involve content written by committee or be subjected to a lengthy approval process. It is not a strategic message carefully worded and reworded to sound off-the-cuff. We can all spot a genuine discussion and we all know when a true exchange of views has taken place.

CAMERAS ROLLING

Technology is not only creating the space to have genuine conversations, it is also enabling us to share these conversations once they have happened. Tools like video mean a conversation that takes place face-to-face between a small group can be shared more widely. Live streaming or video-calls can bridge geographical distances, exploiting the power of face-to-face without the expense of flying people around the world. We have seen clients hosting town halls across continents, allowing employees from multiple countries to participate together as a single community.

Unlike much screen-based communication, video gives you visual cues and emotions that words alone cannot convey. There is a way to capture people on film that is intensely revealing and intimate. We feel we 'know' our favourite characters or celebrities despite only ever seeing them through a camera lens. A careful use of video can foster genuine relationships – essential for productive conversation – between employees even when physical interaction is limited or impossible. It is often the next best thing to being there in person.

Video used to be expensive and cumbersome. It required a whole crew of cameramen, plus sound and lighting engineers. Corporate films were a significant investment, rarely feasible for employee communications. When they were commissioned, communicators spent weeks preparing the perfect script in order to guarantee a worthwhile take. Nowadays almost any camera, and increasingly any phone, can take snippets of film with minimal expense or expertise required. The rise of home videos has also reshaped our expectations. YouTube-style low-budget clips of three minutes or less are now the norm, while apps like Vine allow for just seven seconds of film. We no longer demand our videos be polished and rehearsed – movies like *The Blair Witch Project* and *Paranormal Activity* have made fortunes with low-budget effects and handheld filming. Lack of polish often adds to the authenticity of a message, and something genuine but unrehearsed will achieve a great deal more impact. We like to see behind the curtain and for the corporate mask to slip; it reminds us our leaders are real people.

Aiming the camera at the frontline is a powerful way of capturing the employee voice without a filter. At a conference in 2014, Lisa Wade talked about using video at WaterAid. Employees working on projects around the world used video to share their experiences with colleagues, and at the same time created invaluable marketing material for fundraising teams. Another organisation asked employees to make short films about their teams to improve cross-department relationships. These were informal, often funny, introductions to both the functions of teams and the personalities within them.

HAVING MY SAY

The way we use the internet in our personal lives has shaped our expectations of communication at work. We now expect at least some interactivity – the ability to share, comment, like or review. At this very moment, millions are sharing their view on today's news headlines, whether or not they have any personal knowledge of the topic in question. If the appropriate functionality is not available on one news website, the conversation will just migrate to Twitter or another forum. We are now solicited for reviews on almost everything we buy – from books and items of clothing to restaurant meals and airline journeys. Before going on holiday, the online community will tell you how much the taxi ride will cost from the airport, which part of town to stay in, where to have dinner, what dessert to order and how much to tip afterwards. Sites like Airbnb can even pair you up with a local with a room to rent.

It seems increasingly strange, therefore, that our employers so regularly fail to solicit our opinions and experiences. Given we are free to vote on what burger we want McDonald's to stock or what we want printed on T-shirts, it is odd that on subjects we know so much about – our daily work – there is little opportunity to share our thoughts and ideas. I have heard many diverse views on the significance of social media on employee communications. At one end of the spectrum, there are those who feel that giving their people the opportunity to conduct open conversations on an online forum would be chaotic, even foolish, and lead to unmanageable anarchy or consensus-based mediocrity. Then there are those who believe that greater insight, ideas and opinions are hugely valuable, and that the more organisations can glean from the minds of their people, the better. "We have 161,000 people working for us. Most of them speak to our customers every day. Why wouldn't we want to know what they're thinking about?" says Jacki Connor, retail and logistics HR director at Sainsbury's.

Some wonder whether their employees would ever find the time or the impetus to engage 'socially' at work. My view is the train has already left the station. As Deborah Brambill puts it: "Pandora's box has been opened." We live in a world where we have the right to speak out on anything we choose. Over time, organisations will find it increasingly difficult to stifle the opinions of their employees. We will share our likes, dislikes, first-hand experiences, expert and non-expert opinions, whether officially permitted or not.

COMMUNICATING IN THE MOMENT

Social media has changed our expectations of the speed of interaction and the accessibility of others. While travelling, one of our reporters complained on Twitter to a train operating company about delays to his journey. He received a response before he arrived at his destination explaining that his complaint was being passed to customer services. This prompted an automated email from the customer services team saying he should expect a full response within 10 working days. An important aspect of 'social' is communicating in real time.

Twitter is a conversation happening now – if you are not involved at the time, you have missed it. Around 72 per cent of consumers now expect brands with a Twitter account to respond to their complaints within an hour, according to research by Lithium in 2013.[32] Will we continue to settle for anything less from our own colleagues and superiors?

This instant, responsive nature of social media is in stark

contrast to most internal communication, which is so often carefully choreographed. Plans are important, and there will always be 'set pieces' throughout the year, but there is increasing pressure on practitioners and leaders to jump into a conversation with their employees as events unfold. Deborah Brambill believes the spread of technology has forced communicators to be more 'fleet of foot'. "Employees always have ready access to information, and with smartphones they have that access immediately. If a story about the organisation pops up on the *Daily Mail* or the *Evening Standard*, they will have already read it while the internal communications team is still battling to get sign-off on a response. By the time the official version comes out, is too late." We must not be constantly beaten to the punch by the press, unions or the unofficial rumour mill. Why would employees bother to take note of the bland, albeit 'official', announcement released long after the fact? This need to be more responsive and agile will place greater demands on those communicators who are already feeling overstretched and understaffed. The answer is likely to be less time spent planning and executing large-scale broadcast campaigns and more having local grassroots conversations driven by the audience.

THIS TIME, IT'S PERSONAL

Another challenge for practitioners, perhaps even greater than the lack of resources, is whether they have the authority and confidence to hold an online conversation. Conversation is a person-to-person activity; it is not a person-to-inbox or person-to-communications team activity. For real conversations to take place, organisations will need to rely on articulate individuals, highly conversant with business strategy and trusted to hold an online discussion without an approval process or cascade plan. I can already hear practitioners muttering about inconsistency and the misalignment of messages. How do we ensure everyone representing the organisation's viewpoint 'sings from the same hymn sheet'? The more interesting question may be whether there should be individuals charged with speaking in the voice of 'the organisation'. Organisations, to paraphrase Semple, don't speak, people do. All of those charged with crafting, implementing and promoting strategy should be willing, able, and importantly free, to converse openly about it. Indeed, they should be expected to do so. One individual may not be able to speak at length about every aspect of the organisation, but they should be able respond on their own behalf or enlist the help of an expert.

Josh Bernoff and Ted Schadler believe strongly in such an approach, and argue for it in their *Harvard Business Review* article, 'Empowered: In a world where one angry tweet can torpedo a brand, corporations need to unleash their employees to fight back'.[33] They look primarily at interactions between employees and customers, citing the Best Buy Twelpforce as a successful example of creating a pool of people with the skills and knowledge to interact with customers with minimal central supervision. The US retail giant has enlisted thousands of employees to answer queries and share their expertise on Twitter. Their approach could apply equally to internal problem-solving.

Imagine those senior managers running major change programmes. Traditionally, communication of their initiative to employees might consist of presenting PowerPoint slides to an assembled audience once a month, a weekly conference call and mailing a string of emails; in short, a great deal of broadcast. Imagine instead if everyone involved in the change programme – all 7,500 people – could engage in an online conversation during its lifespan. Here they could raise issues, ask questions, share experiences, seek and give advice to each other. All of a sudden the manager's voice would become just one in the crowd. Could they adapt to being so demonstrably accessible? Could they cope with the speed of an online exchange and the 'always on' nature of the medium? Would they be able to surrender control of the message and rely on others to help spread and promote information related to the project? Despite the challenges posed, in the former model employees are reliant entirely on the senior managers' message. They are told about the programme only at pre-assigned times and in a controlled way. Possibly, much of what they hear is secondhand, not updates directly from the programme manager but information filtered down the chain of command. Raising a question and getting an answer might take days or, more likely, may never happen at all. With an active online forum and thousands of people to speak to, questions would get answered quicker, information would be constantly available and evolving, and employees could speak to their peers about the programme, as well as hearing from their managers. The spread of social media has deeply significant implications for traditional communication methods and the way we do business. As Christopher Locke writes in *The Cluetrain Manifesto*, "the broadcast mentality isn't dead by any means. It's just become suicidal".[34]

FEAR, FALLACIES AND FOIBLES

It is hard to believe that we still need to convince our leaders that empowering workers – not only mobile ones – with smart tools is a business-critical issue. However, we hear of many communicators still trying to build the business case. The widespread use of the web and growth of mobile devices to access it have caught many organisations by surprise. We hear too many frustrating stories of employees being denied access to the same technology as their customers, even when working in marketing or communications teams and tasked with communicating with those outside. This has in some instances resulted in employees using their personal devices surreptitiously under desks or in the toilets just to do their jobs. Others have been told that only one computer in the department will have access to more than a handful of websites. We have designed external sites for clients only to discover their own staff cannot view them in their head office due to old browser software, poor connectivity or restricted access to the web.

There is, of course, a huge financial obstacle in equipping a large workforce with up-to-date technology. While as a consumer we can upgrade overnight, the wholesale roll-out of new hardware takes investment, planning and a great deal of time. As a result, employees often prefer to use their own devices, and are increasingly being encouraged to do so. The rise of bring your own device (BYOD) schemes has long been discussed, and, whether an official policy or not, we find it happening by default. When work tools fail to meet employees' expectations, they use their own. Speaking at the IABC conference in New York in 2013, consultant Shel Holtz said he had observed workers on factory floors breaking a 'no phone' rule to take pictures on their own smartphones of machinery that was malfunctioning and send the images to maintenance departments to speed up the repair process. BYOD may cause headaches for IT departments but it seems they are fighting a losing battle.

We are certainly not making light of risk and security issues. Confidential data can get into the wrong hands and, when it does, the damage can be immense. My concern is that all too often limiting employees' access to the web is less to do with any kind of security risk and far more to do with age-old perceptions of workers as inherently lazy; given half the chance, they will shirk their duties in favour of surfing the web for funny videos of cats. There is no denying that some employees are less productive than others, but with or without access to the internet, these individuals will still find a way to avoid hard work. Restricting access for most employees who are dependable and hardworking is demotivating and this is not the way to deal with a few bad apples. It tells all employees that they are considered untrustworthy or incapable of managing their time.

Workforces with restricted access will quickly create their own workaround. "In this age of smartphones and broadband, employees can't be blocked from doing inappropriate things," write Bernoff and Schadler in their article 'Empowered'. Every manager has a choice; they can "lock down the systems, ask IT to block the sites and ensure that no unauthorised technology-driven activity takes place. Given smartphones, countless free web services, and people who own their own laptops, you're unlikely to succeed. But you will spend a lot of energy proving to employees that you don't trust them and you don't want them to innovate".[35]

Evidence suggests that giving employees access to up-to-date technology actually boosts, rather than hinders, their productivity. A study by Evolv in 2013 tracked workers' use of social media alongside their performance at work and found that digital connectivity appeared to boost productivity and retention. Evolv's study focused on US workers paid by the hour such as call centre staff. From a sample size of nearly 40,000, those employees who used one to four social networking sites a week at work remained in their jobs longer than their peers. In a second experiment with a sample size of nearly 5,000, the ultra social set (those who regularly used more than five social networks) demonstrated higher sales in less time than their colleagues. The study seems to imply, perhaps unsurprisingly, that inherently social people make better contact centre staff. It also suggests that these individuals are able to maintain a level of social activity at work without adversely impacting their performance.[36]

That study was concerned with the use of external social activity, but research by the McKinsey Global Institute into the potential of internal social interaction goes much further. The 2012 research paper 'The Social Economy' argues "social technologies can make significant contributions to raising the productivity of high-skill workers, improving coordination and collaboration with partners, and accelerating innovation through co-creation".[37] McKinsey ultimately estimated that the value of social technologies within organisations could be as much as $900 billion to $1.3 trillion annually.[38] We should be promoting and rewarding social behaviour online, as well as in person, rather than shutting it down.

LOST IN THE FOREST

Each social media tool we choose to use outside of work has a specific purpose. We are perfectly happy to have 50 apps on our smartphones, and we know precisely when and why we use Twitter as opposed to LinkedIn, or why we open iPlayer rather than YouTube. Just as when we walk into a newsagent, unless we choose to browse, we know where to find what we are looking for. The purpose, identity and positioning of our favourite apps, publications and channels are clear – they have an accessibility and familiarity that makes us feel comfortable. Contrast this with both the software and hardware we are given at work. For too many of us, the place where we most need fast, intuitive, connected IT is the very place we do not have it. Instead employees are frustrated by clunky, cumbersome IT, which is neither pleasant nor easy to use. It is not unusual for organisations to have an email system, an intranet, several microsites for discrete departments or activities, at least one social networking tool plus a host of functional software programmes for specific operation tasks. Many of these tools overlap but are incapable of talking to each other, and few have the distinct identity and purpose of consumer apps.

Poorly tagged, categorised and outdated content, together with little or no search functionality, means finding information at work – where we so often need reliable data quickly – is where we tend to draw a blank. There are many reasons why internal technology lags behind the IT developed for customers. Inside most organisations, IT is a cost, not a revenue-generating stream. Although papers are being written at this very moment by IT teams on the increased productivity of the latest technical upgrade, it is almost impossible to make any precise correlation between the tools we give our employees and their eventual output. We should feel some sympathy for our IT colleagues in this regard, as for many years the link between engagement and bottom line performance was equally woolly at best. Despite the work of Towers Watson, Engage for Success and others, some might say it still is. The IT team must compete for a share of the budget just like every other department, and the ideal solution – be it hardware or software – can be prohibitively expensive.

In the early years of the net, when organisations were still grappling with when, how and why to use it, I witnessed a DIY tendency among certain organisations, as if hundreds of years of banking, for example, could equip them to create web and intranet tools. Perhaps there was a reluctance to be beholden to an expensive external supplier. Doing at least part of it yourself helped to minimise and control costs. Whatever the reason, the result was – and often still is – an online experience that turns people off. Too often, in these situations, organisations focus on the control of cost rather than the creation of value. Those employees who have no choice but to use your IT systems will persevere no matter how exasperating they find them. But anyone with a choice will try once, maybe twice and never try again. However fascinating the content we upload to a corporate intranet, if it is frustrating to navigate to, the chance is it will go largely unseen.

The good news is that as mainstream tools become easier to customise and increasingly affordable, the DIY tendency is fading. Unless your organisation actually builds, tests and sells IT solutions, it is probably best not to go it alone. Rather than create a corporate tool from scratch, look to adapt what employees are already choosing to use – unofficially in your organisation, within other companies, or in their private lives. Any solution must test well with user groups and integrate with your existing IT systems, including email. Once built, tools must also be used with consideration to reap the greatest rewards. Neil Jenkins, interim VP for Leadership and Internal Communications for Coca-Cola Enterprises, told us that when it began using Chatter among its sales force, the tool proved to be highly effective for specific types of communication, particularly during events like the 2012 Olympic torch relay. "The field sales leader in Great Britain, who was on the road for the whole of the tour, realised that if he commented on, or complimented something, it would spread instantly." This was the perfect place for informal relationship building, but would not have suited wordy corporate announcements.

As internal communicators, we are becoming more interested and involved in the technology and systems that carry our messages. When we look back, we will think it odd that we wrote our organisation's internal social media strategy but were not part of the debate about the technology itself. To move away from corporate broadcasting, we need to maintain our technological curiosity, so we can understand how tools help, or hinder, conversations among employees.

ASK THE AUDIENCE

With the myriad of online solutions available, from social network sites and social intranets to e-zines and apps, what is the right approach for your audience? The answer will only come if you start asking the right people the right questions. As consultants, we are not in favour of the 'darkened room' approach where experts gather in splendid isolation to ponder great thoughts and create the big idea. We believe not just in James Surowiecki's theory of the wisdom of the crowd, but also in its practical application. With carefully structured and crafted questions, your employees will tell you exactly how, when, and where they like their communication – and, most crucially, why. If they draw a blank at imagining how company information could be better crafted and delivered, they will at least be able to tell you what they are accessing outside work.

Badly conceived research is worse than no research at all, so when planning who to ask, what questions to pose and how to gather answers, we work backwards by identifying what information we will need at the end of the process to move forward. There may be data you can gather without bothering your audience at all. Click rates, downloads, dwell times, most searched words and phrases, for example, can help build a picture of who is reading what – a picture that might be more accurate than the comments of employees who feel obliged to say the right thing. However, it is wise not to rely on data alone. Website analytics will not tell you how many employees tried searching for a document but gave up when they could not find it. The data will not reveal that an entire team was huddled round a screen trying to navigate your SharePoint site. We find that live testing is a much better way to gather this insight. When evaluating one client intranet, we asked employees to locate a series of pages and timed their attempts to do so. Worryingly, more than half the group gave up long before finding the buried content; their endless searching may have appeared in the statistics like a flurry of page visits, but in reality was a frustrated attempt to navigate the labyrinthine site.

Screen-based tools provide a swathe of analytics and in the intangible world of communications we can become overly excited by such hard data. Yet, as we discuss in chapter 10, numbers are rarely as definitive as we might hope. It is all too easy for statistics to mask the true picture or how an audience is thinking and feeling – for that you need a conversation.

MAKE IT PART OF THE DAY JOB

When speaking to those who have pioneered new online channels, such as Neil Jenkins at Coca-Cola Enterprises and Richard Dennison at BT, it becomes clear that they did not try too much too soon, but rather let participation grow organically, knowing that if the channel or platform is useful, people will use it. This is not quite the 'build it and they will come' philosophy. There are plenty of ignored social media tools – building them is not enough. Your new tool needs a purpose. While researching this book, we heard many before-and-after stories that reinforced the point that social media needs to do something useful. We heard about one sales force that once took photographs of display stands with their digital cameras, rushed home, uploaded their pictures and emailed them to supervisors. Once they were given smart devices and access to social media, this task was completed in a matter of moments. Over time momentum builds if the purpose remains clear, the channel accessible and content fresh. This does not mean regular doses of corporate news. This type of content must be carefully streamlined and controlled in favour of letting the people have their say. The new channels we are building are for voices –

real human voices – belonging to individuals, not departments, teams or management strata. Our role as leaders and communicators is to help our colleagues at all levels find their voice and provide tools that encourage them to use it easily across time and space.

In conversation with Richard Dennison

Richard Dennison is intranet and channel strategy manager for BT, one of the world's largest multi-national communications companies. He has pioneered a virtual community so strong, it is now the foundation of the entire company's communications.

BT has a remote workforce spread across the globe, all of which is connected by its intranet, a remarkable tool driven by the innovation of its users. It has its own version of Twitter and Wikipedia, and a blogging platform and hundreds of forums all encouraging personal and professional discussion.

Richard has worked for BT for more than 15 years, in which time he and the team around him have shaped the intranet around its users, making use of collaboration, innovation and conversation.

The origins of this intranet date back to the 1990s, when you worked in the company's sales and marketing division. What sparked your involvement, and its evolution?

The problem with many intranets at that time, ours included, was that they only offered static content from Employee

Communications and HR. We did have things like news groups and forums springing up, but they weren't anything to do with the main parts of the intranet. There was also a frustrating lack of structure.

That's not to say people weren't making use of it. BT is driven by technology, so naturally there were always people collaborating on issues and products online. We found there were small communities developing in the depths of the intranet, offering pockets of niche information and discussion.

The problem was that this wasn't clearly accessible, the structure made it difficult to find things, and easy for content to get lost.

My responsibility was initially just to publish content for my division on the intranet. But taking a quick look at the design of the intranet at the time made it abundantly clear there was a need to apply a more user-friendly structure and architecture.

Fortunately, this idea came at a time when the progression of technology was beginning to gather pace and there were increasingly more tools on offer.

How did you turn the idea of a more collaborative intranet into a reality?

I previously worked at Logica, an IT company, where I helped put together the company's first intranet, so I had some experience in this area. In BT, I was 'centralised' into the corporate communications unit and became part of the small team that planted the seeds for what is the BT Intranet today. It started the way anything like this should: on a small scale involving users and testing constantly.

And what about buy-in on a senior level?

It was easier than you'd think to get buy-in from senior management. We were able to show how disorganised the current structure was, then follow it up with existing examples of idea sharing, where virtual discussions had sparked innovations. It was an easy sell to them after that.

How did you deal with those innovators who were already using the intranet in the way you intended, without alienating them?
Because there was already that established underground network of sorts, where users with specific needs were already working together to innovate, we had to be cautious. We didn't want to uproot all that; therefore, we made a conscious choice to allow that black market of information to continue, while making collaborative tools more accessible to others.

I think over time we succeeded. In 2007, we introduced BTpedia, an enterprise-wide corporate wiki tool, which was easy for everyone to contribute to.

Elsewhere, we have a Twitter-style platform called OfficeTalk, a blogging tool, and My Profile pages for every user. The key to this is integration – these different tools may operate and be viewed independently, but they all interlink in relevant places. Links are critically important in allowing people that easy navigation we wanted when we started.

How did leaders get involved?
In 2007 Ben Verwaayen joined the organisation as the new chief executive. Before him the managerial approach was very hierarchical and traditional, but he was very down to earth and encouraged a more open, flat culture.

We discussed with him how he wanted to do his internal communication. Blogs were all the rage at that time, so there was some pressure for him to blog, but we quickly realised he didn't have the time to do it properly.

Instead, he hosted a 90-minute web chat every six weeks.

He would sit in front of a computer and answer employee questions.

Ben was completely in charge of answering every question. If he couldn't answer it directly, he'd point the person with the question in the direction of whoever could. Very occasionally he would check for feedback on a dubious answer with the internal communication manager, but more often than not go on and publish it anyway.

He was Dutch and didn't waste time using punctuation or grammar. This meant nothing was polished or practised, but it also made everyone instantly aware that the chief executive of the company was sat there, replying to them directly.

This approach made a huge difference to the culture of the organisation.

What challenges did you face during the intranet's evolution?
The biggest pain point was moving from small pilots to enterprise-wide services, particularly where we had used 'open source' tools that weren't officially supported by our internal IT department.

In retrospect, involving them at an earlier stage is something we should have done. It definitely would have smoothed the overall transition.

Could your approach be replicated elsewhere?
There are now so many companies selling wholesale solutions and I think the problem is companies selling these pre-packaged platforms to organisations that aren't culturally ready for them.

Part of the reason our intranet is as widely accepted and embraced as it is now is that the users have been on the same journey as us. People have seen its growth and advancement, and made a conscious decision to go with it.

What's the key to introducing collaborative technology successfully?

The generally accepted culture of work is that people work harder than ever nowadays. They may still have a strong desire to collaborate but they struggle to find the time to do it.

Therefore, whatever we give them to use must be easy and quick, or they will instinctively migrate to less effective tools like email and conference calls.

How vital has your intranet become?

Everything we need to operate is on our intranet. It has to be, we're a global organisation with 15 per cent of our employees working full-time from home. Whoever and wherever they are, our staff must have access to everything they need, and the ease of use must be the same across the board.

I work at home in Devon, but I have the same on-screen experience as everyone else in BT, including those at the head office in London. Everything I do, whether it's ordering pencils and doing reports, or filing expenses and talking in forums, is done on the intranet.

It's the glue that holds everything together in BT and, if our intranet was unplugged, the organisation would implode.

How popular is it with users?

We do biennial research around the intranet and the latest results, from 2012, showed that social interactive functionality has dramatically increased.

For example, 67 per cent of respondents said they had taken part in an online conversation. In 2010, just nine per cent had.

What advice would you give to a company that believes it can get more out of its intranet?

I'd always go back to the basic business need. Every function of the intranet has to support the business strategy. It's very tempting to opt for a flash system with all the bells and whistles, but whatever you're offering your users has to be relevant to their work and your strategy.

Engagement is key, both in development and operation. Ask the people who are going to be using this software every day what they actually want. Then follow through by providing an online community that enables their drive to create and innovate.

Now that our employees have invested in the intranet, they are more likely to feel like a part of the organisation on the whole, which in turn means they're more likely to want to fix or innovate.

We've given them something to lose by walking away. I think a large part of why BT has such low attrition rates is because we've created a kind of family here.

Chapter 9

Face-to-face conversation

ALONE TOGETHER

As consumers, we buy millions of products and services every day without any interaction with another human being. At its busiest, the UK's ATM network processes more than one million transactions an hour[1], and more than 70 per cent of shoppers say that a self-service checkout is more convenient when buying a few items. When we call a helpline or service centre, the option to speak to a 'call representative' is generally the last on the list.

We think of ourselves as living in a highly connected world. During our waking hours, just like our smartphones, we are constantly in send and receive mode. Yet what is the quality of this interaction? "We live in a technological universe in which we are always communicating. And yet we have sacrificed conversation for mere connection,"[2] writes psychologist and Massachusetts Institute of Technology professor Sherry Turkle. In Turkle's view, we have become accustomed to "being alone together". The examples she gives of workers isolating themselves from each other are familiar – such as those who attend meetings but only tune into what interests them between looking at their laptops or checking their smartphones. In one executive team meeting, I witnessed an exasperated vice president firmly ask her colleagues to close their laptops and pay attention, chiding them like naughty school children. I am sure they did not intend to be rude, as Turkle explains we have just become "used to the idea of being in a tribe, loyal to our own party".[3]

THE HUMAN MOMENT

Some believe that interacting only at a distance, and from behind a screen, is detrimental to our wellbeing. Author and renowned psychiatrist Edward Hallowell is "increasingly sought out because people feel lonely, isolated, or confused at work. The treatment I provide invariably involves replenishing the human moments in their lives". These moments of authentic psychological encounter, which can only happen when people are sharing the same physical space, are increasingly rare in modern life. Hallowell predicts their decline could wreak havoc within organisations. "Co-workers slowly but surely lose their sense of cohesiveness. It starts with one person, but distrust, disrespect and dissatisfaction on the job are like contagions… Good people leave. Those who remain are unhappy. Mental health concerns aside, such conditions are not good for business. Indeed, they can be downright corrosive."[4]

Human moments need not be emotionally draining or personally revealing. They can be a brisk and business-like five-minute conversation. But to make them work, "you have to set aside what you're doing, put down the memo you were reading, disengage from your laptop, abandon your daydream, and focus on the person you're with".[5]

We know that face-to-face conversation is richer and often more rewarding than communication of any other kind. It is far easier to gauge sentiment and meaning when an exchange is laden with visual cues. Precisely because it is so revealing, some shy away from discussions in person, preferring to avoid the messy, ungovernable and protracted exchanges that come with it. The quick-fire nature of an email exchange gives the illusion of speed and efficiency – and a protective barrier of distance. Emails are not as forthright as walking up to someone's desk and interrupting their work. The sender is placing the onus on the recipient to decide when, or even if, to respond.

Turkle says these little 'sips of online connection' are no substitute for real conversation, which unfolds slowly and teaches us patience. In our desire get things done and move on, they may feel like a waste of valuable time and resources, not to mention a far riskier proposition than broadcasting a message. However, one meaningful face-to-face conversation – even with its subtleties, nuances and meanderings – has a more lasting and powerful impact than any virtual exchange. Do it right and you will save time, money and frustration in the end.

For an organisation wanting to drive commercial success through greater dialogue, face-to-face is the premium mechanism. Thousands can exchange and generate ideas online but in person there is richness to the feedback received and it is easier to engage those taking part. Stimulating more face-to-face interaction, particularly in a large organisation, is no easy task. The logistical obstacles and costs are prohibitive in some multi-site organisations, not to mention global ones. Yet these exchanges are happening this very moment inside your organisation, and before launching anything new it might be wiser to improve the quality of those conversations already taking place.

This chapter questions how well equipped we are to take advantage of these many interactions. We focus less on large, planned events and more on the exchanges between people, whether formal or informal, throughout an average working day. While we start at the top, looking at a leader's willingness and ability to converse in person, we also examine the essential role line managers play in stimulating and maintaining an effective dialogue with employees. We question whether we adequately support those standing on the frontline of our business in briefing the workforce.

STEPPING AWAY FROM THE PODIUM

When we think of face-to-face senior leadership communication with the frontline, we tend to think of it as one person speaking to the crowd from a podium. At best employees might get a 'Steve Jobs' style presentation, well-delivered and inspiring, but at worst they receive a presentation full of statistics and jargon that mean little to those a long way from the boardroom. However, the tide appears to be turning and the new generation of smart leaders "engage with employees in a way that resembles an ordinary person-to-person conversation more than it does a series of commands from on high"[6]. The work of Boris Groysberg and Michael Slind, authors of *Talk, Inc.*, makes a compelling case for a more conversational approach to leadership communication. "Conversationally adept leaders step down from their corporate perches and then step up to the challenge of communicating personally and transparently with their people."[7] Key to this is building greater intimacy; "distance is a disease that cripples true conversation".[8] Groysberg and Slind acknowledge that what needs to be bridged is more than just a physical gap between a workforce and its leaders. Rather, leaders need to "minimise the distances – institutional, attitudinal, and sometimes spatial – that typically separate them from their employees".[9] While Groysberg and Slind advocate a conversation style across *all* channels, it is most powerful for leaders to create 'intimacy' when standing in the same room as their employees.

At the Post Office, deputy director of communications and engagement Alana Renner has seen the benefits of leaders engaging in a more intimate dialogue with employees. She works with the executive team and senior leaders to create regular opportunities for such interaction, which often take place in small back offices at Post Office branches, and are filmed and made available for other colleagues to watch online. What these clips show are conversations between a small group of staff and senior leaders who are often paired with the CEO. Tough questions are posed – about pay or trade union relations, for example – but because of the setting and atmosphere, these are not ducked or glossed over. By going 'to the people' and meeting on their turf, leaders immediately reduce the distance between their place in the corporate hierarchy, and the daily lives of their frontline staff. The exchange is genuine, the agenda is set by the staff and it is clear that there is as much listening as talking – this is no lecture from the boss. Renner is keenly aware of the reluctance senior leaders often have for such encounters, whether out of a fear of confrontation, or difficulty comprehending their value. However, she tells us that by starting small, and allowing leaders to go in pairs, rather than alone, "they gain great satisfaction from having that conversation. They gain confidence knowing they can do it, and it won't be a disaster". She believes that both the frontline and leaders gain a huge amount from these sessions, "as it allows everyone a chance to be human".

Jacki Connor, Sainsbury's director of HR, Retail and Logistics, thinks that face-to-face communication is especially important in letting people know their leaders really care about them. "Everyone likes to feel like they have the right to an opinion, and that they can share it. Listening is so important – it's why we have a scheme whereby our colleagues can send ideas direct to the CEO, with suggestions to make things simpler or easier in store. Our colleagues are closer to the detail, so it's an excellent way to listen and make the changes that matter." The best way to demonstrate respect for employees' opinions is by placing leaders in a position where they can actively demonstrate they are listening – not just preaching from the pulpit. In order for them to do this, Susan Cain, author of *Quiet*, believes "it is important for companies to groom listeners as well as talkers for leadership roles".[10] The unstructured, intimate exchanges between a leader and a group of employees are given many names – brown bag lunches, chats with the chief or unplugged sessions. One practitioner told us of a CEO who would visit sites across the country at the end of the working day, and take frontline staff out for a beer and a sandwich. It was the only way these employees could directly find out about the organisation's financial performance, but the informal setting also allowed for a broader conversation about the business in general. Everyone involved was able to talk candidly, and it created personal relationships.

I'M GLAD YOU ASKED...

What distinguishes these face-to-face exchanges from a traditional meeting is the lack of a formal agenda. The participants decide, in the room, what to discuss. If the purpose is purely to stimulate dialogue and hear what is on people's minds, there can be no prearranged agenda. This means the chair has to be prepared to relinquish some control and let the conversation be led from the floor. Difficult questions and topics need to be dealt with head on as any evasiveness or perceived deception will cause the discussion to flounder. However, we cannot expect our leaders to be the font of all knowledge. As Margaret Wheatley puts it: "We need to abandon our reliance on the leader-as-hero and invite in the leader-as-host." Instead of seeing themselves as omniscient, "leaders-as-hosts are candid enough to admit that they don't know what to do; they realise that it's sheer foolishness to rely only on them for answers".[11] Leaders need the confidence, and the permission, to admit when they do not know or are not sure. Employees will always prefer an honest response. Promising a fuller reply later, or explaining why you cannot answer, is far better than giving an inaccurate guess or ignoring the question completely.

Even in small and private settings, there may also be reluctance from employees to ask the awkward question. Many fear being seen as a troublemaker. One senior communicator told us his CEO developed a useful solution to the 'tumbleweed' moment when the room falls silent. He would say, "I'll start by asking the most difficult question you're probably all thinking about…" Then he would start talking about their pay deal. This usually sparked additional questions and comments as employees realised that nothing was out of bounds.

We would warn against the alternative approach of planted questions. Employees can usually spot a prearranged question and, when they do, it feels embarrassingly phony. It dents the credibility of any leader who wants to be seen as open and accessible. If the conversation is especially difficult to get going, employees could be encouraged to raise questions and issues beforehand – anonymously if necessary. Leaders must be open to the views of others, even when they are uncomfortable. "It seems counterintuitive, but the act of engaging with people, of accepting that they have power, can actually put you in a position to counter negative behaviour. In fact, it's really the only chance you have of being able to influence the outcome,"[12] says Charlene Li, author of *Open Leadership*. Better leaders want to hear feedback 'warts and all' because understanding and acknowledging a problem are the first steps to solving it.

As well as soliciting views from the floor, it can be just as powerful to have leaders ask their own questions. By starting with an open question, leaders are less likely to be seen as distant and all-knowing. It is humbling to admit *I don't know, can you help me understand?* Author Edgar Schein believes "subordinates are always in a vulnerable position and must, therefore, first be reassured before they will fully commit to open communication and collaboration".[13] Asking what is important to colleagues, and for their views and impressions, recognises the vital role they play. Co-founder of Pixar Ed Catmull believes "the best managers acknowledge and make room for what they do not know – not just because humility is a virtue but because until one adopts that mindset, the most striking breakthroughs cannot occur".[14] This rarely comes instantly, and reassurance may need to be given to leaders who feel deflated by the initially parochial nature of employees' concerns. It is worth listening to complaints about minor irritants in the short term, to build the trust that ultimately allows for a major conversation.

A LEADERLESS CONVERSATION

Sometimes the best thing an organisation can do for its frontline is 'shut up and listen'. This became the internal codename for the HSBC Exchange programme, launched in 2013. Exchange is a series of team meetings, led by employees and without a fixed agenda. Pierre Goad, Global Head of Communications, told us "although the manager hosts the event, he or she is not expected to say anything – just record the issues, ideas and opinions of the room".

HSBC Exchange is still in its infancy. It is a worldwide initiative to encourage open dialogue between employees. In its first year, 46 per cent of the organisation (130,000 people) attended an Exchange event. The ambition is to have the entire organisation attend once a quarter. "If we set an agenda, the Exchange becomes just another meeting. This is the employees' event – they decide how to use the time and what to say," explained Goad. Exchange is part of a cultural change in the organisation and stems from a conscious desire to move away from an over-adherence to hierarchy and a reliance on cascade.

Exchange does not just look to spark new conversations, but to unearth and highlight those already happening in the corridors – "it's a way of shining a light on issues that existed, but were never taken up or addressed". Managers are obliged to report back on topics discussed. This formal capturing of informal discussions provides leaders with "insight they didn't have before, so that the topics that are of most concern to HSBC people are at the top of their agenda".[15] By participating, employees are "actually influencing the conversation… And all because they spoke up, and we listened".[16]

EARNING THE RIGHT TO GOVERN

"If you are among the many executives who long for the 'good ol' days' when rules and roles were clear, indulge yourself in that kind of thinking for just a few more minutes – then it's time to get to work. This is a fad that will not fade, but will only grow stronger, with or without you,"[17] believes Charlene Li. Relationships must shift from those that are "transactional, short-term, and impersonal in nature to ones that are more long-term focused, personal, and intimate".[18] In order to have the conversations we believe are essential for a business to flourish in the modern world, leaders need to build trust. This is no easy feat, trust is hard to establish and easy to destroy. It takes consistency, fairness, a desire to listen and a willingness to share openly.

Not everyone agrees leaders should even try. "On the surface, the idea that leadership is a conversation is interesting, logically seductive, and well intentioned. The danger is that this can be misleading, misunderstood, and be potentially dangerous,"[19] writes blogger Lawrence Serewicz. "In some situations, there are no questions to ask or to answer because the commands need to be followed. To put it bluntly, leadership in a war zone is not a debating club."[20] The critics of open, inclusive leadership believe at some point the discussion has to end. In some cases, a debate is out of the question; and at times, an instruction or command is the most effective form of communication. The non-believers remind us leadership is not a popularity contest or 'a crowdsourced function'. "Leaders may use conversations to achieve their ends. However, leadership is not a conversation. A conversation is an unguided exchange between equals. Leaders, by their nature, are unequal within the organisation and they must not confuse their organisational or work persona with their private or informal persona."[21] In Serewicz's view – and I suspect many others – a genuine conversation is impossible between an employee and a leader.

Yet strip away the job titles and other paraphernalia, and we *are* all equals. Deference is in decline. We are more likely than ever before to question those in authority, and live in an era of unprecedented transparency in which organisations and those who govern them are thrown into an ever brighter spotlight. A fundamental gap between who we are and who we claim to be – whether at work or anywhere else – is risky. "Transparency is non-negotiable. Provide it voluntarily and build trust, or it will be imposed on you."[22] That is the conclusion of Ketchum's Leadership Communication Monitor, which in 2014 polled the views of 6,509 respondents across 13 global markets. For three consecutive years between 2012 and 2014, the survey found 'communicating in an open, transparent way' was a leading attribute when it comes to effective leadership. Yet, in 2014, only 40 per cent of respondents felt leaders communicate in this way. The message to those at the top is clear: leave the ivory tower, step away from the podium, put down the speaking notes and say it with candour, honesty and authenticity. In short, be you.

ONCE MORE WITH FEELING

We rarely train our leaders to have conversations. For some, open debate comes naturally, but for others, it is more of a challenge. "Many people think of communication as talking *at* someone rather than having a dialogue. I've seen new starters be genuinely surprised at the depth of the work we do to listen to, and engage with, our colleagues," says Jacki Connor. Daniel Goleman, author of *Working with Emotional Intelligence*, believes "the rules for work are changing. We're being judged by a new yardstick: not just by how smart we are, or by our training and expertise, but by how well we handle ourselves and each other".[23] In his view there is now a hard case for soft skills. His research shows that the more senior the star performer, the more emotional intelligence was identified as the reason for his or her effectiveness

In Goleman's view, too much communication training focuses on improving analytical and technical ability rather than feelings, impulses and drives. A two-day seminar, a spot of role-play or a presentation skills workshop is not what is needed. There is no quick fix for boosting the emotional intelligence that allows for a meaningful conversation. "It's important to emphasise that building one's emotional intelligence cannot – will not – happen without sincere desire and concerted effort."[24] In short, we have to *want* to change. For some, the fear of getting left behind might be motivation enough. "The world is full of well-trained, once promising men and women who have plateaued in their careers – or worse, derailed – because of crucial gaps in emotional intelligence."[25]

"It's time to stop leaving the emotional side of leadership

to chance,"[26] believes Nick Morgan, author of *Power Cues, The Subtle Science of Leading Groups, Persuading Others, and Maximizing Your Personal Impact*. Like Goleman, his advice to those of us seeking to improve our ability to communicate is to become more self-aware. "Every communication is two conversations. The first conversation is the one you're aware of – the content. The second conversation is the one that you're an unconscious expert on – the non-verbal one,"[27] explains Morgan. People decode emotions primarily through gesture and tone of voice, so we need to work just as hard at perfecting our non-verbal communication as we do at crafting content. His advice is to develop greater self-awareness and a heightened awareness of the emotions of others. This may come naturally to some, but others may need help to know when lowering their voice might help defuse a situation, or when leaning in could appear more aggressive than enthusiastic. Just as the content and language we use will change according to who we are talking to, so our body language and tone should alter to be appropriate for the setting. This is not about 'acting' or playing a part, but recognising the behaviours that will enable us to get the most from any conversation.

We tend to think leaders need to be gregarious. But according to Jim Collins, "we don't need giant personalities to transform companies. We need leaders who build not their own egos but the institutions they run".[28] If your CEO is an introvert, this need not be a barrier to developing better face-to-face communication skills. Susan Cain, author of *Quiet*, believes extroversion has wrongly become the cultural ideal. "Introverts are uniquely good at leading initiative-takers. Because of their inclination to listen to others and lack of interest in dominating social situations, introverts are more likely to hear and implement suggestions."[29] Whatever the natural disposition of your leader, they are capable of holding interesting, meaningful conversations with employees. What it takes is a genuine desire to reach out and listen; respecting the insight someone has to offer more than their place in an artificial hierarchy.

AND YOUR POINT IS?

Aside from 'set piece' communication activities, which are carefully orchestrated and usually involve staging and lights, many leaders do not rub shoulders with the hundreds or thousands who make their organisations tick. Too many leaders find themselves forever in meetings, buildings and even countries a long way from frontline operations. There are many reasons for this, the most obvious being logistics. How can one busy man or woman converse face-to-face with a global, or even national, workforce? Their time is precious. But is the lack of time given to this type of communication really a matter of necessity? It may just be the commercial benefit of clearing space in the diary for speaking informally with the workforce is unclear. Rather than 'how can I fit this in?', are leaders in your organisation more likely to be thinking 'why should I bother to fit this in?'?

Jacki Connor told us "there is a risk that people can be sceptical about being truly open with people, and that engagement is seen as 'fluffy'. We actively challenge this using our own data that shows a clear link between higher colleague engagement scores and store sales performance". For some, it will take this kind of hard data to be convinced. Other leaders will understand the value of a closer relationship with the frontline instinctively, or will be convinced by successful pilots or anecdotal evidence. As communicators, we must address any leader reticence appropriately, using *their* values to make *our* point.

Often, it is easier to win leaders round to the power of informal face-to-face conversation if there is a clear strategic focus.

The questions can still be broad and open, and employees can still guide a conversation, but confine discussion to the issue that is keeping your leaders awake at night. An hour discussing health and safety with the frontline will be far more palatable – and effective – for your Quality, Health, Safety and Environment (QHSE) director than a free-for-all. Certain boundaries around a discussion can also help employees feel at ease. Particularly where an open culture has not previously existed, staff will be happier sharing their views on specific operational matters than spontaneously revealing their innermost thoughts and feelings. Build trust on both sides by demonstrating the value of a focused discourse and broader conversations, and insight will follow.

CHANGING THE CULTURE ONE CONVERSATION AT A TIME

If it is impossible to squeeze extra meetings into executives' diaries for new face-to-face conversations, it is worth considering how many people they already speak with during an average week. Let us assume your CEO has four meetings a day attended by at least five other people. Granted some of these individuals will be the same, but in an average week he or she could be seeing with well over 100 people. What if he or she dedicated at least some of that time to a genuinely open conversation?

I remember being told by the CEO at a British bank, "I wish they'd say to me in the meeting what they say to each other in the corridor afterwards". It is not just the frontline that can feel disconnected from the conversations driving their organisation. If your leader wants to avoid a respectful silence potentially masking an unpalatable truth, they need to make clear their willingness to listen and desire for honesty. Goleman reminds us, "the emotional tone set by any leader ripples down with remarkable precision".[30] If the CEO makes clear the value they place on open discussion, this behaviour will likely percolate further. What would happen if senior leaders demonstrated this with middle managers, who in turn exhibited this style of communication with their colleagues and direct reports? Without clearing space in anyone's diary, a new type of conversation can start to take place across the organisation.

By institutionalising an open discursive culture throughout the organisation, rather than simply initiating frontline-CEO forums, leaders can ensure their middle management do not feel bypassed. One practitioner in a particularly long-established and hierarchical public body told me when her chief executive started to meet frontline employees informally over a working lunch, this middle layer were openly hostile. They felt this undermined them and interrupted the accepted flow of information through the hierarchy. By encouraging middle managers to hold open discussions, both with their employees and their own supervisors, they will discover for themselves the potential power of a conversation. If you create a culture where the value of a contribution matters more than role or rank and anyone is free to speak up, the only people who will be threatened are those whose authority comes from their job title alone.

IN THE FACE OF MAJOR CHANGE

TJ and Sandar Larkin's *Communicating Change: Winning Employee Support for New Business Goals* landed on our desks at an interesting time. In the mid-1990s, in the UK at least, internal communicators were gaining more respect from our leaders. We were beginning to advise executive teams during times of crisis and change. I was helping to plan the kind of major initiative that was springing up across the corporate world. We were putting our CEO on the road, to address internal audiences of several thousand. Our objective was for frontline employees to hear about the new strategy straight from the top. In the middle of these programmes, a few of us read Larkin and Larkin's book. It implied that, to a large extent, we were wasting everyone's time.

"Most advice given to executives about communicating change is wrong. The advice usually boils down to more: more values, missions, and vision; more videos, publications, and meetings; more executive road shows. This communication is not working. Why would anyone want more of it?"[31] Larkin and Larkin asked. Their solution was seductively simple; target frontline superiors with the facts and do not let executives introduce change to frontline employees. The authors were advising us on communicating major change – "the sort of change that most companies face every five to ten years"[32] – to the people making the product or delivering the service. "If you want these people to change the way they do their jobs, then you must change the way you communicate with them."[33] The trouble for internal communicators, as TJ Larkin saw it, is that most of what we were producing – newsletters, intranet sites, emails and blogs – raised awareness but did not change behaviour. "If you want to change behaviour there has to be a face-to-face conversation because that's where the persuasion takes place."[34]

"Communication professionals are wedded to the big bang theory of communication," Larkin and Larkin observed. It is what communicators call 'sheep dipping' – the notion that several thousand people can attend the same Big Event, be submerged in the organisation's new strategy for the day, and somehow leave the venue more informed and capable. These events might generate excitement, even awareness, but in reality they do little to affect behavioural change. For that, Larkin and Larkin told us to turn to the experts in frontline communication – those who are constantly conversing with employees at the sharp end of our businesses – the supervisors. "No matter what the change – merger, restructuring, downsizing, re-engineering, the introduction of new technology, or a customer service campaign – the first words frontline employees hear about a change should come from the person to whom they are closest: their supervisor."[35]

Supervisors vary greatly in their ability to communicate, but according to Larkin and Larkin we hamper their capabilities by giving them the wrong kind of messages. We tend to send evasive, overwritten and overly corporate press releases rather than providing them with the facts. The reason a manager's face-to-face communication with his or her team does not happen as it should is because we formalise the content, turning it into something that no one can deliver, understand or believe – we give them a 50-slide PowerPoint presentation or a video of the CEO, rather than the time to speak directly with their staff, in team meetings or one-to-one. Larkin and Larkin suggest a compelling alternative. Give supervisors 'high demand' content – factual information only – and allow them to communicate this as they see fit, drawing on their personal experience of liaising with their teams. This approach taps in to the insight supervisors have into their teams' communication needs and preferences.

Larkin and Larkin's book contained examples of briefing notes for supervisors. The approach was to avoid hoopla, corporate speak and glossy marketing messages. The brief summary then becomes a guide for face-to-face communication between senior managers and supervisors, and between supervisors and frontline employees. Without slogans, threats or hyperbole.

Speaking at an IABC conference in 2011, TJ Larkin explained how a simple drawing was given to supervisors to explain Boeing's strategy after its merger with McDonnell

Douglas. This drawing did not replace the 96-page strategy document on which it was based, but middle managers used it to have informal conversations with supervisors who, in turn, used it to explain the company's strategy to their teams.

FROM THE HORSE'S MOUTH

Are the lessons of *Communicating Change* still relevant, given the last two decades of dramatic social, technological and economic upheaval? We are now in the era of the knowledge worker. A report from McKinsey Global Institute suggests that there are now 230 million knowledge workers around the world.[36] As communicators, we know that knowledge workers can be hard to reach, they are likely to be engaged in projects, often working from home, a client's office or an airport lounge. These are networked individuals, with a high degree of independence, managing their own workloads and using technology to share data and ideas with others. They are unlikely to be having regular, face-to-face meetings with a supervisor. Knowledge workers have managers to monitor their workloads and provide guidance, but not to 'supervise' in quite the same way. This relationship is less central to the lives of employees and these self-motivated, independently minded individuals form their own opinions by consulting their network both inside and outside the organisation. No doubt there will be people these employees trust to look them in the eye and explain 'the facts' of a major change initiative, but they will not necessarily be confined to the next level up in the corporate hierarchy. They might look to senior leaders, peers, union representatives or even external sources. As communicators, rather than focus all our efforts on supervisors, we need to find the real opinion influencers.

In an age of declining deference, we no longer wait to be told by a line manager and make do with second hand or unsatisfactory information. We seek out the truth, from wherever we feel we will get it. When it comes to strategic information, as opposed to something strictly operational, we are far more likely to look to senior leaders than our direct supervisors. As Kevin Ruck has found, "employees want to hear about high-level strategy from the senior managers, because they know these are the people actually controlling it". Pierre Goad, from HSBC, puts it this way: "The only person who can talk about our strategy in the way our CEO does is the CEO."[37] The past two decades have seen growing scrutiny paid to corporate boardrooms, forcing greater transparency. There are no hiding places left for those in authority. Employees expect their leaders to look them in the eye, and tell them the truth. Personal and corporate reputations suffer when those at the top fail to be open and honest.

HOLDING THE LINE

Just as we expect leaders to have the best grasp of the strategic direction of an organisation, so we expect our line managers to have the best understanding of our operational needs and practices. Employees look to the top for news about a shiny new acquisition, but to local management for explanation of the impact of this on shift patterns and changes in procedure. Communicators have learnt how to communicate the unveiling of a major initiative. But as the fanfare dies, those in operational roles may have yet to feel the first ripples of that change. The real impact for them comes later, when leaders have moved on to something new, and it is supervisors who will be managing the change – all too often with insufficient skills or support.

In research we often find line managers are often the most stressed, frustrated and misunderstood individuals in a business. They feel pressure from above, anger from below and are often isolated from their peers. Promoted for operational achievements rather than their communication abilities, many feel ill equipped to cope with the demands of the role. Internal communicators may be sending out detailed PowerPoint presentations or long lists of FAQs for them, forgetting the raft of other messages this group are asked to communicate to their teams – from health and safety procedures and human resources information to new product changes and operating processes. With so much resting on the shoulders of local managers, it is to time to acknowledge their importance. The first step is listening to their communication needs, preferences and personal challenges. The next step is to provide materials and support crafted around their needs rather than designed to satisfy the predilections of head office.

A PLACE FOR EVERYTHING

In the drive to stimulate more meaningful face-to-face conversations at work, we may have to reconsider the layout and design of our offices. Although we know chance encounters and conversations promote co-operation and innovation, "when companies craft their floor plans and cultures with this in mind, the results have been surprising – and often disappointing"[38] say Anne-Laure Fayard and John Weeks, writing in the *Harvard Business Review*. They cite the experience of Scandinavian Airlines, which in 1987 redesigned its headquarters around a central 'street' with a café, shops, medical, sports and other facilities. "The new design was explicitly intended to promote informal interactions, and management broadcast the message that employees should find opportunities in the new space for 'impromptu meetings' and 'creative encounters'."[39] Yet a later study found that just nine per cent of employee interactions were happening in the 'street'. Two-thirds of interactions were still confined to private offices.

"Common sense, it turns out, is a poor guide when it comes

to designing for interaction," they concluded. While there is evidence that suggests removing physical barriers and bringing people closer together fosters casual conversation, roughly the same amount of research proves the opposite; employees in open-plan spaces "knowing that they may be overheard or interrupted, have shorter and more superficial discussions than they otherwise would," say Fayard and Weeks. The answer is a space that "brings people together and removes barriers while also providing sufficient privacy that people don't fear being overheard or interrupted".[40] We need to feel we have permission to convene and speak freely. Fayard and Weeks reference the work of architect Christopher Alexander, who describes the alcove as the ideal space for informal interactions – being sufficiently public for casual encounters, but providing enough privacy for confidential conversations. "People are afraid to talk about intimacy in the workplace because of the implications. But we need to make space for it,"[41] says Susan Cain, author of *Quiet*. If we want to encourage more collaborative working relationships, we need to provide the space for them to develop.

The construction and style of the space will differ depending on the culture of the organisation. Not every business could – or would want to – take video games developer Valve's approach. In its employee handbook, this games company explains why everyone's desk is on wheels: "Think of those wheels as a symbolic reminder that you should always be considering where you could move yourself to be more valuable. But also think of those wheels as literal wheels, because that's what they are, and you'll be able to actually move your desk with them."[42]

Many of us would find this type of office environment chaotic, but it suits Valve's unusually flat, highly participative culture. The lesson for the rest of us is not to emulate others but to create an environment that is suited to the tasks performed by our people. What matters most is outcomes, not reinforcing status or traditions. This approach will ultimately facilitate more productive conversations – both casual and planned – because it creates environments more conducive to what we do and how we do it.

BACK TO BASICS

Conversation works best face-to-face, and outside the artificial constructs of corporate organisation we do it without thinking. We naturally understand the value of informal dialogue when it comes to communicating with our friends and family. Unfortunately, when it takes place within office walls, conversations are too often impeded by hierarchical concerns, unsuitable environments and a fear of speaking up. We find it hard to quantify their value, and they are dismissed as time-consuming, logistically complex and unstrategic.

Until you master the art of an open, honest exchange of views while sitting in the same room, all the trappings of the digital age or impressive engagement strategies will come to nothing. Productive and meaningful face-to-face conversations are the acid test of your internal communication. Decades of cascading a message down, and keeping the frontline at arm's length, have embedded behaviours that might be hard to throw off. Yet, we believe open dialogue is the foundation of collaborative working, employee engagement and ultimately of organisational success.

In conversation with Richard Davies

Richard Davies has worked with industry giants London Underground and eBay.

He now leads world class engagement at Crossrail, the rail infrastructure project that is tunnelling 42km under London.

At the heart of Crossrail's engagement story is a team of senior leaders who realise the value of an engaged workforce and who are committed to creating a culture of inclusion through face-to-face communication.

Can you describe the Crossrail organisation?

Our core workforce is an integrated client delivery organisation consisting of 1,200 people from nine different employers, all working in a 'single use vehicle' that will dissolve following the project's completion.

Its role is to oversee delivery from more than 20 principal contractors, each with their own supply chain. At its peak, the project has an overall workforce of 14,000 people. The team is highly diverse, ranging from technical office-based roles to site-based construction roles, located across more than 40 separate projects.

How do you keep up face-to-face communication with such a disparate workforce?

The senior leaders regularly visit our project sites to conduct safety tours and meet staff. Each project team has a quarterly 'all hands' event, at which a member of the leadership team gives an open and honest 'big picture' status report on how the project is going.

We think it's important that everyone understands how their work contributes to the overall programme and how they are helping to move London forward.

How do you stop these being just a lecture from the boss?

The events are PowerPoint-free, which encourages a more personal style of engagement. At least half the time is devoted to a frank question-and-answer session.

The events work well because we have credible and authentic leaders who have worked hard to create an open environment where employees feel able to speak up and have opinions that matter.

Our 'Big Dig' survey in 2013 showed that 97 per cent of employees understood our vision, and 94 per cent felt that leadership had a clear sense of direction for the project. I believe that good face-to-face communication is essential to achieving these high levels of engagement.

Do your leaders understand the value of face-to-face engagement?

Andrew Wolstenholme, our Chief Executive Officer, is very committed to a highly visible and open style of leadership. Prior to Crossrail, he worked on the Terminal 5 construction at Heathrow, where he championed high standards of workforce engagement. Andrew is a former Army officer, so standing up and talking to people directly comes naturally to him.

Andrew also likes to visit a different project team every month for a breakfast session with around a dozen people. These groups are usually split between office-based staff and contractor staff, including people who are 'on the tools'. The main purpose is to find out what it's like to work there – is it a safe site and how can it be made safer?

He also takes time to find out about the people working on the project. When the CEO talks to you over breakfast about your job, the previous projects you've worked on and how you feel about working on Crossrail, it definitely helps build engagement. Staying in touch with what people on the project are thinking is at the heart of his authentic leadership style.

Do you find any downsides of having such an open and visible leadership?
It's important to beware of inadvertently bypassing and undermining line management. While it's great that frontline employees can voice their concerns and suggestions directly to senior leaders, we have to respect the roles of local managers.

Senior leaders need an instinct for what they should take away with them and what they should leave with the local line managers to address.

The key to managing this successfully is for leaders to have a preliminary session with local line managers to understand what's on people's minds and the issues likely to come up during the interactive session. That helps ensure that staff feel listened to without treading on local managers' toes.

Working with employees who come from so many different organisations must be a challenge. How do you make them feel like part of Crossrail?
We've invested a lot of effort in building a culture based on a shared vision, mission and values.

New starters on the programme spend their first day at head office for an induction session. They receive a copy of our pocket-sized booklet, known as 'The Little Pink Book'.

The message printed on the back sums up our approach: "Whatever role we do, wherever we work, whoever we work for, we are all part of the same project, sharing common values and working towards the same goals."

During the induction, they will meet one of our senior directors, who will talk to them in person about why these values are important. I'm a great believer that written communication can inform people, but if you really want to engage people and change how they feel about something, you have to do it face to face.

Apart from the leadership tours, how else do you keep this remote, diverse workforce engaged?

We have invested a lot of effort in creating what we call 'I was there' experiences. The best example of this was when we arranged for 600 people in mainly desk-based roles to witness a tunnel breakthrough at our Woolwich station site. The chance to watch one of our giant tunnel boring machines come through the wall and then have your photograph taken in front of it was an unforgettable moment for everyone who experienced it.

Similarly, to mark reaching the halfway stage of the programme, we held more than 40 small group tours and open day events for people on the programme to visit other project sites and see the progress for themselves, with expert guidance from their colleagues. This included a friends and family day in which 800 people experienced a unique train ride along a completed section of tunnel.

As a government-funded organisation, we don't have the budget of private sector corporate companies to throw lavish events, but we can still give our staff incredible memories and experiences. The cost of the Woolwich breakthrough event was installing a temporary staircase and giving everyone a bottle of water, but the feedback was off the scale. For our 'halfway there' events, 96% of people said they came away feeling inspired by Crossrail and our achievements. Bringing people together in this way can have a huge impact on employee morale and team spirit.

Why do you think creating an open and engaged culture is so important?

If we want to get the best out of people, they need to feel they are part of something special and that their contribution is valued. Having an open and engaged culture is at the heart of this. Making it happen requires leaders who can listen and empathise, so that people feel able to speak honestly and openly. As communicators and leaders, we can't afford to have a workforce that keeps its ideas and opinions to itself.

Chapter 10

Measurement through conversation

PROVING OUR WORTH

"My first day as a communication vice president started with my new employer's chief financial officer stopping by my office to welcome me to the company in a rather disturbing way: 'I have no idea why Michael [the CEO] created your position,' he said. 'As far as I can tell, you're just a drag on my bottom line. But welcome to the company anyway'."[1] Angela Sinickas, author, speaker and employee communications consultant, recalls an experience that is probably familiar to many of us – whether or not the scepticism was quite so blatant.

While some understand the value of what we do as communicators, there are plenty who believe that communication should just happen, without the need for additional budgets or dedicated resources. The need to prove our worth and justify our activities has been partly responsible for the adoption of more robust and meaningful assessment of our work. The practice is a useful one, and evidence demonstrates that companies managed using balanced performance measurement systems outperform and have superior share prices to those that are not 'measure managed'.[2] While businesses as a whole might be benefiting from such metrics, in the world of internal communications I believe that research and measurement is not yet achieving its full potential. This chapter explores attempts to quantify the value of something as intangible as employee communications. We consider what measurement can provide, not only when it comes to impressing our bosses and winning budget, but more importantly for gaining greater insight and understanding of our audience, and serving them better as a result. We look at the role conversation has to play in not only producing such insight, but making measurement more rewarding for those taking part.

WHAT TO MEASURE

"Throughout history, performance measures have been used to assess the success of organisations,"[3] say Mike Kennerley and Andy Neely in their paper 'Measuring performance in a changing business environment'. By the 1980s, the nature of this measurement was moving away from pure financials, as organisations began to recognise this kind of data was historical in nature; encouraged short termism; provided little indication of future performance; was internally rather than externally focused; and lacked strategic focus and insight. Measurement tools became more sophisticated with the introduction of balanced scorecards and key performance indicators that measured the company in more rounded and dynamic ways than simply an assessment of profit or loss.

In our field, we adopted more sophisticated research methodologies, thanks partly to the influence of market researchers. From the 1980s, "corporate leaders began to express an interest not only in what their customers were thinking but also in the opinions of their employees".[4] Until this point, employee surveys had tended to focus on specific issues employee parking or benefits, for example. Breakthroughs like Gallup's

Q12, which aims to measure overall employee engagement, "occurred when corporate leaders actually committed themselves and their organisations to studying basic employee attitudes that affect workplace morale, and ultimately, overall productivity".[5] As communicators, we similarly became more thoughtful in our measurement. We were learning it was possible to be more holistic and rounded in our measurement, and no less robust.

QUANTIFYING THE UNQUANTIFIABLE

When pitching for a major new account – one of the biggest in AB's history – we were told that proving our return on investment (ROI) would be key. So I went back to basics, starting with the obvious question, what is ROI? The general equation is as follows:

$$\% \ ROI = (Net \ gain/Investment) \ x100$$

Applying this equation to our communications activities would have been effectively impossible. While the cost to the business, the investment required, would be clear, how would we agree on the gain – in solid financial terms – as a result of our work? We could look to reduced costs in hiring if engagement rose and attrition fell, or similar performance and people metrics, but proving an exclusive relationship between our activity and a rise or fall in these numbers would be trickier.

"Measurement of the positive causal relationship has not been well established in terms of how top communicators link their organisation's internal communication efforts with business performance,"[6] writes Dr Juan Meng. Even organisations with woeful communications can generate a healthy profit thanks to fortunate market conditions such as poor competition or entrenched customers. The effect of communication – good or bad – on a business is not easily quantifiable. As communicators, our success is in affecting what employees think, feel and do. This in turn will impact almost every business and performance metric an organisation tracks. But proving a communications programme has led to a rise in sales is complicated. We would have to prove the programme led directly to employee engagement that then influenced the greater discretionary effort and better customer service that resulted in the spike in sales. As Baruch Lev, author of *Intangibles: Management, Measurement and Reporting*, explains, despite an "apparent link between, say, employee training and productivity, it isn't always possible to confirm a causal relationship between the investment and the positive result, given the variety of factors – information technology and so on – that affect employee productivity".[7]

Even when you ask people why they think, feel or behave in a certain way – which we invariably recommend – the answers are never entirely straightforward. Our attitudes and actions stem from a complex set of beliefs, assumptions and influences – sometimes even we are not entirely clear what drives our actions or opinions.

Organisations like Towers Watson are long established and well regarded in the measurement of intangibles like employee engagement, communications and change. It presents findings that appear robust and statistically grounded, such as the conclusion to its 2013-2014 'Change and Communication ROI Study Report': "Organisations with effective change and communication are 3.5 times as likely to significantly outperform their peers."[8] The study was certainly thorough, surveying more than 650 organisations from a broad range of industry sectors and from a cross-section of regions. But while it successfully establishes a link between effective communication and superior financial performance, it does not prove *causality* – nocturnal animals may come out at night, but they do not bring about the sunset. "Correlation is important. You can't have causation without it. But selling one for the other is survey snake-oil, a statistical confidence game. It may be true that engaged employees make for profitable companies, but it may also be true, and more than likely is, that profitable companies make for engaged employees,"[9] says 'The (statistical) confidence game of employee engagement surveys', an intriguing report by Converge Consulting Group based in Alberta, Canada.

Given the difficulty in measuring the 'net gain' of something as intangible as communication, I am deeply sceptical of any fixed numerical value placed on any piece of work, unless cause and effect are blindingly obvious and irrefutably certifiable. Of course, I believe strongly in the commercial value of what we do, but the average chief financial officer, trained to work in facts and stats, will shoot holes through the assumptions and suppositions that need to be made when measuring what cannot be clearly seen and counted. However, John Hayes, chief marketing officer of American Express, highlights the challenge of moving away from hard statistics. "We tend to overvalue the things we can measure, and undervalue the things we cannot".[10] Lev finds hard evidence to support Hayes' theory. He writes that "in an era when physical assets have essentially become commodities, the benefits intangible investments yield – increased productivity, improved margins, and, most importantly, innovative products and processes – are the only means companies can use to escape intensifying competitive pressures".[11] Yet, his research indicates, "investors systematically misprice the shares of intangibles-intensive enterprises"[12] due to the difficulty of accurately valuing these elusive facets of an organisation.

Technology is one of the intangibles Lev considers. Mark Hall, the opinions editor of Computerworld, is scathing of attempts to measure ROI in this field. "The best, most innovative IT improvements have no ROI. There was no decent ROI on installing the first Wang word processor in the 1970s or the first PC to run VisiCalc in the 1980s or the first Linux server for corporate websites in the 1990s."[13] Hall believes "if you're jumping through ROI hoops for every IT project on your whiteboard these days, you're wasting your time. It may sound ironic, but the simple truth is that there's no ROI in analysing the ROI on everything. At the risk of being labelled a blasphemer, I suggest you rid yourself of the fancy-schmancy, spreadsheet-happy blather of ROI gurus and use your own wisdom to evaluate IT projects. If it makes sense to you, do it. If not, don't. You know the business. You know the technology. You know your crew. You know your budget. You know if it's feasible or not. What else do you need?"[14] My guess is that many internal communicators feel the same way about their profession.

MEASURING OUTCOMES NOT OUTPUTS

The difficulty of quantifying the impact of our work means many communicators slip into the practice of documenting output, rather than the outcome of our efforts. The fact we can prove 76 per cent of employees have seen or even read a communication might be interesting, but it is of relatively little consequence. "The worst mistake communicators (and others) make when measuring the effectiveness of online communication is measuring hits. Hits, according to one communication management guru, is an acronym for 'how idiots track success',"[15] writes Shel Holtz in *Corporate Conversations*. Angela Sinickas has found organisations tend to measure "satisfaction, rather than effectiveness".

As professionals, the very minimum asked of us is to create readable communications that arrive on time, get opened and read. We must hold ourselves to a more consequential definition of success – did the communication change opinions, prompt action or deepen understanding? To even attempt to measure such success, we need to be clear from the outset about the shift in thought, behaviour or attitudes we are seeking. Taking this more strategic approach to measurement forces us to ask the difficult questions at the outset – *Why are we doing this? What is it for?* Defining a clear outcome for every communication activity is not as simple as it might sound, but asking these questions forces a pause for thought. It can reduce the noise inside organisations by scrapping communication not tied to a clear commercial gain.

Too much of our activity is explained as 'raising awareness', a catch-all term that can excuse sloppy communication practice. The problem is, an employee can be fully aware of their organisation's values – seeing them plastered on everything from office stationery to the back of the toilet door – and behave in a completely contradictory manner. You may achieve 100 per cent awareness among the workforce, but employees may remain unsure about why or even how these values should impact their behaviour. As practitioners, we need to identify the 'what's in it for me?' – the compelling reason men and women outside the C-suite should be listening. Then, we need to translate strategy into a set of tasks – *do less of that, but more of this*. This translation into actions is often the missing piece of the puzzle and where even the most compelling messages fail.

Public health campaigns offer clear examples of communication that actually focuses on a change in behaviour. In the UK, the strategy developed to fight obesity is translated into a message to 'eat five a day'. In the US, the campaign preaching that 'Friends don't let friends drive drunk' has been cited as instrumental in achieving a 10 per cent decrease in alcohol-related fatalities between 1990 and 1991: the single largest one-year drop ever recorded.[16] Identifying a clear outcome for your activity is an essential first step, not just for meaningful measurement but meaningful communications.

MAKING IT TANGIBLE

When the outcome you are aiming for is as tangible as a decline in alcohol-related driving deaths, then one clear measure of your success is clear. If an internal campaign asked employees to 'think twice about every journey', then a reduction in travel expenses would be an obvious mark of its success. These kinds of statistics will already be generated within your organisation and can provide the data your budget-holders may be hungry for. Proving causation can still be tricky, although a clear aim, and the ability to map data over time, can help strengthen your case – for instance, if a new communications initiative was the only thing that changed in January, and it was since February that executives began cutting down on long-haul flights for the first time in years, then you can claim at least some involvement with confidence.

By piloting your communication in one area of the business, you have a control group to monitor as well. If change *only* occurs, or is more significant, in your pilot area, then causation is more effectively demonstrated. Pilots have a host of other benefits, allowing you to discover potential issues and refine practices before they are rolled out on a broader scale. They are often less scary to managers, requiring less financial investment and providing greater protection from potential failure. A happy test group, who are one step ahead on the change curve, can also prove invaluable if initiatives are later expanded more widely. While testing ideas in theory with an audience provides some insight, this will not provide as accurate a picture as a live trial.

YOUR OPINION MATTERS TO US

Observing changes in behaviour is one way of measuring impact. But restricting ourselves purely to monitoring actions limits our insight to what is clearly visible. If communication has failed to result in the desired outcome, we need to ask why, and the only people to ask are the target audience. In fact, even if communication has proved wildly successful and achieved everything we had hoped for, it is still worth discussing it with the audience – *What was it that was so effective in this case? Could anything have been improved further? What lessons can we take from this campaign to future projects?*

A communications plan that does not have some kind of audience feedback as a critical step will be open to challenge. Yet "a survey with badly designed questions, with no clear sponsor or purpose, and no attempt to communicate or take action on the results, will increase the 'disempowering distance' between management and employees",[17] warns Towers Watson. Many of us have experienced a poorly conceived survey as a respondent – the frustration of not being able to answer accurately, or not understanding the thrust of a question. We have seen staff extend scales with extra options or scrawl comments in a margin because the existing design did not allow them space to express their true feelings.

Employees all too often feel that internal surveys are 'tickbox' exercises in both a literal and figurative sense. The organisation is asking because it feels it has to, not with any real conviction and with no desire or intention of taking meaningful action as a result. We have met many employees over the years who believe that negative opinions will simply be swept under the carpet. They are not always mistaken. If, after answering a long list of questions, nothing much happens, then the process is less than worthless; it is a frustrating waste of your time. This is when participation rates for subsequent research drops – a metric that tells you everything you need to know about how valued and regarded a workforce feels.

Giving feedback and having it ignored is worse than not being asked for it in the first place. Take two scenarios. In the first, you order duck at a swanky French restaurant and the waiter says: "Our chef likes to cook the duck as he feels it should be served. Are you happy with that?" You agree. After all, the chef should know. When your duck arrives, slightly less well done than you prefer, you accept it without complaint. Compare that to second scenario and the waiter who asks: "How would you like your duck this evening?" You say: "Well done, please". When it arrives, a shocking pink, you feel distinctively put out and ready to complain. "Pretending to listen is worse than not listening at all," says Deborah Dorman, Head of Great Place to Work at Sainsbury's. "If you are going to listen you have to demonstrate that you did, even if it is to say no; it's much better to explain why."[18]

Before being asked to undertake any measurement exercise, we like to be clear why it is happening. *Because it's been 12 months since the last survey* is not a good enough reason. What did the measurement a year ago change? Has it impacted your communication this year? Research and measurement must be driven by a genuine desire to improve performance through better understanding. If there is no real desire to act differently, or use feedback to inform future decision-making, do not ask.

If you do intend to act on what you hear, then it is vital to make clear to employees that their views have shaped your actions. It is all too easy for a response to become disconnected from the measurement or feedback that originally prompted it. Sinickas told us that every time a company announces a change, they should ask how it relates to any research – if employee input has played any role in prompting the decision. When this does not happen, communicators miss a perfect opportunity to prove their listening credentials, and encourage greater audience involvement in the future. 'You said, we did' features should be part of the campaign before any survey – clearly showing the results from previous questioning. While it takes a little more bravery, it is also important to include details of feedback that could not be acted upon, along with clear reasoning for things remaining the same. It is very hard to filter what employees have told you without destroying your credibility; employees know what feedback you received – it was they who provided it.

TWO TABLETS, TWICE A DAY

What happens *after* the research is what really matters – asking but not responding is worse than futile. Yet, far too often we see research and measurement that provides all manner of conclusions without any plans for action. The sign of poor or inadequate research is that no one is sure what should happen next – it is like a diagnosis from the doctor without a prescription.

Asking your audience for answers and not just problems makes your job easier and empowers them as individuals. It encourages participants to think hard about the practicalities of the issues they are raising. In face-to-face research we often ask, 'How would you solve that problem?', prompting some employees to rethink a complaint – *I suppose they are probably doing all that they can. There isn't really another option.* If you do not ask for a solution, you can unduly panic over a worrying statistic, without knowing it would take very little to turn the number around. What might appear to be a massive problem around unmanageable workloads could be fixed with a simple tweak to a process.

This approach works well at the end of focus groups, which can sometimes spiral into moaning sessions. Angela Sinickas cautions that the complaints of the few can soon infect others and leave participants feeling worse about the organisation than when a session began. Our approach is to capture the issues that most frustrate those in the room, and ask *them* for the solutions; forcing the group to be proactive. It is more empowering to solve an issue than simply raise one, and it is easier to believe that action will follow if you have created the plan for it yourself. As communicators, we can test our own ideas for remedies with an audience – *Would this solve your issue? Would that make it better?*

When we report our findings, we are in a much stronger position if we bring clear next steps that we know will make a difference. It takes bravery to present difficult results, but we are far more likely to get a positive response if each issue identified comes with a plan of action. Faced with a long to-do list, it can be helpful to differentiate between those initiatives that are quick wins, and those requiring longer-term investment. Indeed, if your plan is ultimately for a wholesale cultural shift – hard to cost, difficult to achieve and a long time in the making – it can be valuable to purposely create more attainable goals along the way. Planning in the small successes builds momentum and reassures both leadership and research participants their efforts have been worthwhile and change is truly afoot.

QUANT VERSUS QUAL

Practitioners tend to split approaches to audience research broadly into qualitative and quantitative. Qualitative methods are used extensively in psychology, sociology and anthropology. The emphasis is on understanding – on unpicking thoughts, feelings and motivations. Those gathering and analysing the data are themselves an integral part of the research process, particularly when information is collected face-to-face during in-depth interviews or focus groups. Researchers need high emotional intelligence to gather real insight, and 'read' the answers they are receiving. Questions posed are open, and allow participants to respond in their own words, unrestricted by artificial scales and weightings. Misunderstandings and inferences can be checked and verified during the process. If an answer is incomplete, the researcher has the chance to probe further. The result is a huge wealth of data that is often difficult to categorise and sort through. While sentiment analysis tools continue to improve, and we can now easily scan for key words and trends, open answers tend to need human interpretation. We find reading through each and every open response in a survey paints a very different picture to a computerised analysis.

Quantitative data is focused on the numbers, and usually asks closed questions, where findings can easily be translated into pie charts and bar graphs. In typical engagement surveys, participants are asked to plot their views on a Likert scale or similar – specifying their level of agreement or disagreement to a series of statements. By producing hard figures rather than open comments, quantitative research provides findings that are easier to track over time and compare with other companies. They can appear more definitive – '90 per cent' is often more persuasive than 'a clear trend in comments'. The relative speed and subsequent cost of analysing numerical data means sample sizes are typically greater. Once again, this can bestow a certain weight to findings.

"There has probably been more energy expended on debating the differences between and relative advantages of qualitative and quantitative methods than almost any other methodological topic in social research,"[19] writes professor William Trochim of Cornell University. In his view, the differences between the two approaches have been overplayed. "All numerical information involves numerous judgements about what the number means."[20] It is hard to find an absolute and certain truth in any survey data completed by human beings; the participant, researcher or both have likely made some kind of interpretation or assumption. Used appropriately, these two approaches can both provide valuable insight.

MAKING UP THE NUMBERS

Quantitative research gives us the reassurance of being able to say '85 per cent' of employees responded. Closed questions are easier to ask and analyse en masse, and, when open to an entire organisation, offer everyone equal opportunity to take part. A common criticism levied at those undertaking qualitative research is the typically smaller sample size. How can the answers of 40 people possibly tell me what my 30,000 employees feel? The importance of size can be overplayed. "In much the same way that a chef can judge a large vat of soup by tasting just one spoonful, providing that the soup has been well stirred, so that the spoonful is properly 'representative', one spoonful is sufficient,"[21] says the British Polling Council.

Great care needs to be taken to ensure that a sample is truly diverse and simply making it bigger does not guarantee it becomes more representative. "A biased sample is a biased sample, however large it is."[22] To ensure your sample is representative, you cannot leave the process to chance or self-selection, blindly analysing whatever responses come in. Head office staff with easy access to a PC are likely to be disproportionately represented. Does this make their views any more valid? Demographic information, and appropriate weighting when it comes to analysis, can help, but findings must always be read with care. There may be a thousand different stories between every percentage point.

We strongly believe opinions and suggestions are equally valid, no matter where they come from – your most junior recruit might have the freshest ideas. However, it would be naïve not to acknowledge certain employees hold greater sway over an organisational mood and culture than others. If your CEO is deeply dissatisfied and disengaged, it will have a deeper impact than similar sentiment from a single individual on the frontline. Senior leaders have the power to shine a light or cast a shadow over colleagues, and yet our attempts to survey the audience rarely touches them. Few CEOs or executives consider whole staff surveys relevant for them to complete. Even if they do participate, by viewing their response as just one among many, we miss the critical insight and specific implications of their feedback. A robust measurement process needs to provide even the upper echelons of your workforce the space to air their views in confidence. Analysis cannot treat every response as entirely equal. Not because certain opinions are more valid than others, but because they have undeniably greater influence.

STANDARDISED TESTING

When it comes to quantitative surveys, organisations typically fall back on standard, off-the-shelf solutions, at best augmenting these with a few tailored questions. These are seen as the stock solution, used across industry and providing easily comparable benchmarks. While your score might prove useful when applying to schemes like 'Top 100 Companies', in reality they provide limited insight. Unless you can find two organisations with the same heritage, workforce, culture and management style at the same point in their evolution, comparisons are likely to be futile.

These kinds of surveys, brimming with statistical data, encourage us to focus on questions with the greatest drop in performance or the poorest result against an industry mean. "If it's statistically significant, then it's deemed important. No judgement is required. Statistical significance provides an air of

scientific rigour and legitimacy to the conclusions simultaneously stifling critical thinking and common sense,"[23] says Converge Consulting Group. Numbers can be a distraction from
the real issues, which might not manifest themselves in stark
drops in performance, but could have a dramatic impact on the
business. Never rely on a report that tells you only the five top
and bottom performing areas – with the full results hidden on
page 1,034. In narrowly focusing on the most dramatic statistics, you can be blinded to more dramatic issues. You may also
miss the opportunity to pre-empt embryonic problems from
escalating.

Generalised surveys with generalised questions tend to
lead to generalised conclusions and recommendations. Angela
Sinickas described to us a client who had received poor scores
around workplace stress. Based on the results, it would have
been easy to initiate a well-being campaign, complete with
yoga classes or massages at desks. Each division looked
again at their scores, and while stress was high in a number
of them, the reasons behind this were different in every case.
For some it was a matter of high workloads and a need for
additional resource, in another a demanding leader was
causing tension with last-minute demands to cancel employees' time off due to his own lack of planning. A blanket solution would have addressed nothing, and in failing to deal with
the underlying issues may have acted only to exacerbate the
frustration of employees. "In the case of employee engagement, it would appear that what gets measured is not necessarily the right thing and that the results generated do not
lead to effective management of what is required to deliver
enhanced engagement,"[24] says John Smythe in *The Velvet
Revolution at Work*.

The standard staff engagement survey does at least offer
organisations an objective, third party assessment. The

anonymity these should provide is highly valuable. However, we have seen companies so determined to guarantee a high response rate that managers have stood over staff as they answered – hardly providing an environment for honesty and openness. Equally, some managers say they have to be on hand, as too often staff cannot understand what is being asked of them. In these cases, the interpretation of each employee, or manager, is unlikely to be consistent, and may be a whole world away from what the questioner intended.

MEASURING IN THE MOMENT

One typical feature of whole-staff engagement surveys is the long delay between completion and receiving results. It can take months to receive anything more than headline findings; by the time they are cascaded to employees, their issues may well have changed. One client told us of a recent survey rendered essentially useless before they had even received the report. A new director had so dramatically affected the mood of the office that they could no longer rely on the findings.

In an effort to combat the delay, and capture sentiment in the moment, many have initiated 'pulse' programmes. These are intended to be short, frequent checks that allow us to monitor continuously. Yet, we have seen 'pulse' surveys that are only run annually, or that might run bi-monthly but contain 40 separate questions. Taking a pulse should be regular and easy. It will never provide an in-depth diagnosis, but a quick check-up on the health of your organisation. 'Pulse' research tends to work best when it follows on from something more substantial. After setting a benchmark, they work well to track progress, alerting us to any hiccups along the way.

Travellers going through security at Heathrow are simply asked to press a button on their way out, a choice of three faces – happy, ok or unhappy. The process is painless to complete and provides real-time trackable data. When used in retail stores, similar systems have alerted managers of the need to adjust staffing levels at particular times of the day. In measuring our emotional response to a specific issue or event, timeliness is important. Clients have asked us to undertake large-scale telephone polls, providing results within a few hours to gauge immediate reactions to a new initiative. Findings provided a benchmark for future research, enabling us to monitor changes in sentiment from the launch date onwards. This way research can not only evaluate the success of a project but also actively influence the ongoing approach. If something lands well one day, communicators can put their foot down, while a negative response might prompt us to change gear.

If we are going to ask people to invest their time in helping us to monitor organisational health, we need to give them something in return. In the long run, this will come in the form of improvement initiatives, but we can also provide something more instant. I am far more likely to respond to a poll online if I get to see the live results afterwards. I can see how my view compares, and what the crowd is thinking. This level of transparency might worry some – no time to massage the numbers or filter responses, but it is much more likely to make what could otherwise be a tedious process engaging. It also means outliers can see themselves as such. If they are the only one per cent of the business complaining about a process, they might be more understanding when it does not get addressed. Providing a sneak preview of results might be a preferable incentive for organisations uncomfortable with the idea of offering prize draws.

WHY CONVERSATIONS MEASURE UP

Quantitative research, in the form of polls, surveys and questionnaires is used more widely and regularly to assess the value and outcomes of communications than qualitative approaches. Indeed, Angela Sinickas does not believe that 'qual' can be considered measurement at all – for her, the measurement implies numbers and anything else is 'insight', 'evaluation' or 'research'. She says: "For example, to measure an object's size, we need a yardstick. However, you could just eyeball the item to make a rough estimate, but it wouldn't be called measurement." Yet, in our experience, many quantitative surveys are blunt instruments that can result in more questions than answers. A survey might tell you that 'x' went up or 'y' went down, but rarely tells you why. Standard engagement surveys often have more than 40 questions, and many clients find it hard to decide which results matter most. Often, we are called in after a whole-staff survey to dig deeper into numerical findings with qualitative research. This gives the numbers meaning and clarity; and ultimately gives the client something concrete to act on.

Mark Twain reportedly told us that "facts are stubborn things, but statistics are more pliable". Even when a statistical finding appears clear-cut – *78 per cent of respondents understand the direction of the organisation* – it can be masking the truth, that one-third of this 78 per cent has in mind a different direction than you. It does not tell you that 45 per cent of respondents misinterpreting the direction of your organisation speak with customers every day. The challenge in measuring shifts in behaviour and the imparting of knowledge is that it is hard to capture in a tick-box survey.

The question 'Do you understand the organisation's business strategy?' requires self-analysis and evaluation on behalf of the participant, which may or may not be accurate. As Donald Rumsfeld said: "There are known knowns. There are things we know that we know. We also know there are known unknowns. That is to say, there are things we know we do not know. But there are also unknown unknowns. There are things we don't know we don't know."[25] In a face-to-face conversation, researchers can ask, 'What does the organisation's business strategy mean to you?', and test not only the interviewee's knowledge, but their confidence, belief and personal investment in the strategy. Experienced researchers will use a face-to-face meeting to assess not only what people say, but how they say it and when. They will note the words people use, their underlying attitudes and subtle shifts in behaviour that signal when things need to be explored further.

In some cases where an open exchange of views is rare, or participants doubt anonymity, they may feel wary of being *too* honest. In person, researchers can tell when someone is holding back, which is often a message in itself. By ensuring research is carried out with employees at all levels in the corporate hierarchy, differences between departments and grades can be keenly observed. It becomes clear if certain levels are being particularly cagey with researchers, or if they are discussing particular issues in markedly different terms. When we undertook individual, confidential face-to-face interviews in one large manufacturing company, we found that many members of the senior team were proud that every month they managed to issue team briefs to line managers, full of business performance information. However, the line managers told us they felt embarrassed giving these briefings to their staff because of how they were written. One told us: "The language at the top is so different. We need simple messages to cascade down. Talk in terms of 'pallets sold'. That's something my guys recognise, it's what they work with every day – not market share points and percentages!" This kind of tip is gold dust to an internal communicator who wants to get inside the mind of the workforce and develop more impactful communications for specific segments of an audience.

HOW WAS IT FOR YOU?

Very little of the literature on measurement considers how participants feel about the process. Response rates have been sinking fast in traditional public opinion phone polls, as we get more unsolicited calls than ever. Scott Keeter, the Pew Research Centre's survey director, and president of the American Association for Public Opinion Research, has seen Pew's response rates falling from about 36 per cent in 1997 to just nine per cent in 2012.[26] The volume of product and service suppliers asking for feedback after every transaction, however small, exacerbates the problem of 'survey fatigue' among consumers. William Grimes of *The New York Times* rather eloquently refers to these constant requests that follow every purchase, call or click of a mouse as "relentless tugs on the sleeve".[27] At work, we see a similar fatigue resulting in declining response rates. The problem is not that we are unwilling to share our views and opinions, but how we are being asked to do this. Completing a tick box survey is a dull, repetitive exercise, which rarely makes the respondent feel valued, understood or unique. Instead we need to make the process of measuring engagement an engaging activity – turning the method itself into a message.

Such engagement is attainable. One employee we interviewed face-to-face as part of a qualitative research project told us: "That was like an hour of therapy, I feel much better. Thank you so much for listening." When we ask participants at the end of an interview whether they believe their organisation truly values internal communication, part of the answer we invariably receive is: "Well you're here aren't you? That must mean something." Sitting with an independent, interested researcher concerned with what you have to say regardless of your pay grade, and asking open-ended questions, is a far more rewarding process than being made to complete a tickbox survey. The employee *knows* they have been listened to because they have seen someone listening. They can be confident they have been understood because the questioner can ask for clarification and check what they have heard. When qualitative research is done well, it should be rewarding for everyone, not least the participant who should be left feeling that his or her organisation values their opinion and is seeking to truly understand them.

Once you have spent time listening to employees in person, whether one-on-one or in small groups, the resulting information is far richer that pure statistics. Respecting the confidentiality of feedback, while identifying key themes and findings, is more of an art than a science and undeniably requires substantial time and effort. Maintaining confidentiality is essential, but if you can use the words of employees in ways that do not identify them, these can be hugely powerful. Verbatim quotes that explain weaknesses or opportunities add a depth and authenticity to a final report that make it harder for sceptics to dismiss.

SEEING IS BELIEVING

Ultimately, Angela Sinickas managed to change the opinion of her sceptical CFO without an elaborate ROI calculation. "A few months after I joined the company, he was named interim CEO of one of our business units. While there, he had a chance to experience the bottom-line value of the communication manager I had hired for his unit – including one safety communication campaign that was so successful in the pilot locations it was implemented that it reduced the company's vehicle insurance premium by US$1 million. When the communicator announced she was getting married, the former CFO's panicked comment to me was: 'What if she decides to stay home and have children? How will I be able to run my company without her?'" Devoting hours trying to prove our value through statistics is a misdirection of our efforts. It will be far more persuasive for leaders to personally experience value from your communications activity. "The fact is that people, even those driven by numbers, are not swayed by them if they contradict the world they believe in,"[28] writes Charlene Li, author of *Open Leadership*.

Measurement should help us to improve, not prove, our worth. We must aim to make our value clear, tangible and irrefutable without the need for elaborate calculations or swathes of data. Any piece of research – quantitative or qualitative – should be done to learn something new, not merely to justify budget. If leaders expect a number will be able to convey the full value of good communication, or employee engagement, they will be disappointed. While we might be able to measure the impact of a specific campaign, we can never quantify the ROI of every email, telephone call, meeting or conversation.

In organisations where employee opinions are being stifled, formal measurement can be the only way of capturing the views of the frontline. Communicators have adopted it in earnest in an attempt to listen rather than broadcast. Yet too many suggestion schemes and feedback channels remain essentially one-way. It is just the direction that changes. In a world beyond cascading opinions – up or down – where everyone participates in regular, meaningful conversations, having our say is not a discrete activity. It is not once a year, it is not ticking a box, it is not 'measurement'. It is a genuine dialogue that drives constant improvement, makes us better connected, and ultimately more successful.

In conversation with employees

Throughout this book we have urged leaders and communicators to speak directly to their people. Middle managers and frontline employees often get excluded from the conversations that affect them the most.

We have spoken with many practitioners and experts, but in the spirit of practising what we preach, it is time to hear from employees themselves.

We asked three, from very different organisations, to describe the impact of a shift from cascade to conversation.

Stella Giles: shop floor worker at Iceland Foods
in its Bulwell store, in Nottingham.

The thing that has really created a feeling of local community for stores is how the company has encouraged us to get store-specific groups on Facebook.

They are closed groups not open to the public, and each page has a nominated administrator. We put news and achievements up there, but also use them to organise events.

Anyone from the team can post and quite often you'll find employees like me uploading stuff every working day.

When people are acknowledged for their hard work, it helps to motivate them, and because it's Facebook everyone is instantly notified when something positive is said. We're all very familiar with social media, so it was easy to get used to because we were all already using it.

Facebook is a social thing, not a work tool, and we still see it that way. It's just that it has helped to give work some of those social benefits.

You'll find people having a laugh on there, but also genuinely praising each other.

We don't just rely on Facebook for praise, and the store manager will regularly send out text messages praising us individually.

Of course, texting and Facebook aren't the best ways of telling us when things go wrong, but because we have these good relationships with our teammates and line managers, it doesn't feel scary to talk openly when problems come up.

We don't have big stores like many of our competitors, so it makes sense for us to create a close, local community where employees and the management team get on very well. We're still connected to the rest of Iceland through an elected representative who regularly attends area Talking Shop meetings and relays news back to their store. I've been the rep for ours for more than three years and it has definitely helped us.

It's just great for other employees to know they can come to me with an issue and I'll take it to a manager and then can let them know something is being done. Their issue might only be small, personal issues in the wider scheme of things, but it really matters to them. So to see something being done to rectify it is very important.

Dionne Clark: learning and communities manager at AzkoNobel, Ashington.

The factory here in Ashington is a newly built, first-rate facility that is one of the most sustainable paint manufacturing sites in the world. But it's pointless having technology and environments of that quality if the culture and the engagement don't match it.

A big part of my job is creating a culture where people can openly say what's wrong and put their name to their opinions. We want to speak to people as adults and get their feedback, because we genuinely value it and recognise their experience.

As a member of the Inspire Leadership Group, which comprises 100 nominated people managers from across the UK decorative paints business, I attend quarterly meetings where we're given updates on everything across the business.

Each member also receives *OneTalk* each month, a briefing pack full of snippets of need-to-know news that we then deliver to our staff.

At Ashington, we hold a monthly town hall-style meeting with everyone at the factory to go through everything from *OneTalk* and the quarterly meetings, and open it up for discussion. Not only does it mean everyone is receiving a consistent message, but they also have the opportunity to give feedback.

It's a very transparent culture, and there's no such thing as 'for your ears only' news any more.

It's improved since I joined AzkoNobel 12 years ago, because the company has embraced an open culture based on discussions and employee involvement.

We don't currently have a union representing employees in Ashington and we hope to keep it that way. Instead, we have regular open forums in the workplace where people can raise anything they want. It's the right kind of environment and encourages people to speak honestly.

Natalie Lake: call centre operator for Admiral
Insurance in Swansea.

For me, face-to-face is the most effective form of communication, but we also have a fantastic intranet, called 'Atlas', that is a one-stop shop for everything we need for the business.

Admiral is based in three offices in the UK, where all staff have access to Atlas. Each department has its own section featuring content relevant to them.

It's full of business news and people stories that you can comment on. It's a great way of communicating with others in the businesss and bringing people together. I find myself quite trigger happy on the comments because it's a fun way of engaging with people in other departments.

Although our communications team drives content on the site, anyone can submit ideas and stories. It's something I've done in my eight years here. I think it works because so many people are keen to showcase and share good work. It's become a part of our culture.

We also get *The Column*, a monthly magazine packed with interesting stories, fun things like recipes and non-work-related interviews with senior members of staff. This makes them seem more like normal people, especially to those of us who don't often or ever see them, so they feel more approachable.

Every two years we also have an Admiral staff party at different venues with a headline music act. It's always a fantastic experience and a good way of showing how everyone is treated as equal.

This culture of motivation, engagement and reward is a big part of what Admiral is about. You can tell those running the organisation believe in helping and supporting their staff. It's a great place to come to work.

Afterword

This book is intended to kickstart a new conversation about the power of employee participation and involvement. To help the dialogue continue, we have created a website to accompany this book at www.cascadetoconversation.co.uk. It is home to the many examples of great practice we have found during our research. It has some of our favourites that made it to the book, and others we lost along the way. It has the content that cannot live in print, and ideas we could not reproduce in full. We hope it provides further food for thought, and welcome your contributions and suggestions.

Acknowledgements

The process of writing this book is a message itself about the power of dialogue and collaboration. *From Cascade to Conversation* is the result of many fascinating exchanges with people who generously shared their views, ideas and experience. I am very grateful for their contribution and guidance. I will not try to name everyone, but a few must receive special recognition.

By my side throughout this process, keeping me on track, testing my thinking and generally spurring me on was Eloise Hindes. Her dedication to this project, along with an insight and wisdom far beyond her years, has made this a much better book. 'Thank you' hardly seems adequate.

Ben Hall took on the challenge of interviewing a diverse range of individuals for the 'in conversation' pieces. These come alive due to his infectious enthusiasm and journalistic nose for a great story. Throughout the writing process, we submitted each chapter to Ken Hunter for review. His long and varied career, plus his warmth and vivacity, meant our review sessions were both informative and entertaining.

Alison Harmer and Duncan Mills did an amazing job of

proofreading each chapter. I am grateful for their attention to detail while having to work at speed. When the fact-checking, rewriting and editing finally stopped, I needed someone fresh to the project to read every word before the manuscript went to print. That 'honour' went to my co-director at AB, Anthony Naughton. I am yet to meet anyone with better laser-like vision when it comes to checking copy. However, any mistakes you may find are entirely my own.

Under the guidance of AB's head of creative, Joel O'Connor, designers Andy Stanford and Hampus Gunnarsson turned our words into a book. Seeing typeset pages for the first time was a memorable moment.

Tracy Gallagher, AB's head of production, created and managed the schedule from beginning to end. The book you are holding today is thanks to her freakish attention to detail and supreme organisational abilities.

AB is a family firm in every sense of the word. I am grateful to our chairman Tim Buckley and everyone in the team for their unwavering support and encouragement.

We interviewed a number of individuals as part of our research to understand how this shift from cascade to conversation works in practice. Thank you to Neil Jenkins, Jacki Connor, Kevin Ruck, Andrew Lord, Angela Sinickas, Deborah Brambill, Alana Renner and Pierre Goad. In addition, my thanks to those who agreed to share a specific first-person experience – Neil Taylor, Carol Miller, Tony Buckley, Richard Davies, Richard Dennison, Richard Mullender, Saskia Jones, Wendy Jordan and Caroline Thomas. Everyone mentioned gave generously of their time and spoke with insight and candour. Having listened to their collective passion and creativity, I am in no doubt we work in an extraordinary profession capable of scaling even greater heights.

A special mention also to those employees of Admiral,

AzkoNobel and Iceland who gave us the audience's perspective for Chapter 10. Thank you too to John Abulafia who showed me what good communication looks like in person and Steve Doswell, chief executive of the Institute of Internal Communication, who suggested we include the voices of practitioners throughout the book. It was a good call. The majority of this book was written each day on the 8.14am train from Alton to Waterloo. To my fellow commuters, hopefully this book confirms we are truly the 'media carriage'.

Although the book has been a year in the writing, it's been 24 years in the making. I am very fortunate to have worked with many incredible colleagues, clients and leaders during that time. That experience has been the real inspiration for this book. It taught me what communication can achieve when it's considered, genuine and inclusive.

Acknowledgements always seem to end with a thank you to family and friends. Before writing this book, I wondered if this was merely a polite custom. Now I realise it is not. Writing a book is a time-consuming, absorbing and solitary experience. My heartfelt thanks to Barker for his patience, to Dave and my mother who, as always, supported me every step of the way.

KATIE MACAULAY
AUGUST 2014

Endnotes

INTRODUCTION

1.   Christopher Locke et al, *The Cluetrain Manifesto: The End of Business as Usual*, 10th Anniversary edition (New York: Basic Books, 2009), p.173

2.   David Weinberger, *Small Pieces, Loosely Joined: A unified theory of the web* (New York: Basic Books, 2002), p. 126

3.   Don Tapscott and Anthony D Williams, *Wikinomics: How mass collaboration changes everything* (Croydon: Portfolio/Atlantic Books, 2006), p.314

4.   *The Cluetrain Manifesto*, p.141

5.   Quoted in H James Harrington and Frank Voehl, *The Five Pillars of Organisational Excellence: Knowledge Management Excellence* (California: Paton Press LLC, 2007), p.xxi

6.   Peter Drucker, *Landmarks of Tomorrow: A Report on the New 'Post-Modern' world* (New Jersey: Harper & Row, 1996), p.94

CHAPTER 1
IN THE BEGINNING THERE WAS BROADCAST

1.   'What is employee engagement?', www.engageforsuccess.org/about/what-is-employee-engagement/ [accessed 23 January 2014]

2.   E.A.M Gale, 'The Hawthorne Studies – a fable for our times?', *QJ Med* (Vol.97, No. 7, 2004), p. 441

3.   'The Hawthorne Studies', p.441

4.   Jeffrey Sonnenfeld, 'Shedding Light on the Hawthorne Studies', *Journal of Occupational Behaviour* (Vol. 6, No. 2, April 1985), p.113

5.   Quoted in foreword to Abraham Maslow, *Maslow on Management*, with Deborah Stephens and Gary Heil (New York: John Wiley and Sons Inc., 1998), p.viii

6.   Douglas McGregor, with J. Cutcher-Gershenfeld, *The Human Side of Enterprise: Annotated Edition* (New York: McGraw Hill, 2006), p.11

7.   *The Human Side of Enterprise*, p.154

8.   *The Human Side of Enterprise*, p.201

9.   Quoted in *The Human Side of Enterprise*, p.xxxii

10.   *The Human Side of Enterprise*, p.xv

11.   William Kahn, 'Psychological conditions of personal engagement and disengagement at work', *Academy of Management Journal* (Vol. 33, No. 4, Dec 1990), p.692

12.   'Psychological conditions of personal engagement', p.692

13.   'Psychological conditions of personal engagement', p.711

14.   Tom Peters and Robert H Waterman Jr., *In Search of Excellence: Lessons from America's Best Run Companies* (New York: Harper and Row, 1982), p.6

15.   Quoted in *In Search of Excellence*, p.58

16.   *In Search of Excellence*, p.87

17.   *In Search of Excellence*, p.318

18.   *In Search of Excellence*, p.322

19.   *In Search of Excellence*, p.xxiii

20.   *The Human Side of Enterprise*, p.39

21.   Donald Campbell, 'The Proactive Employee: Managing Workplace Initiative', *The Academy of Management Executive* (Vol. 14, No. 3, August 2000), p.55

22.   Quoted in *In Search of Excellence*, p.259

23.   McKinsey Global Institute, 'The Social Economy: unlocking value and productivity through social technologies' (white paper, McKinsey Global Institute, July 2012), p.2

24.   Euan Semple, *Organisations Don't Tweet, People Do: A Manager's Guide to the Social Web* (Padstow: Wiley and Sons, 2012), p.10

25.   Heron's argument, paraphrased in Vanita, *Effective Communication in Human Resource Development* (New Delhi: Atlantic Publishers and Distributors, 2003), p.3

26.   Alexander Heron, *Sharing Information with Employees: Toward Understanding in Industry* (California: Stanford University Press, 1942), p.79

27.   Kevin Ruck and Heather Yaxley, 'Tracking the rise and rise of internal communication from the 1980s' (conference paper, History of PR Conference in Bournemouth, August 2013), p.14

28.   Kevin Ruck, 'The rise and rise of internal communications', www.exploringinternalcommunication.com/2013/04 [published 29 April 2013, accessed 24 January 2014]

29.   Michael Bland, *Employee Communications in the 1980s: A Personnel Manager's Guide* (London: Kogan Page, 1980), p.68

30.   *Employee Communications in the 1980s*, p.30

31.   *Employee Communications in the 1980s*, p.145

32.   Quoted in Michael Silverman, Elmira Bakhshalian and Laura Hillman, 'Social media and employee voice: the current landscape (white paper, CIPD, Silverman Research, March 2013), p.11

33.   *In Search of Excellence*, p.50

34.   Janet Fulk and Gerardine DeSanctis, 'Electronic Communication and Changing Organisational Form', *Organisational Science* (Vol. 6, No.4, Jul-Aug 1996), p.339

35.   *Organisations Don't Tweet*, p.66

36.   'The Social Economy', p.16

37.   *Organisations Don't Tweet*, p.28

38.   John Smythe, *The Velvet Revolution at Work: The Rise of Employment Engagement, the fall of Command and Control* (Dorchester: Gower, 2013), p.50

CHAPTER 2
WHY CONVERSATION WORKS

1.   Boris Groysberg and Michael Slind, *Talk, Inc.: How Trusted Leaders use Conversation to Power their Organisations* (Boston: Harvard Business Press, 2012)

2.   William Kahn, 'Psychological conditions of personal engagement and disengagement at work', *Academy of Management Journal* (Vol. 33, No. 4 Dec 1990), p.707

3.   James Surowiecki, *The Wisdom of Crowds: Why the Many are Smarter than the Few* (London: Abacus, 2004), p.30

4.   Rick Levine, Christopher Locke, Doc Searls and David Weinberger, *The Cluetrain Manifesto: The end of business as usual*, 10th Anniversary edition (New York: Basic Books, 2009), p.195

5.   Keith Sawyer, *Group Genius: The Creative Power of Collaboration* (New York: Basic Books, 2007), p.57

6.   Tom Peters and Robert H Waterman Jr., *In Search of Excellence: Lessons from America's Best-Run Companies* (New York: Harper and Row, 1982), p.193

7.   *Talk, Inc.*, p.24-25

8.   Nancy Klein, *Time To Think: Listening to Ignite the Human Mind* (London: Cassell Illustrated, 1999), p.37

9.   Edgar H Schein, *Humble Inquiry: The Gentle Art of Asking Instead of Telling* (San Francisco: Berrett-Koehler Publishers Inc., 2013), p.2

10.   *Humble Inquiry*, p.8

11.   *Humble Inquiry*, p.19

12.   Chade-Meng Tan, *Search Inside Yourself: Increase productivity, creativity and happiness* (St Ives: Collins, 2012)

13.   *Search Inside Yourself*, p.59

14.   *Search Inside Yourself*, p.59

15. Dick Mullender, *Dispelling The myths and Rediscovering the Lost Art of Listening: Communication secrets of a hostage negotiator* (ebook: Griffin Professional Business and Training Services, October 2012)
16. *Search Inside Yourself*, p.61
17. *Dispelling the myths*
18. *Dispelling the myths*
19. Daniel Goleman, *Working with emotional intelligence* (London: Bloomsbury, 1998) p.141
20. Aristotle, *Nichomachean Ethics*, Book I, 1094.a18
21. David Weinberger, 'Is there an echo in here?', www.salon.com/2004/02/21/echo_chamber [published 21 February 2004, accessed 2 January 2014]
22. Quoted in *Talk, Inc.*, p. 22
23. Quoted in Stephen van Belleghem, *The Conversation Company: Boost your Business through Culture, People, and Social Media* (London: Kogan Page, 2012), p.57
24. *The Conversation Company*, p.2
25. Quoted in *Talk, Inc.*, p.33
26. *Group Genius*, p.140
27. *Talk, Inc.*, p.2
28. *Talk, Inc.*, p.3
29. Quoted in *Talk, Inc.*, p.35
30. *Talk, Inc.*, p.9

CHAPTER 3
NO ONE IS AS SMART AS EVERYONE

1. James Surowiecki, *The Wisdom of Crowds: Why the Many are Smarter than the Few* (London: Abacus, 2005), p.205
2. *The Wisdom of Crowds*, p.xix
3. Keith Sawyer, *Group Genius: The Creative Power of Collaboration* (New York: Basic Books, 2007), p.140
4. *Group Genius*, p.7
5. Francis Galton, *Memories of My Life* (London: Methuen, 1908), p.246
6. Francis Galton, 'Vox Populi', *Nature* (Vol.75, March 7 1907), p.451
7. *The Wisdom of Crowds*, p.xiii
8. Quoted in *The Wisdom of Crowds*, p.16. See also Sergey Brin and Larry Page, 'The Anatomy of a Large-Scale Hypertextual Web Search Engine', infolab.stanford.edu/~backrub/google.html [accessed 2 July 2014]
9. Rob Howard, 'The Community is Right 91% of the Time', www.cmswire.com/cms/social-business/the-community-is-correct-91-of-the-time-013714.php [published 6 December 2011, accessed 2 July 2014]
10. *The Wisdom of Crowds*, p.221
11. Donald Campbell, 'The Proactive Employee: Managing Workplace Initiative', *The Academy of Management Executive* (Vol. 14, No. 3, Aug 2000), p.52
12. Charles Heckscher and Laurence Prusack, 'Building a Collaborative Enterprise: Four Keys to Creating a Culture of Trust and Teamwork', *Harvard Business Review* (Reprint R1107G, July-August 2011), p.9
13. Sid Joynson and Andrew Forrester, *Sid's Heroes: Uplifting Business Performance and the Human Spirit* (London: BBC Books, 1995), p.6
14. *Sid's Heroes*, p.6
15. *Sid's Heroes*, p.31
16. *Group Genius*, p.5
17. Morten Hansen, *Collaboration: How Leaders Avoid the Traps, Create Unity and Reap Big Results* (Boston: Harvard Business Press, 2009), p.27
18. *Collaboration*, p.30
19. Quoted in *Collaboration*, p.7
20. Quoted in *Collaboration*, p.8

21. IBM Invests $100 Million in Collaborative Innovation Ideas', IBM Press releases, www-03.ibm.com/press/us/en/pressrelease/20605.wss [published 14 November 2006, accessed 15 January 2014]

22. Steve Van Belleghem, *The Conversation Company: Boost Your Business Through Culture, People and Social Media* (London: Kogan Page, 2012), p.5

23. Jacques Bughin, James Manyika and Andy Miller 'Building the Web 2.0 Enterprise' (McKinsey Global Survey Results, June 2008)

24. 'Open Innovation', www.unilever.com/innovation/collaborating-with-unilever/open-innovation/ [accessed 2 July 2014]

25. Quoted in Jan Moye, 'Rethinking R&D: How Coke Uses Its Global Scale to Take Innovations Further, Faster', www.coca-colacompany.com/stories/rethinking-r-d-how-coke-uses-its-global-scale-to-take-innovations-further-faster [published 19 November 2013, accessed 2 July 2014]

26. Don Tapscott and Anthony D Williams, *Wikinomics: How Mass Collaboration Changes Everything* (Croydon: Portfolio/Atlantic Books, 2006), p.128

27. At the 'Conversation with transformative CEOs' panel at the IABC's World Conference, New York City, New York, June 2013

28. David Weinberger, *Too Big To Know: Rethinking Knowledge Now that the Facts aren't Facts, Experts are Everywhere, and the Smartest Person in the Room is the Room* (New York: Basic Books, 2011), p.170

29. Scott Page, *The Difference: How the Power of Diversity Creates Better Groups, Firms, Schools and Societies* (New Jersey: Princeton Press, 2007), p.137

30. *The Wisdom of Crowds*, p.10

31. Luke Visconti, 'Did the Fed's Stunning Lack of Diversity Cause the Housing Crisis?', *Ask the White Guy*, www.diversityinc.com/ask-the-white-guy/the-housing-crisis-and-the-business-case-for-diversity/ [accessed 13 January 2014]

32. 'Did the Fed's Stunning Lack of Diversity Cause the Housing Crisis?'

33. *The Difference*, p.363

34. *The Difference*, p.366

35. *The Difference*, p.364

36. *Group Genius*, p.72

37. *The Wisdom of Crowds*, p.41

38. *Collaboration*, p.155

39. *The Difference*, p.50

40. *Group Genius*, p.61

41. *Collaboration*, p.19

42. 'The Proactive Employee', p.58

43. *The Wisdom of Crowds*, p.75

44. *Collaboration*, p.51

45. Quoted in *Collaboration*, p.12

46. *Group Genius*, p.45

47. Stephen Shapiro, '10x Innovation ROI on your Internal Collaboration' (white paper, InnoCentive, October 2013), p.1

48. *Collaboration*, p.49

49. *Collaboration*, p.97

50. *Group Genius*, p.37

51. Michael Silverman, Elmira Bakhshalian and Laura Hillman, 'Social Media and Employee Voice: the current landscape' (research report, CIPD, Silverman research, March 2013), p.21

52. Tammy Johns and Lynda Gratton, 'The Third Wave of Virtual Work: Knowledge workers are now untethered, able to perform tasks anywhere at any time. What do the best of them want from your organisation?', *Harvard Business Review* (Reprint R1301D, Jan-Feb 2012), p.5

53. *Wikinomics*, p.37

54. *Too Big to Know*, p.52

55. *Too Big to Know*, p.52

56. Quoted in Howard Rheingold, *Smart Mobs: the Next Social Revolution, Transforming Cultures and Communities in the Age of Instant Access* (Boston: Basic Books, 2002), p.54

57. *Group Genius*, p.219

58.   *Wikinomics*, p.12
59.   *Too Big To Know*, p.64
60.   *Group Genius*, p.129

CHAPTER 4
WHAT DOES SUCCESS LOOK LIKE?
1.   James Surowiecki, *The Wisdom of Crowds: Why the Many are Smarter than the Few* (United States: Abacus, 2004), p.212
2.   Peter Drucker, *Management: Tasks, Responsibilities, Practices* (New York: Harper and Row, 1973), p.44
3.   Patrick Lencioni, *The Advantage: Why Organisational Health Trumps Everything Else in Business* (San Francisco: Jossey-Bass, 2012), p.5
4.   Jennifer Reingold and Ryan Underwood, 'Was "Built to Last" Built to Last?', *Fast Company*, www.fastcompany.com/50992/was-built-last-built-last [published 1 November 2004, accessed 24 July 2014]
5.   Ed Catmull with Amy Wallace, *Creativity, Inc.: Overcoming the unseen forces that stand in the way of true inspiration* (London: Random House, 2014), p.xi
6.   Tony Hsieh, 'Why I Sold Zappos', www.inc.com/magazine/20100601/why-i-sold-zappos.html [published 1 June 2010, accessed 31 July 2014]
7.   Tony Hsieh, 'CEO Letter', www.zappos.com/ceoletter [published 22 July 2009, accessed 31 July 2014]
8.   Bill Taylor, 'Why Amazon is Copying Zappos and Paying Employees to Quit', *HBR blogs*, blogs.hbr.org/2014/04/why-amazon-is-copying-zappos-and-paying-employees-to-quit/ [published 14 April 2014, accessed 31 July 2014]
9.   Simon Sinkek, 'How great leaders inspire action', TED talk, Sept 2009, at TEDx Puget Sound, Washington
10.   'Why I Sold Zappos'
11.   'Was "Built to Last" Built to Last?'
12.   'Why Amazon is Copying Zappos'
13.   'Why Amazon is Copying Zappos'
14.   Arie de Geus, 'The Living Company', *Harvard Business Review* (March 1997)
15.   'The Living Company'
16.   'The Living Company'
17.   'How great leaders inspire action'
18.   'The Living Company'
19.   Laszlo Bock, 'Passion, Not Perks', www.thinkwithgoogle.com/articles/passion-not-perks.html [published September 2011, accessed 31 July 2014]
20.   Paul Adler, Charles Heckscher and Laurence Prusack, 'Building a Collaborative Enterprise: Four keys to creating a culture of trust and teamwork', *Harvard Business Review* (July-Aug 2011), p.5
21.   John Lewis Partnership,'The Constitution of the John Lewis Partnership: Introduction, Principles and Rules' (May 2014), p.7
22.   'Our Constitution', www.johnlewispartnership.co.uk/about/our-constitution.html [accessed 31 July 2014]
23.   'The Constitution of the John Lewis Partnership, p.3
24.   'Company philosophy: 'The way we do things around here', book excerpt, *McKinsey Quarterly*, from Marvin Bower, *The Will to Manage: Corporate Success Through Programmed Management*, www.mckinsey.com/insights/leading_in_the_21st_century/company_philosophy_the_way_we_do_things_around_here [published May 2003, accessed 31 July 2014]
25.   Ori Brofman and Rod Beckstrom, *The Starfish and the Spider: The Unstoppable Power of Leaderless Organisations*, p.90
26.   Keith Sawyer, *Group Genius: The Creative Power of Collaboration* (New York: Basic Books, 2007), p.153
27.   *Group Genius*, p.155
28.   Ricardo Semler, 'Managing without managers', *Harvard Business Review* (Reprint 89509, Sept-Oct 1989), p.5
29.   'Managing without managers', p.10

30. 'Managing without managers', p.5
31. Ricardo Semler, *Maverick! The Success Story Behind the World's Most Unusual Workplace* (St Ives: Arrow Books, 1993), p.4
32. Daniel Pink, *Drive: The Surprising Truth About What Motivates Us* (London: Penguin Group, 2009)
33. 'Managing without managers', p.3
34. Christopher Locke et al, *The Cluetrain Manifesto: The End of Business as Usual*, 10th Anniversary edition (New York: Basic Books, 2009), p.192
35. Warren Bennis and Patricia Ward Biederman, *Organising Genius: The Secrets of Creative Collaboration* (New York: Basic Books, 1997), p.164
36. *The Cluetrain Manifesto*, p.158
37. Ed Catmull, 'How Pixar Fosters Collective Creativity', *Harvard Business Review* (Reprint R0809D, September 2008), p.9
38. *The Cluetrain Manifesto*, p.93
39. 'Managing without managers', p.4
40. 'Passion, not perks'
41. 'Managing without managers', p.4
42. James O'Toole and Warren Bennis, 'A Culture of Candour', *Harvard Business Review* (Reprint R0906F, June 2009), p.2
43. 'A Culture of Candour', p.2
44. 'How do you execute internal announcements that also reach out to external audiences?', *PR Week*, www.prweek.com/article/1278215/execute-internal-announcements-reach-external-audiences [published 1 September 2012, accessed 31 July 2014]
45. 'A Culture of Candour', p.3
46. Ram Charan, 'Home Depot's Blueprint for Culture Change', *Harvard Business Review* (Reprint R0604C, April 2006), p.5
47. Weber Shandwick, 'Employees Rising: Seizing the Opportunity in Employee Activism' (white paper, Weber Shandwick and KRC Research, 2 April 2014), p.23
48. 'A Culture of Candour', p.3
49. Edgar H Schein, *Humble Inquiry: The Gentle art of asking instead of telling* (San Francisco: Berrett-Koehler Publishers Inc., 2013)
50. Cass Business School, 'Roads to Ruin: the analysis, A Study of Major Risk Events: Their origins, impact and implications' (research report, Cass Business School on behalf of Airmic, July 2011), p.5
51. 'Roads to Ruin', p.5
52. 'Roads to Ruin', p.15
53. 'Roads to Ruin', p.9
54. 'Roads to Ruin', p.9
55. 'Home Depot's Blueprint for Culture Change', p.9
56. Helen Deverell, 'The power of Jam - live blogging at our partner conference', *Just the way IC it*, http://helendeverell.wordpress.com/2014/05/11/the-power-of-jam-live-blogging-at-our-partner-conference/ [published 11 May 2014, accessed 31 July 2014]
57. Booker T. Washington, *Up From Slavery: An Autobiography*, http://www.literaturepage.com/read/upfromslavery-32.html [accessed 31 July 2014], p.32
58. 'Roads to Ruin', p.15

CHAPTER 5
PREPARING ORGANISATIONS FOR CONVERSATION

1. Steven Van Belleghem, *The Conversation Company: Boost your Business through Culture, People and Social Media* (London: Kogan Page, 2012), p.xiii
2. Tom Peters and Robert H Waterman Jr., *In Search of Excellence: Lessons from America's Best Run Companies* (New York: Harper and Row, 1982), p.8
3. Anthony Salz, 'Salz Review: An Independent Review of Barclays' Business Practices', (report document, April 2013), p.92
4. Bruce Rayton, Tanith Dodge and Gillian D'Analeze, 'The Evidence: Employee Engagement Task Force "Nailing the evidence" workgroup' (white paper, Engage for Success, 12 November 2012)

5.   Daniel Goleman, *Working with Emotional Intelligence* (London: Bloomsbury, 1998), p.198

6.   *In Search of Excellence*, p.6

7.   Charlene Li, *Open Leadership: How Social Technology can Transform the way you Lead* (San Francisco: Jassey Bass, 2010), p.76

8.   Morten Hansen, *Collaboration: How Leaders Avoid the Traps, Create Unity and Reap Big Results*, (Boston: Harvard Business Press, 2009), p.167

9.   James Suroweicki, *The Wisdom of Crowds: Why the Many are Smarter than the Few* (London: Abacus, 2004), p.208

10. Shel Holtz, *Corporate Conversations: a Guide to Crafting Effective and Appropriate Internal Communications* (AMACOM Div American Management Association, 2004), p.10

11. Rick Levine, Christopher Locke, Doc Searls, and David Weinberger, *The Cluetrain Manifesto: The End of Business as Usual*, 10th anniversary edition (New York: Basic Books, 2009), p.87

12. *The Cluetrain Manifesto*, p.xvii

13. Ron Thomas, Joshua Bellin, Claudy Jules and Nandani Lynton, 'Leadership Ensembles: orchestrating the global company' (research report, Accenture institute for high performance, October 2012), p.4

14. *Working with Emotional Intelligence*, p.32

15. 'Leadership Ensembles', p.9

16. *Collaboration*, p.15

17. *Collaboration*, p.147

18. Ram Charan, 'Conquering a culture of indecision', *The Harvard Business Review* (Reprint R06J, 2006), p.2

19. Carol L Bernick, 'When your culture needs a makeover', *The Harvard Business Review* (Reprint R0106B, June 2001), p.9

20. McKinsey Global Institute, 'The Social Economy: unlocking value and productivity through social technologies' (white paper, McKinsey Global Institute, July 2012), p.47

21. Chade-Meng Tan, *Search Inside Yourself: Increase Productivity, Creativity and Happiness* (St Ives, HarperCollins, 2012)

22. *Collaboration*, p.155

23. 'The Social Economy', p.52

24. IPA and Tomorrow's Company, 'Releasing Voice for Sustainable Business Success' (white paper, November 2012), p.20

25. 'The Social Economy', p.124

26. Stephen Shapiro, '10X innovation ROI on your internal collaboration' (white paper, InnoCentive, October 2013), p.7

27. Donald Campbell, 'The Proactive Employee: Managing Workplace Initiative', *The Academy of Management Executive* (Vol. 14, No.3, August 2000), p.65

CHAPTER 6
FROM THE CORPORATE TO THE EMPLOYEE VOICE

1.   'Going Underground', www.goingunderground.net/#heroes [accessed 19 February 2014]

2.   'JFK assassination: Cronkite informs a shocked nation', www.youtube.com/watch?v=6PXORQE5-CY [published, 17 November 2013, accessed 19 February 2014]

3.   'CBS News Moon landing coverage with Walter Cronkite, www.youtube.com/watch?v=_3vVjyqkwrw [published 20 July 2013, accessed 19 February 2014]

4.   'Remarks by the president at memorial service in honor of Walter Cronkite', Lincoln Centre, New York, The White House press release, www.whitehouse.gov/the_press_office/Remarks-by-the-President-at-Memorial-Service-in-Honor-of-Walter-Cronkite [published 9 September 2009, accessed 19 February 2014]

5.   Philip Kennicott, 'Whom Can We Trust Now?', *The Washington Post* (21 July 2009)

6.   Rick Levine, Christopher Locke, Doc Searls and David Weinberger, *The Cluetrain Manifesto: The End of Business as Usual*, 10th Anniversary edition (New York: Basic Books, 2009), p.xv

7.   *The Cluetrain Manifesto*, p.ix

8.   *The Cluetrain Manifesto*, p.x

9.   Deborah Jermyn and Su Holmes, 'The Audience is Dead, Long Live the Audience! Interactivity, 'Telephilia', and the contemporary television audience', *Critical Studies in Television: The International Journal of Television Studies* (Manchester University Press, Vol 1., No. 1, Spring 2006), p.49

10.   Charles Leadbeater, *We-Think: Mass Innovation, not Mass Production* (London: Profile Books Ltd, 2008), p.30

11.   TJ Larkin and Sandar Larkin, *Communicating Change: Winning Employee Support for New Business Goals* (New York: McGraw Hill, 1994), p.162

12.   Angela Sinickas, 'Employees prefer intranets to supervisors 2 to 1', *SCITI* (Vol. 13, Issue 6, Oct/Nov 2009), p.11

13.   Cited in Shel Holtz, *Corporate Conversations: A Guide to Crafting Effective and Appropriate Internal Communications* (New York: American Management Association, AMACOM, 2004), p. 196

14.   Quoted in Boris Groysberg and Michael Slind, *Talk, Inc.: How Trusted Leaders use Conversation to Power their Organisations* (Boston: Harvard Business Review Press, 2012), p.33

15.   Douglas McGregor, *The Human Side of Enterprise: Annotated Edition* (New York: McGraw Hill, 1994), p.xxii

16.   *The Human Side of Enterprise*, p.55

17.   James Suchan and Robert Colucci, 'The High Cost of Bureaucratic Written Communications', *Business Horizons* (Vol 34, No.2, 1991), p.68-73

18.   111th Congress Public Law 274

19.   Stephen Poole, *Unspeak: How Words Become Weapons, How Weapons Become a Message, and How that Message Becomes Reality* (New York: Grove Press, 2006)

20.   IPA and tomorrow's company, 'Releasing Voice for sustainable business success' (white paper, November 2012), p.4

21.   'The Audience is Dead, Long Live the Audience', p.52

22.   David Weinberger, *Too Big to Know: Rethinking Knowledge Now That the Facts aren't Facts, Experts are Everywhere, and the Smartest Person in the Room is the Room* (New York: Basic Books, 2011), p.x

23.   Boris Groysberg and Michael Slind, 'Want to Build Engagement? Be Inclusive', *HBR blogs*, blogs. hbr.org/2012/06/want-to-build-engagement-be-in [published 28 June 2012, accessed 28 February 2014]

24.   'Want to Build Engagement? Be Inclusive'

25.   'Want to Build Engagement? Be Inclusive'

26.   'Releasing Voice", p.36

27.   Quoted in *Talk, Inc.*, p.138

28.   Jeff Howe, *Crowdsourcing: How the Power of the Crowd is Driving the Future of Business* (New York: Random House Business Books, 2009), p.231

29.   Sohaib Athar (Really Virtual), 1 May 2011, 8:58pm, tweet

30.   Sohaib Athar (Really Virtual), 1 May 2011. 9.09pm, tweet

31.   *The Economist*, 'The people formerly known as the audience', www.economist.com/node/18904124 [published 7 July 2011, accessed 17 March 2014]

32.   Quoted in 'The people formerly known as the audience'

33.   Quoted in Shayne Bowman and Chris Willis, 'We Media: How audiences are shaping the future of news and information', edited by J.D. Lasica (white paper, The Media Centre at the American Press Institute, July 2003), p.vi

34.   Andrew Keen, *The Cult of the Amateur: How blogs, MySpace, YouTube and the Rest of Today's User-generated Media are Killing our Culture and Economy* (London: Nicholas Brearly Publishing, 2008), p.3

35.   Quoted in 'The people formerly known as the audience'

36.   Quoted on 'The Working Mother Experience book is released!', www.facebook.com/notes/emc-careers/the-working-mother-experience-book-is-released/194603205416 [published 14 April 2009, accessed 18 March 2014]

37.   Vineet Nayar, *Employees First, Customers Second: Turning Conventional Management Upside Down* (Boston: Harvard Business Review, 2010) p.97

38. *Employees First, Customers Second*, p.10

39. Boris Groysberg and Michael Slind, 'Leadership is a Conversation: How to Improve Employee Engagement and Alignment in Today's Flatter, More Networked Organisations', *Harvard Business Review* (Reprint R1206D, June 2012), p.5

CHAPTER 7
WHY PAPER ISN'T DEAD

1.   'Innovation' (report handed out to NYT employees, The New York Times, March 24, 2014), www.scribd.com/doc/224608514/The-full-New-York-Times-Innovation-Report [accessed 9 June 2014], p.81

2.   '60 years of daily newspaper circulation trends (1950-2010): will there be a plateau?' (discussion paper, Communication Management Inc., 6 May 2011)

3.   'ABCs: National daily newspaper circulation April 2014, *The Guardian*, www.theguardian.com/media/table/2014/may/09/abcs-national-newspapers [published 9 May 2014, accessed 9 June 2014]

4.   'BuzzFeed Reaches More than 130 Million Unique Visitors in November', www.buzzfeed.com/buzzfeedpress/buzzfeed-reaches-more-than-130-million-unique-visitors-in-no [published 2 December 2013, accessed 9 June 2014]

5.   Elinor Hayes, 'The Employees' Publication', *The University Journal of Business* (University of Chicago Press, Vol. 1, No. 1. November 1922), p.81

6.   'The Employees' Publication', p.81

7.   Quoted in Mark Hooper, 'Who says print is dead?', *The Guardian*, www.theguardian.com/media/2012/Jun/03/who-says-print-is-dead [published 3 June 2012, accessed 12 June 2014]

8.   *Delayed Gratification*, www.dgquarterly.com [accessed 12 June 2014]

9.   'Who says print is dead?'

10. Quoted in Ferris Jabr, 'The reading brain in the digital age', *Scientific American*, www.scientificamerican.com/article/reading-paper-screens [published April 11 2013, accessed 12 June 2014]

11. 'Consumers' Environmental Perceptions of Print and Paper: Two Sides' European and US Consumer Survey Results' (report, Two Sides, September 2011)

12. TJ Larkin and Sandar Larkin, *Communicating Change: Winning Employee Support for New Business Goals* (New York: McGraw Hill, 1994), p.117

13. *Communicating Change*, p.124

14. *Communicating Change*, p.152

15. *Communicating Change*, p.122

16. Alan Rusbridger, 'Harold Evans: We have to keep doing it', *The Guardian*, www.theguardian.com/media/2009/oct/05/harold-evans-interviewed-alan-rusbridger [published 5 October 2009, accessed 17 June 2014]

17. 'The Employees' Publication', p.90

18. 'Innovation', p.24

19. 'Print edition of Ariel to close', *BBC website*, www.bbc.co.uk/ariel/15376161 [published 9 October 2011, accessed 9 June 2014]

20. Quoted in Tim Kenneally, 'TheGrill: USA Today Publisher - Newspapers Must be Conversation-Starters in the Digital Age', *The Wrap*, www.test.thewrap.com/thegrill-usa-today-publisher-larry-kramer-on-journalism-and-advertising-in-the-digital-age/ [published 24 September 2013, accessed 26 June 2014]

21. Quoted in 'Newspapers Must be Conversation-Starters'

CHAPTER 8
CONVERSATIONS VIA A SCREEN

1.   Daniel Morrison, 'Meet Downside, our first iPhone game!', www.collectiveidea.com/blog/archives/2013/04/30/meet-downside/ [published 30 April 2013, accessed 11 June 2014]

2.   Sherry Turkle, 'The flight from conversation', *Sunday Review, The New York Times*, www.nytimes.com/2012/04/22/opinion/sunday/the-flight-from-conversation.html?pagewanted=all&_r=0 [published April 21 2014, accessed 11 June 2014]

3.   Susan Tardanico, 'Is Social Media Sabotaging Real Communication?', *Forbes*, www.forbes.com/sites/susantardanico/2012/04/30/is-social-media-sabotaging-real-communication/ [published 30 April 2012, accessed 21 May 2014]

4.   Sara Radicati and Justin Levenstein, 'Email Statistics Report, 2013-2017' (research report, The Radicati group Inc, April 2013), p.3

5.   Ryan Holmes, 'Email is the new Pony Express – and it's time to put it down', *Fast Company*, www.fastcompany.com/3002170/email-new-pony-express-and-its-time-put-it-down [published 16 October 2012, accessed 21 May 2014]

6.   Paul Lancaster, 'No Email Day', www.slideshare.net/lordlancaster/no-email-day-by-paul-lancaster [published 11 August 2011, accessed 21 May 2014]

7.   Mark Hurst *Bit Literacy: Productivity in the age of information and email overload* (New York: Good Experience Press, Kindle edition, 2007), Ch. 8: Creating Bits

8.   Christopher Locke et al, *The Cluetrain Manifesto: The End of Business as Usual*, 10th Anniversary edition (New York: Basic Books, 2009), p.xvii

9.   Toby Ward, 'State of the Social Intranet: Results of 2012 Social Intranet Survey' (summary report, Prescient digital media, January 2013), p.5

10. Jeff Seacrist, 'Using Analytics to Measure Your Intranet' (white paper, Webtrends, June 2012), p.2

11. Steven Tellen, 'The IntraNet Architecture: Managing information in the new paradigm' (research paper, Amdahl Corporation, June 1996)

12. 'The IntraNet Architecture'

13. 'The IntraNet Architecture'

14. *The Cluetrain Manifesto*, p.95

15. *The Cluetrain Manifesto*, p.91

16. *The Cluetrain Manifesto*, p.93

17. *The Cluetrain Manifesto*, p.86

18. Euan Semple, *Organisations Don't Tweet, People Do: a manager's guide to the social web* (Padstow: Wiley and Sons, 2012), p.28

19. *Organisations Don't Tweet, People Do*, p.30

20. 'State of the Social Intranet', p.4

21. *Organisations Don't Tweet, People Do*, p.164

22. *The Cluetrain Manifesto*, p.145

23. Sam Jones, 'HMV workers take over official Twitter feed to vent fury over sacking', *The Guardian*, www.theguardian.com/business/2013/jan/31/hmv-workers-twitter-feed-sacking [published 31 January 2013, accessed 29 May 2014]

24. *Organisations Don't Tweet, People Do*, p.24

25. Patty McCord, 'How Netflix Reinvented HR: Trust people, not policies. Reward candour. And throw away the standard playbook', *Harvard Business Review* (Reprint R1401E, Jan-Feb 2014), p.4

26. Don Tapscott and Anthony Williams, *Wikinomics: How mass collaboration changes everything*, (Croydon: Portfolio, 2006), p.xi

27. *The Cluetrain Manifesto*, p.141

28. *The Cluetrain Manifesto*, p.141

29. Andrew Keen, *The Cult of the Amateur: How blogs, MySpace, YouTube and the rest of today's user-generated media are killing our culture and economy* (London: Nicholas Brealey publishing, 2008), p.30

30. *Organisations Don't Tweet, People Do*, p.110

31. *The Cluetrain Manifesto*, p.195

32. 'Consumers will punish brands that fail to respond on Twitter quickly', www.lithium.com/company/news-room/press-releases/2013/consumers-will-punish-brands-that-fail-to-respond-on-twitter-quickly [published 29 October 2013, accessed 30 May 2014]

33. Josh Bernoff and Ted Schadler, 'Empowered: in a world where one angry tweet can torpedo a brand, corporations need to unleash their employees to fight back', *Harvard Business Review* (Reprint R0117H, Jul-Aug 2010)

34.   *The Cluetrain Manifesto*, p.89

35.   'Empowered', p.8

36.   Jeanne Meister, 'Want to be a more productive employee? Get on social networks', *Forbes*, www.
      forbes.com/sites/jeannemeister/2013/04/18/want-to-be-a-more-productive-employee-get-on-
      social-networks/ [published 18 April 2013, accessed 15 July 2014]

37.   McKinsey Global Institute, 'The Social Economy: unlocking value and productivity through social
      technologies' (white paper, McKinsey Global Institute, July 2012), p.93

38.   James Manyika, Michael Chui and Hugo Sarrazin, 'Social Media's productivity payoff', *HBR blogs*,
      blogs.hbr.org/2012/08/social-medias-productivity-pay [published 21 August 2012, accessed
      30 May 2014]

CHAPTER 9
FACE-TO-FACE CONVERSATION

1.   'LINK, the UK ATM network', www.link.co.uk/AboutLINK/Pages/LINK.aspx [accessed 17 July 2014]

2.   Sherry Turkle, 'The Flight from Conversation', *The New York Times*, www.nytimes.com/2012/04/22/
      opinion/sunday/the-flight-from-conversation.html?pagewanted=all&_r=0 [published 21 April 2012,
      accessed 17 July 2014]

3.   'The Flight from Conversation'

4.   Edward Hallowell, 'The Human Moment at work', *Harvard Business Review* (Reprint 99104, Jan-Feb
      1999), p.4

5.   'The Human Moment at work', p.4

6.   Boris Groysberg and Michael Slind, 'Leadership is a conversation: how to improve employee
      engagement and alignment in today's flatter, more networked organisations', *Harvard Business
      Review* (Reprint R1206D, June 2012) p.4

7.   'Leadership is a conversation', p.4

8.   Boris Groysberg and Michael Slind, *Talk, Inc.: how trusted leaders use conversation to power their
      organisations* (Boston: Harvard Business Review Press, 2012), p.13

9.   'Leadership is a conversation', p.4

10.   Susan Cain, *Quiet: The power of introverts in a world that can't stop talking* (St Ives: Penguin, 2012),
      p.58

11.   Margaret Wheatley with Debbie Frieze, 'Leadership in the Age of Complexity: From Hero to Host',
      Resurgence Magazine (Winter, 2011)

12.   Charlene Li, *Open Leadership: How social technology can transform they way you lead* (San
      Francisco: Jossey-Bass, 2010), p.9

13.   Edgar H. Schein, *Humble Inquiry: the gentle art of asking instead of telling* (San Francisco:
      Berrett-Koehler Publishers Inc., 2013), p.65

14.   Ed Catmull with Amy Wallace, *Creativity Inc.: overcoming the unseen forces that stand in the way of
      true inspiration* (London: Random House, 2014), p.xvi

15.   Pierre Goad, 'The Employee Communication revolution: ripping up the rule book at HSBC', *The
      Journal or Internal Communication* (Gatehouse, Volume 5), p.41

16.   'The Employee Communication revolution', p.41

17.   *Open Leadership*, p.8

18.   *Open Leadership*, p.56

19.   Lawrence Serewicz 'Leadership is not a conversation', http://thoughtmanagement.org/2012/06/23/
      leadership-is-not-a-conversation/ [published 23 June 2012, accessed 17 July 2014]

20.   'Leadership is not a conversation'

21.   'Leadership is not a conversation'

22.   'Ketchum Leadership Communication Monitor' *(white paper, Ketchum, May 2014)*, p.2

23.   Daniel Goleman, *Working with Emotional Intelligence* (London: Bloomsbury, 1998), p.3

24.   Daniel Goleman, 'What makes a leader?', *Harvard Business Review* (Reprint R0201H, Best of HBR
      1998), p.5

25.   Daniel Goleman, *Working with Emotional Intelligence* (London: Bloomsbury, 1998), p.12

26.   Nick Morgan, 'How to master your gestures to become a more effective communicator', http://
      publicwords.com/how-to-master-your-gestures-to-become-a-more-effective-communicator/
      [published 1 October 2012, accessed 21 July 2014]

27.   'How to master your gestures'

28.   Cited in *Quiet*, p.55

29.   *Quiet*, p.57

30.   *Working with Emotional Intelligence*, p.189

31.   TJ and Sandar Larkin, 'Reaching and changing frontline employees', *Harvard Business Review* (Reprint 96304, May-June 1996), p.95

32.   Reaching and changing frontline employees', p.95

33.   'Reaching and changing frontline employees', p.96

34.   IABC Conference 2011, Seattle

35.   'Reaching and changing frontline employees', p.101

36.   McKinsey Global Institute, 'Ten IT-enabled business trends for the decade ahead' (white paper, McKinsey Global Institute, May 2013)

37.   'The Employee Communication revolution', p.38

38.   Anne-Laure Fayard and John Weeks, 'Who Moved My Cube? Creating workspaces that actually foster collaboration', *Harvard Business Review* (Reprint R1107H, July-August 2011), p.3

39.   'Who Moved My Cube?', p.3

40.   'Who Moved My Cube?', p.4

41.   Quoted in Mimi Zeiger, 'Steelcase and Susan Cain Design Offices for Introverts', www.fastcodesign. com/3031341/steelcase-and-susan-cain-design-offices-for-introverts?partner=rss&utm_ source=feedburner&utm_medium=feed&utm_campaign=feedburner+fastcodesign&utm_ content=feedburner [accessed 29 July 2014]

42.   'Valve: Handbook for new employees' (2012), http://assets.sbnation.com/assets/1074301/Valve_ Handbook_LowRes.pdf [accessed 29 July 2014], p.6

CHAPTER 10
MEASUREMENT THROUGH CONVERSATION

1.   Angela Sinickas, 'Help CEOs See Communication as a Business Process', CW Bulletin, www.sinicom. com/Sub Pages/pubs/articles/article141.pdf [published 5 August 2011, accessed 3 July 2014]

2.   Lingle and Schieman (1996) and Gates (1999) cited by Mike Kennerley and Andy Neely in 'Measuring performance in a changing business environment', *International Journal of Operations and Production Management* (Vol. 25, No. 2, 2003), p.213

3.   'Measuring performance in a changing business environment', p.214

4.   'Corporate History', www.gallup.com/corporate/1357/corporate-history.aspx [accessed 31 July 2014]

5.   'Corporate History'

6.   Juan Meng and Bruce K. Berger, 'How Top Business Communicators Measure the Return on Investment (ROI) of Organisation's Internal Communication Efforts' (white paper, International Public Relations Research Conference, 2010), p.1

7.   Baruch Lev, 'Sharpening the Intangibles edge', *Harvard Business Review* (Reprint R0406H, June 2004), p.5

8.   Towers Watson, 'Change and Communication ROI – The 10th Anniversary Report: How the fundamentals have evolved and the best adapt' (study report, Towers Watson, December 2013), p.5

9.   Converge Consulting Group, 'The (Statistical) Confidence Games of Employee Engagement Surveys' (white paper, Converge Consulting Group Inc., August 2012), p.8

10.   Quoted in Charlene Li, *Open Leadership: How social technology can transform the way you lead* (San Francisco: Jossey Bass, 2010), p.76

11.   'Sharpening the Intangibles edge', p.8

12.   'Sharpening the intangibles edge', p.1

13.   Mark Hall, 'Forget ROI', Computerworld, www.computerworld.com/s/article/78516/Forget_ROI [published 17 February 2003, accessed 15 July 2014]

14.   'Forget ROI'

15.   Shel Holtz, *Corporate Conversations: A Guide to Crafting Effective and Appropriate Internal Communications* (New York: American Management Association, AMACOM, New York, 2004), p.252

16.   Nancy R Lee and Philip Kotler, *Social Marketing: Influencing Behaviors for Good* (Los Angeles: Sage publications, 2011), p.377

17.   Towers Watson, 'Employee voice: Releasing voice for sustainable business success' (white paper, Towers Watson, February 2014), p.4

18.   IPA and tomorrow's company, 'Releasing Voice for sustainable business success', IPA and tomorrow's company (white paper, November 2012), p.17

19.   William M. K. Trochim, 'The Qualitative Debate', www.socialresearchmethods.net/kb/qualdeb.php [published 20 October 2006, accessed 18 July 2014]

20.   The Qualitative Debate'

21.   Peter Kellner, 'A Journalist's Guide to Opinion Polls', www.britishpollingcouncil.org/a-journalists-guide-to-opinion-polls/ [accessed 22 July 2014]

22.   'A Journalist's Guide to Opinion Polls'

23.   'The (Statistical) Confidence Games of Employee Engagement Surveys', p.8

24.   John Smythe, *The Velvet Revolution at Work: The rise of employee engagement, the fall of command-and-control* (Gower: Farnham, 2013), p.190

25.   Donald Rumsfeld, 'Donald Rumsfeld Unknown Unknowns!', www.youtube.com/watch?v=GiPe1OiKQuk [published 7 August 2009, accessed 21 July 2014]

26.   'Pollsters face Challenges in Getting Survey Responses', www.pewresearch.org/daily-number/pollsters-face-challenges-in-getting-survey-respondents/ [published 24 May 2012, accessed 22 July 2014]

27.   William Grimes, 'When Businesses Can't Stop Asking, 'How Am I Doing?', *New York Times*, www.nytimes.com/2012/03/17/business/onslaught-of-surveys-is-fraying-customer-patience.html?pagewanted=all&_r=0 [published 16 March 2012, accessed 22 July 2014]

28.   Charlene Li, *Open Leadership: How social technology can transform the way you lead* (San Francisco: Jossey-Bass, 2010), p.79

Bibliography

111th Congress Public Law 274

'60 years of daily newspaper circulation trends (1950-2010): will there be a plateau?' (discussion paper, Communic@tion Management Inc., 6 May 2011)

'ABCs: National daily newspaper circulation April 2014, *The Guardian*, www.theguardian.com/media/table/2014/may/09/abcs-national-newspapers [published 9 May 2014, accessed 9 June 2014]

'Accenture Technology Vision 2013: Every Business Is a Digital Business' (white paper, Accenture, 2013)

Adler, Paul, Charles Heckscher and Laurence Prusack, 'Building a collaborative enterprise: Four keys to creating a culture of trust and teamwork', *Harvard Business Review* (Reprint R1107G, July-Aug 2011)

Alfes, Kerstin, Catherine Truss, Emma C Soane, Chris Rees and Mark Gatenby, 'Creating an Engaged Workforce: Findings from the Kingston Employee Engagement Consortium Project' (research report, CIPD, January 2010)

Anderson, John D, 'Qualitative and Quantitative research' (research report, Imperial COE, 2006)

Aristotle, *Nichomanchean Ethics*, Book I, 1094.a18

Bennis, Warren and Patricia Ward Biederman, *Organising Genius: The Secrets of Creative Collaboration* (New York: Basic Books, 1997)

Bernick, Carol Lavin, 'When your culture needs a makeover', *Harvard Business Review* (Reprint R0106B, June 2001)

Bernoff, Josh and Ted Schadler, ' Empowered: In a world where one angry tweet can torpedo a brand, corporations need to unleash their employees to fight back', *Harvard Business Review* (Reprint R1007H, July-Aug 2010)

Brien, Andrew, 'Professional ethics and the culture of trust', *Journal of Business Ethics* (Springer, Vol. 17 No.4, March 1998), pp.391-409

Bland, Michael, *Employee Communications in the 1980s: A Personnel Manager's Guide* (London: Kogan Page, 1980)

Bock, Laszlo, 'Passion, Not Perks' www.thinkwithgoogle.com/articles/passion-not-perks.html [published September 2011, accessed 31 July 2014]

Booker T. Washington, *Up From Slavery: An Autobiography*, www.literaturepage.com/read/upfromslavery-32.html [accessed 31 July 2014],

Boudreau, Kevin J. and Karim R. Lakhani, 'Using the crowd as an innovation partner: for certain types of problems, crowds can outperform your company. You just need to know when – and how – to use them', *Harvard Business Review* (Reprint R1304C, April 2013)

Bower, Marvin, *The Will to Manage: Corporate Success Through Programmed Management* (McGraw-Hill, The Marvin Bower Trust, 1966)

Bowman, Shayne and Chris Willis, 'We Media: How audiences are shaping the future of news and information', ed. J.D Lasica, (white paper, The Media Centre at the American Press Institute, July 2003)

Brin, Sergey and Larry Page, 'The Anatomy of a Large-Scale Hypertextual Web Search Engine' http.//infolab.stanford.edu/~backrub/google.html [accessed 2 July 2014]

Bughin, Jacques, James Manyika, Andy Miller, 'Building the Web 2.0 Enterprise' (McKinsey Global Survey Results, June 2008)

'BuzzFeed Reaches More than 130 Million Unique Visitors in November', www.buzzfeed.com/buzzfeedpress/buzzfeed-reaches-more-than-130-million-unique-visitors-in-no [published 2 December 2013, accessed 9 June 2014]

Brofman, Ori and Rod Beckstrom *The Starfish and the Spider: The Unstoppable power of Leaderless Organisations* (New York: Portfolio, 2006)

Cain, Susan, *Quiet: The power of introverts in a world that can't stop talking* (St Ives: Penguin, 2012)

Campbell, Donald. J, 'The Proactive Employee: Managing Workplace Initiative', *The Academy of Management Executive* (Vol. 14 No. 3, Aug 2000), pp.52-66

Campbell, Andrew, Jo Whitehead and Sydney Finkelstein, 'Why Good Leaders Make Bad Decisions', *Harvard Business Review* (Reprint R0902D, February 2009)

Cass Business School, 'Roads to Ruin: the analysis, A Study of Major Risk Events: Their origins, impact and implications' (research report, Cass Business School on behalf of Airmic, July 2011)

Catmull, Ed, 'How Pixar Fosters Collective Creativity', *Harvard Business Review* (Reprint R0809D, September 2008)

Catmull, Ed with Amy Wallace, *Creativity, Inc.,: Overcoming the unseen forces that stand in the way of true inspiration* (London: Random House, 2014)

'CBS News Moon landing coverage with Walter Cronkite' www.youtube.com/watch?3vVjyqwrw [accessed 19 February 2014]

Charan, Ram, 'Conquering a culture of indecision', *Harvard Business Review* (Reprint R0601J, January 2006)

Charan, Ram, 'Home Depot's Blueprint for Culture Change', *Harvard Business Review* (Reprint R0604C, April 2006)

Collins, James C and Jerry I Porras, *Built to Last: Successful Habits of visionary companies* (New York: HarperCollins, 2002)

'Consumers' Environmental Perceptions of Print and Paper: Two Sides' European and US Consumer Survey Results' (report, Two Sides, September 2011)

'Consumers will punish brands that fail to respond on Twitter quickly', www.lithium.com/company/news-room/press-releases/2013/consumers-will-punish-brands-that-fail-to-respond-on-twitter-quickly [published 29 October 2013, accessed 30 May 2014]

Converge Consulting Group, 'The (Statistical) Confidence Game of Employee Engagement Surveys' (white paper, Converge Consulting Group Inc., August 2012)

'Conversation with transformative CEOs' panel at the IABC's World Conference, New York City, New York, June 2013

'Daily newspaper circulation trends, 2000-2013: can daily newspaper 'brands' survive the decline (and likely disappearance) of the printed product?' (discussion paper, Communic@tion Management Inc, 28 October 2013)

De Geus, Arie, 'The Living Company', *Harvard Business Review* (March 1997)

Deal, Terrence E. and Allan A. Kennedy, *Corporate Cultures: the rites and rituals of corporate life* (Reading, Massachusetts: Addison-Wesley Publishing Company, Inc., 1982)

Delayed Gratification, www.dgquarterly.com [accessed 12 June 2014]

Deverell, Helen, 'The power of Jam – live blogging at our partner conference', *Just the way IC it*, helendeverell.wordpress.com/2014/05/11/the-power-of-jam-live-blogging-at-our-partner-conference/ [published 11 May 2014, accessed 31 July 2014]

'Donald Rumsfeld Unknown Unknowns!', www.youtube.com/watch?v=GiPe1OiKQuk [published 7 August 2009, accessed 21 July 2014]

Drucker, Peter, *Management: Tasks, Responsibilities, Practices* (New York: Harper and Row, 1973)

Fayard, Anne-Laure and John Weeks, 'Who Moved My Cube? Creating workspaces that actually foster collaboration', *Harvard Business Review* (Reprint R1107H, July-August 2011)

Ferrazzi, Keith, 'Candor, Criticism, Teamwork', *Harvard Business Review* (Reprint F1201F, Jan-Feb 2012)

Friedman, Jacob, 'Blogging vs. Journalism: The Ongoing Debate', the next web, thenextweb.com/us/2010/08/18/blogging-vs-journalism-the-ongoing-debate/ [published 18 August 2010, accessed 31 July 2014]

Fulk, Janet and Gerardine DeSanctis, 'Electronic Communication and Changing Organisational Form', *Organisation Science* (Vol. 6, No. 4, July-Aug 1995) pp.337-349

Gale, E.A.M., 'The Hawthorne Studies – a fable for our times?', *QJ Med* (Vol. 97 No. 7, 2004) pp.439-449

Gallo, Carmine, *Talk like TED: the nine public speaking secrets of the world's top minds* (New York: St Martin's Press, 2014)

Galton, Francis, *Memories of my life* (London: Methuen, 1908)

Galton, Francis, 'Vox Populi', *Nature* (Vol.7, March 1907), pp.450-451

Goad, Pierre, 'The Employee Communication revolution: ripping up the rule book at HSBC', *The Journal of Internal Communication* (Gatehouse, Vol. 5)

'Going Underground', www.goingunderground.net/#heroes [accessed 19 February 2014]

Goleman, Daniel, *Emotional Intelligence: Why it can matter more than IQ* (St Ives: Bloomsbury, 1996)

Goleman, Daniel, *Working with Emotional Intelligence* (London: Bloomsbury, 1998)

Goleman, Daniel, 'What Makes a Leader?', *Harvard Business Review* (Reprint R0401H, 1998)

Greendale, Roy, 'Newspaper sales plunge over the decade', *The Guardian*, www.guardian.com/media/2009/dec/14/national/newspapers/sales/decade [published 14 Dec 2009, accessed 9 June 2014]

Grimes, William 'When Businesses Can't Stop Asking, 'How Am I Doing?', *New York Times*, www.nytimes.com/2012/03/17/business/onslaught-of-surveys-is-fraying-customer-patience.html?pagewanted=all&_r=0 [published 16 March 2012, accessed 22 July 2014]

Groysberg, Boris and Michael Slind, *Talk, Inc.: how trusted leaders use conversation to power their organisations* (Boston: Harvard Business Press, 2012)

Groysberg, Boris and Michael Slind, 'Leadership is a conversation: how to improve employee engagement and alignment in todays flatter, more networked organisations', *Harvard Business Review* (Reprint R12061, June 2012)

Groysberg, Boris and Michael Slind, 'Want to Build Engagement? Be Inclusive', *HBR blogs*, blogs.hbr.org/2012/06/want-to-build-engagement-be-in/ [accessed 28 February 2014]

Hall, Mark, 'Forget ROI', *Computerworld*, www.computerworld.com/s/article/78516/Forget_ROI [published 17 February 2003, accessed 15 July 2014]

Hallowell, Edward M., 'The Human Moment at Work', *Harvard Business Review* (Reprint 99104, Jan-Feb 1999)

Hansen, Morten, *Collaboration: How Leaders Avoid the Traps, Create Unity and Reap Big Results* (Boston: Harvard Business Press, 2009)

Harter, James K, Frank L Schmidt, Emily A Killham and James W Asplund, 'Q12 Meta-Analysis' (white paper, Gallup Consulting, 2006)

Hayes, Elinor, 'The Employees' Publication', *The University Journal of Business* (University of Chicago Press, Vol. 1, No. 1, November 1922), pp.81-94

Heckscher, Charles and Laurence Prusack, 'Building a collaborative enterprise: four keys to creating a culture of trust and teamwork', *Harvard Business Review* (Reprint R1107G, July-August 2011)

Henderson, Iain, *Human Resource Management: For MBA Students*, second edition (CIPD, 2011)

Heron, Alexander, *Sharing information with employees: toward understanding in industry* (California: Stanford University Press, 1942)

Holmes, Ryan, 'Email is the new Pony Express – and it's time to put it down', www.fastcompany.com/3002170/email-new-pony-express-and-its-time-put-it-down [published 16 October 2012, accessed 21 May 2014]

Holtz, Shel, *Corporate Conversations: A Guide to Crafting Effective and Appropriate Internal Communications* (New York: American Management Association, AMACOM, 2004)

Hooper, Mark, 'Who says print is dead? Is the internet really killing print publishing – or could it prove to be its unlikely saviour, with niche magazines thriving in the digital era?', *The Guardian*, www.theguardian.com/media/2012/June/03/who-says-print-is-dead [published 3 June 2012, accessed 12 June 2014]

House of Commons Treasury Committee, 'Women in the City: Tenth Report of Session 2009-2010' (committee report, HC 482, Incorporating HC 967 i-ii, Session 2008-2009, 3 April 2010)

'How do you execute internal announcements that also reach out to external audiences?', *PR Week*, www.prweek.com/article/1278215/execute-internal-announcements-reach-external-audiences [published 1 September 2012, accessed 31 July 2014]

'How leadership must change to meet the future' (research report, PricewaterhouseCoopers, 2009)

Howard, Rob, 'The Community is Right 91% of the Time', www.cmswire.com/cms/social-business/the-community-is-correct-91-of-the-time-013714.php [published 6 December 2011, accessed 2 July 2014]

Howe, Jeff, *Crowdsourcing: How the Power of the Crowd is Driving the Future of Business* (New York: Random House Business Books, 2009)

Howell, Chris, *Trade Unions and the State: The construction of industrial relations institutions in Britain, 1890-2000* (Princeton, New Jersey: Princeton University Press, 2005)

Hsieh, Tony, 'Why I Sold Zappos', www.inc.com/magazine/20100601/why-i-sold-zappos.html [published 1 June 2010, accessed 31 July 2014]

Hurst, Mark, *Bit Literacy: Productivity in the age of information and email overload* (New York: Good Experience Press, 2007, Kindle Edition)

IBM, 'IBM Invests $100 Million in Collaborative Innovation Ideas', IBM Press releases, www-03.ibm.com/press/us/en/pressrelease/20605.wss [published 14 November 2006, accessed 15 January 2014]

'IBM Social Computing Guidelines: blogs, wikis, social networks, virtual worlds and social media', www.ibm.com/blogs/zz/en/guidelines.html [accessed 31 July 2014]

IPA and tomorrow's company 'Releasing Voice for Sustainable Business Success' (white paper, November 2012)

Jabr, Ferris, 'The reading brain in the digital age: the science of paper versus screens', *Scientific American*, www.scientificamerican.com/article/reading-paper-screens/ [published 11 April 2013, accessed 12 June 2014]

Jermyn, Deborah and Su Holmes, 'The Audience is Dead, Long live the Audience! Interactivity, 'Telephilia' and the contemporary television audience', *Critical Studies in Television: The International Journal of Television Studies* (Manchester University Press, Volume 1 Number 1, Spring 2006), pp.49-57

'JFK assassination: Cronkite informs a shocked nation', www.youtube.com/watch?v=^PXORQES-CY [published 17 November 2013, accessed 19 February 2014]

John Lewis Partnership, 'The Constitution of the John Lewis Partnership: Introduction, Principles and Rules' (May 2014)

Johns, Tammy and Lynda Gratton 'The Third Wave of Virtual Work: Knowledge workers are now untethered, able to perform tasks anywhere at any time. What do the best of them want from your organisation?', *Harvard Business Review* (Reprint R1301D, Jan-Feb 2012)

Jones, Sam, 'HMV workers take over official Twitter feed to vent fury over sacking;, *The Guardian*, www.theguardian.com/business.2013/jan/31/hmv-workers-twitter-feed-sacking [published 31 January 2013, accessed 29 May 2014]

Joynson, Sid and Andrew Forrester, *Sid's Heroes: Uplifting Business Performance and the Human Spirit* (London: BBC Books, 1995)

Kahn, William A, 'Psychological Conditions of Personal Engagement and Disengagement at Work', *The Academy of Management Journal* (Vol. 33 No. 4, Dec 1990) pp.692-724

Keen, Andrew, *The Cult of the Amateur: How blogs, MySpace, YouTube and the rest of today's user-generated media are killing our culture and economy* (London: Nicholas Brealey Publishing, 2008)

Kellner, Peter, 'A Journalist's Guide to Opinion Polls', www.britishpollingcouncil.org/a-journalists-guide-to-opinion-polls/ [accessed 22 July 2014]

Kenneally, Tim, 'The Grill: USA Today Publisher – Newspapers Must be Conversation-Starters in the Digital Age', *The Wrap*, www.test.thewrap.com/thegrill-usa-today-publisher-larry-kramer-on-journalism-and-advertising-in-the-digital-age/ [published 24 September 2013, accessed 26 June 2014]

Kennerley, Mike and Andy Neely, 'Measuring performance in a changing business environment', *International Journal of Operations and Production Management* (Vol. 25, No. 3, 2003), pp.213-229

Kennicott, Philip, 'Whom Can We Trust Now?', *The Washington Post* (21 July 2009)

'Ketchum Leadership Communication Monitor' (white paper, Ketchum, May 2014)

Klein, Nancy, *Time to Think: Listening to ignite the human mind* (London: Cassell Illustrated, 1999)

Lancaster, Paul, 'No Email Day', www.slideshare.net/lordlancaster/no-email-day-by-paul-lancaster [published 11 August 2011, accessed 22 May 2014]

Larkin, TJ and Sandar Larkin, *Communicating change: winning employee support for new business goals* (New York: McGraw Hill, 1994)

Larkin, TJ and Sandar Larkin, 'Reaching and Changing Frontline Employees', *Harvard Business Review* (Reprint 96304, May-June 1996)

Larkin, TJ, 'Communicating Big Change', IABC Seattle 2011, 17 February 2011, IABC Seattle: Communications Innovation: Be Heard in an Age of Information Overload [26 May 2011]

Leadbeater, Charles, *We-Think: Mass innovation, not mass production* (London: Profile Books Limited, 2008)

Lencioni, Patrick, *The Five Dysfunctions of a Team: A Leadership Fable* (San Francisco: Jossey-Bass, 2002)

Lencioni, Patrick, *The Advantage: Why Organisational Health Trumps Everything Else in Business* (San Francisco: Jossey-Bass, 2012)

Lev, Baruch, 'Sharpening the Intangibles Edge', *Harvard Business Review* (Reprint R0406H, June 2004)

Levering, Robert and Marcus Erb, 'Emerging trends in people management', *Swiss Business* (Jan/Feb 2011), pp.30-33

Levine, Rick, Christopher Locke, Doc Searls, David Weinberger and others, *The Cluetrain Manifesto: The End of Business as Usual*, 10th Anniversary edition (New York: Basic Books, 2009)

'LINK, the UK ATM network', www.link.co.uk/AboutLINK/Pages/LINK.aspx [accessed 17 July 2014]

Maslow, Abraham H, *Maslow on Management*, with Deborah Collins Stephens, D, and Gary Heil (New York: John Wiley and Sons Inc., 1998)

Manyika, James, Michael Chui and Hugo Sarrazin, 'Social media's productivity payoff', *HBR blogs*, blogs.hbr.org/2012/08/social-medias-productivity-pay [published 21 Aug 21 2012, accessed 30 May 2014]

McChrystal, Stanley, 'Listen, learn…then lead', TEDTalks, March 2011 at TED2011, Long Beach, California [22 May 2014]

McChrystal, Stanley, 'The military case for sharing knowledge', TEDTalks, March 2014 at TED2014, Vancouver BC [22 May 2014]

McCord, Patty, 'How Netflix Reinvented HR: Trust People, Not Policies. Reward Candour. And Throw away the standard Playbook', *Harvard Business Review* (Reprint R1401E, Jan-Feb 2014)

McGregor, Douglas, *The Human Side of Enterprise: Annotated Edition*, with Joel Cutcher-Gershenfeld (New York: McGraw Hill, 2006)

McKinsey Global Institute, 'The Social Economy: unlocking value and productivity through social technologies' (white paper, McKinsey Global Institute, July 2012)

McKinsey Global Institute, 'Ten IT-enabled business trends for the decade ahead' (white paper, McKinsey Global Institute, May 2013)

Meister, Jeanne, 'Want to be a more productive employee? Get on social networks', *Forbes*, www.forbes.com/sites/jeannemeister/2013/04/18/want-to-be-a-more-productive-employee-get-on-social-networks/ [published 18 April 2013, accessed 15 July 2014]

Meng, Juan and Bruce K. Berger, 'How Top Business Communicators Measure the Return on Investment (ROI) of Organisation's Internal Communication Efforts' (white paper, International Public Relations Research Conference, 2010)

Moody, Glyn, *Rebel Code: Inside Linux and the Open Source Revolution* (Cambridge MA: Basic Books, 2001)

Morgan, Nick 'How to master your gestures to become a more effective communicator', publicwords.com/how-to-master-your-gestures-to-become-a-more-effective-communicator/ [published 1 October 2012, accessed 21 July 2014]

Morrison, Daniel 'Meet downside, our first iPhone game', www.collectiveidea.com/blog/archives/2013/04/30/meet-downside/ [published 30 April 2013, accessed 11 June 2014]

Moye, Jan, 'Rethinking R&D: How Coke Uses its Global Scale to Take Innovations Further, Faster', www.coca-colacompany.com/stories/rethinking-r-d-how-coke-uses-its-global-scale-to-take-innovations-further-faster [published 19 November 2013, accessed 2 July 2014]

Mullender, Richard, *Dispelling the Myths and Rediscovering the Lost Art of Listening: Communication Secrets of a Hostage Negotiator* (ebook: Griffin Professional Business and Training Services, October 2012)

Nayar, Vineet, *Employees First, Customers Second: Turning Conventional Management Upside Down* (Boston: Harvard Business Review Press, 2010)

'Innovation' (report handed out to NYT employees, *The New York Times*, March 24, 2014), www.scribd.com/doc/224608514/The-full-New-York-Times-Innovation-Report [accessed 9 June 2014]

Obama, Barack, 'Remarks by the president at memorial service in honor of Walter Cronkite', Lincoln Centre, New York, The White House press release, www.whitehouse.gov/the_press_office/Remarks-by-the-President-at-Memorial-Service-in-Honor-of-Walter-Cronkite [published 9 September 2009, accessed 19 February 2014]

'Open Innovation', www.unilever.com/innovation/collaborating-with-unilever/open-innovation/ [accessed 2 July 2014]

O'Dell, Jolie, 'How to tell a journalist from a blogger', jolieodell.wordpress.com/2010/07/21/how-to-tell-a-journalist-from-a-blogger/ [published 21 July 2010, accessed 31 July 2014]

O'Toole, James and Warren Bennis 'A Culture of Candor', *Harvard Business Review* (Reprint R0906F, June 2009)

'Our Constitution', www.johnlewispartnership.co.uk/about/our-constitution.html [accessed 31 July 2014]

Page, Scott. E, *The Difference: How the Power of Diversity Creates Better Groups, Firms, Schools, and Societies* (New Jersey: Princeton Press, 2007)

Parker, Monica, 'The Myths of Activity Based Working', *The Huffington Post*, www.huffingtonpost.co.uk/monica-parker/the-myths-of-activity-bas_b_3859841.html [published 3 September 2013, accessed 31 July 2014]

Parmar, Belinda, *The Empathy Era: Women, Business and the new pathway to profit* (Lady Geek, 2014)

Peters, Tom J and Robert H Waterman Jr., *In Search of Excellence: Lessons from America's Best-Run Companies* (New York: Harper & Row, 1982)

Pink, Daniel, *Drive: The Surprising Truth About What Motivates Us* (London: Penguin Group, 2009)

'Pollsters face Challenges in Getting Survey Responses', www.pewresearch.org/daily-number/pollsters-face-challenges-in-getting-survey-respondents/ [published 24 May 2012, accessed 22 July 2014]

Poole, Stephen, *Unspeak: how words become weapons, how weapons become a message, and how that message becomes reality* (New York: Grove Press, 2006)

'Print edition of Ariel to close', www.bbc.co.uk/ariel/15376161 [published 9 October 2011, accessed 9 June 2014]

Radicati, Sara and Quoc Hoang, 'Email Statistics Report, 2011-2015' (research report, The Radicati group inc., May 2011)

Radicati, Sara and Justin Levenstein, 'Email Statistics Report, 2013-2017' (research report, The Radicati group inc., April 2013)

Raymond, Eric. C, 'The Cathedral and the Bazaar', Thyrsus Enterprises, version 3.0 (2000) https://docs.google.com/document/preview?hgd=1&id=1O7LgcL8r8VNXzDQTlhK4MnamZuTKmwI620QLthgLJwQ [accessed 27 January 2014]

Rayton, Bruce, Tanith Dodge, and Gillian D'Analeze, 'The Evidence: Employee Engagement Task Force "Nailing the evidence" workgroup' (white paper, Engage for Success, 12 November 2012)

Reingold, Jennifer and Ryan Underwood, 'Was "Built to Last" Built to Last?', *Fast Company*, www.fastcompany.com/50992/was-built-last-built-last [published 1 November 2004, accessed 24 July 2014]

Rheingold, Howard, *Smart Mobs: The Next Social Revolution: Transforming Cultures and Communities in the Age of Instant Access* (Boston: Basic Books, 2002)

Rheingold, Howard, 'The new power of collaboration', TED2005, February 2005 at TED2005, Monterey, California [accessed 23 June 2014]

Ruck, Kevin, 'The rise and rise of internal communication', www.exploringinternalcommunication.com/2013/04 [published 29 April 2013, accessed 24 January 2014]

Ruck, Kevin, and Heather Yaxley 'Tracking the rise and rise of internal communications from the 1980s' (conference paper, History of PR Conference in Bournemouth, August 2013)

Rusbridger, Alan, 'Harold Evans: We have to keep doing it', *The Guardian*, www.theguardian.com/media/2009/oct/05/harld-evans-interviewed-alan-rusbridger [published 5 Oct 2009, accessed 17 June 2014]

Salz, Anthony, 'Salz Review: An Independent Review of Barclay's Business Practices' (report document, April 2013)

Sawyer, Keith, *Group Genius: The Creative Power of Collaboration* (New York: Basic Books, 2007)

Schein, Edgar H, *Humble Inquiry: the gentle art of asking instead of telling* (San Francisco: Berrett-Koehler Publishers Inc., 2013)

Schrage, Michael, 'The Real Power of Enterprise Social Media platforms', *HBR blogs*, blogs.hbr.org/2013/07/the-real-power-of-enterprise-s/ [published July 26 2013, accessed 27 May 2014]

Seacrist, Jeff, 'Using analytics to measure your intranet' (white paper, Webtrends, June 2012)

Semler, Ricardo, 'Managing without managers', *Harvard Business Review* (Reprint 89509, Sept-Oct 1989)

Semler, Ricardo, *Maverick! The Success Story Behind the World's Most Unusual Workplace* (St Ives, Arrow Books, 1993)

Semple, Euan, *Organisations Don't Tweet, People Do: A Manager's Guide to the Social Web* (Padstow: Wiley and Sons, 2012)

Serewicz, Lawrence 'Leadership is not a conversation', http://thoughtmanagement.org/2012/06/23/leadership-is-not-a-conversation/ [published 23 June, accessed 17 July 2014]

Shapiro, Stephen, '10X Innovation ROI on Your Internal Collaboration' (InnoCentive white paper, InnoCentive, October 2013)

Silverman, Michael, Elmira Bakhshalian, and Laura Hillman, 'Social Media and employee voice: the current landscape' (white paper, CIPD , Silverman research, March 2013)

Sinek, Simon, 'How great leaders inspire action', TEDTalks, September 2009 at TEDx Puget Sounds, Washington [accessed 22 May 2014]

Sinek, Simon, 'Why good leaders make you feel safe', TEDTalks, March 2014 at TED2014, Vancouver BC [accessed 22 May 2014]

Sinickas, Angela 'Employees prefer intranets to supervisors 2 to 1', *SCITI* (Vol. 13, Issue 6, Oct/Nov 2009)

Sinickas, Angela, 'Yes, We've Heard About the Cascade. But Is It Always the Best Tactic?', *The Journal of Internal Communication* (Gatehouse Group, May 2012)

Sinickas, Angela, 'Help CEOs See Communication as a Business Process', *CW Bulletin*, www.sinicom.com/Sub%20Pages/pubs/articles/articles141.pdf [published 5 August 2011, accessed 3 July 2014]

Sirolli, Ernesto, 'Want to help someone? Shut up and listen!', TEDx, September 2012, at TEDxEQChCh, Christchurch New Zealand [accessed 23 June 2014]

Smythe, John, *The CEO - Chief Engagement Officer: Turning the Hierarchy Upside Down to Driver Performance* (Farnham: Gower, 2007)

Smythe, John, *The Velvet Revolution at Work: The Rise of Employee Engagement, the Fall of Command and Control* (Dorchester: Gower, 2013)

Stone, Douglas and Sheila Heen, *Thanks for the Feedback: The science and art of receiving feedback well, even when it is off base, unfair, poorly delivered, and, frankly, you're not in the mood* (London: Portfolio Penguin, 2014)

Sonnenfeld, Jeffrey, 'Shedding Light on the Hawthorn Studies', *Journal of Occupational Behaviour* (Vol. 6 No. 2, April 1985) pp.111-130

Suchan, James and Robert Colucci, 'The High Cost of Bureaucratic Written Communications', *Business Horizons* (Vol 34, No.2, 1991), pp.68-73

Surowiecki, James, *The Wisdom of Crowds: Why the Many are Smarter than the Few* (London: Abacus, 2005)

Tan, Chade-Meng, *Search Inside Yourself: Increase productivity, creativity and happiness* (St Ives: Collins, 2012)

Tapscott, Don and Anthony Williams, *Wikinomics: How mass collaboration changes everything* (Croydon: Portfolio/Atlantic Books, 2006)

Tardanico, Susan 'Is Social Media Sabotaging Real Communication?', *Forbes*, www.forbes.com/sites/susantardanico/2012/04/30/is-social-media-sabotaging-real-communication/ [published 30 April 2012, accessed 21 May 2014]

Taylor, Bill, 'Why Amazon us Copying Zappos and Paying Employees to Quit', *HBR blogs*, blogs.hbr.org/2014/04/why-amazon-is-copying-zappos-and-paying-employees-to-quit/ [published 14 April 2014, accessed 31 July 2014]

Taylor, Paul, 'Atos' 'zero email initiative' succeeding': enterprise social networking platforms replace internal email', *Financial Times*, www.ft.com/cms/s/0/11384220-8761-11e2-bde6-00144feabdc0.html#axzz32MuCraGB [published 7 March 2014, accessed 22 May 2014]

Tellen, Steven L., 'The IntraNet Architecture: Managing information in the new paradigm' (research paper, Amdahl Corporation, June 1996)

'The people formerly known as the audience', *The Economist* (7 July 2011)

'The Working Mother Experience book is released!', www.facebook.com/notes/emc-careers/the-working mother-experience-book-is-released/194603205416 [published 14 April 2009, accessed 18 March 2014]

Thomas, Ron, Joshua Bellin, Claudy Jules and Nandani Lynton, 'Leadership Ensembles. Orchestrating the Global Company' (research report, Accenture institute for high performance, October 2012)

Towers Watson, 'Change and Communication ROI – The 10th Anniversary Report: How the fundamentals have evolved and the best adapt' (study report, Towers Watson, December 2013)

Towers Watson, 'Employee voice: Releasing voice for sustainable business success' (white paper, Towers Watson, February 2014)

Trochim, William M K, 'The Qualitative Debate' www.socialresearchmethods.net/kb/qualdeb.php [published 20 October 2006, accessed 18 July 2014]

Turkle, Sherry, 'The flight from conversation', *The New York Times*, www.nytimes.com/2012/04/22/opinion/sunday/the-flight-from-converation.html?pagewanted=all&_r=0 [published 21 April 2012, accessed 14 June 2014]

Tutty, Jeremy I. and James D. Klein, 'Computer mediated instruction: a comparison of online and face-to-face collaboration', *Educational technology research and development* (Vol. 56, No. 2, April 2008), pp.101-124

'Valve: Handbook for new employees' (2012), assets.sbnation.com/assets/1074301/Valve_Handbook_LowRes.pdf [accessed 29 July 2014],

van Belleghem, Steve, *The Conversation Company: Boost Your Business Through Culture, People and Social Media* (London: Kogan Page, 2012)

Vanita, *Effective Communication in Human Resource Development* (New Delhi: Atlantic Publishers and Distributors, 2003)

Visconti, Luke 'Did the Fed's Stunning Lack of Diversity Cause the Housing Crisis?' *Ask the White Guy*, www.diversityinc.com/ask-the-white-guy/the-housing-crisis-and-the-business-case-for-diversity [accessed 13 January 2014]

Ward, Toby, 'State of the social intranet: results of 2012 Social Intranet Survey' (summary report, Prescient digital media, January 2013)

Weber Shandwick, 'Employees Rising: Seizing the Opportunity in Employee Activism' (white paper, Weber Shandwick and KRC Research, 2 April 2014)

Weeks, John and Anne-Laure Fayard, 'Blurring Face-to-Face and Virtual Encounters', *HBR blogs*, blogs.hbr.org/2011/07/blurring-face-to-face-and-virt/ [published 18 July 2011, accessed 31 July 2014]

Weinberger, David, *Too Big To Know – Rethinking Knowledge Now that the Facts aren't Facts, Experts are Everywhere, and the Smartest Person in the Room is the Room* (New York: Basic Books, 2011)

Weinberger, David, *Small Pieces Loosely Joined: A unified theory of the web* (New York: Basic Books, 2002)

Weinberger, David, 'Is there an echo in here?', www.salon.com/2004/02/21/echo_chamber {published 21 February 2004, accessed 2 January 2014]

'What is employee engagement?', *Engage for success*, www.engageforsuccess.org/about/what-is-employee-engagement/ [accessed 23 January 2014]

Wheatley, Margaret with Debbie Frieze, 'Leadership in the Age of Complexity: From Hero to Host', *Resurgence Magazine* (Winter, 2011)

Zeiger, Mimi, 'Steelcase and Susan Cain Design Offices for Introverts', www.fastcodesign.com/3031341/steelcase-and-susan-cain-design-offices-for-introverts?partner=rss&utm_source=feedburner&utm_medium=feed&utm_campaign=feedburner+fastcodesign&utm_content=feedburner [accessed 29 July 2014]

About the authors

KATIE MACAULAY'S career in corporate communications spans more than 20 years. After working as a consultant and on staff for a number of public and private organisations, she now runs the London-based communication agency AB. She lives in Hampshire with her partner Barker and two sons, Sam and Harry.

After graduating in history from Oxford University, ELOISE HINDES joined AB in 2012. Her work as a consultant involves fascinating conversations with employees from a whole range of organisations. She is grateful to her dad for countless discussions and insights that have informed her work on this book.

BEN HALL graduated in journalism from Staffordshire University and worked on a regional newspaper before joining AB in 2011. He now produces written content and video for clients in print and online, striving to represent the employee voice and champion employee engagement. He lives in London with his partner Jenny.